ENGLISH ITEMS:

OR,

MICROSCOPIC VIEWS

OF

ENGLAND AND ENGLISHMEN.

BY

MATT. F. WARD,

AUTHOR OF "LETTERS FROM THREE CONTINENTS."

NEW-YORK:
D. APPLETON AND COMPANY,
200 BROADWAY.
M.DCCC.LIII.

TO

J. J. HUGHES, ESQ.,

This Work is Dedicated,

AS

A SLIGHT TESTIMONIAL OF SINCERE FRIENDSHIP

AND

HIGH RESPECT.

MATT. F. WARD.

CONTENTS.

ENGLISH ITEMS.

CHAPTER I.

OUR INDIVIDUAL RELATIONS WITH ENGLAND.

ENGLISHMEN, and their admirers, have so carefully stowed away English supremacy in a nice glass box, guarded at every angle by portentous "hands off," as successfully to protect it from the too close scrutiny of the masses. Indeed, whilst it continues the custom of the Miss Nancies, and old women of the fashionable and literary worlds of America extravagantly to extol every thing English, it will be deemed reprehensible temerity in any man, to refuse to acknowledge the received superstition. The American, daring enough to assail England's claims to superiority, will be pronounced guilty of outrage by those of his countrymen, too indolent or too dastardly to think for themselves. His sacrilege will be thought no greater by these Anglicized Republicans, than that of the conqueror Antiochus, in the opinion of the Jews, when he boldly entered their temple —ordered a great sow to be sacrificed on the altar for burnt-offerings—and polluted the Holy of Holies, by having the blood of the unclean animal scattered about the sacred edifice.

Before I had ever travelled beyond the confines of the

United States, I had grown weary of the thraldom to English dictation of public opinion in America. I entertained no great love for Englishmen, and all that I saw during my first visit to Europe, and what I have seen since, has not served to increase my affection for them. Yet I must confess that I experienced, a year or two ago, certain aguish sensations at my own rashness, in expressing a somewhat unfavorable opinion of Englishmen and their manners. It might have been, as a distinguished Review sagely remarked, an unbearable degree of impudence in an unknown individual from Arkansas, to pretend to pronounce judgment on the refinements of English society. But being accustomed to attack rampant bears at home, I suppose the innocent cavortings of the British Lion seemed much less terrible to me, than to some of my more civilized countrymen, who had never seen angry beasts out of cages. Although the roar of this pampered Lion of England has long since ceased to affect us as a nation, yet no one can doubt that his complaining growls make those individuals quake amongst us, who pretend to a refined excess either of fashion or gentility. I am sorry to observe that it is becoming more and more the fashion, especially among "travelled" Americans, to pet the British beast. In defiance of his surly ways, they are eternally trying by flattery to coax him into good humor, as the boys throw apples and gingerbread to his prototype of the menagerie. He never fails to repay their officious kindness with snarling disapprobation, and always attacks the hand that pats him. But instead of treating him like other refractory brutes, they pusillanimously strive to soothe him by a forbearance he cannot appreciate. They never laugh so loudly, as when suffering from his bite, and good-naturedly designate his ruthless clawings the facetious indications of a playful disposition.

What beast-tamer, in his senses, ever dreamed of subduing an angry lion by soothing him? Beasts are ruled through fear, not kindness. They submissively lick the hand that wields the lash, not the one that feeds them. So long as we attempt to pacify the British Lion by patting him, we shall be clawed and bitten. He must be treated according to his nature. Seize him fearlessly by the throat, and once strangle him into involuntary silence, and the British Lion will hereafter be as fawning as he has hitherto been spiteful.

It is a melancholy fact, which I am most reluctant to acknówledge even to myself, that there is a growing inclination towards flunkeyism, in what are termed the higher classes of society in America. We too frequently find the American recently returned from Europe, whose powers of observation should be quick'ened by foreign associations, and whose mind should be so enlarged by studying the institutions of other countries, as to enable him better to understand the inestimable blessings of our own, expressing a captious dissatisfaction with his own country. Sneering at America—finding fault with her people—ridiculing her manners—and objecting to her customs; he professes to find nothing good enough for him, with the eminently flunkey hope, that those of his countrymen who have remained at home, will be inspired with awful respect for his improved taste, and travelled cultivation. If our travelled countrymen can derive no higher evidence of improvement from a European tour, than a servile imitation of every thing they have seen in England, even to fault-finding with America, I sincerely hope they may for ever remain in the republican simplicity which they received from our Fathers. If no more valuable lesson is to be learned by Americans abroad, than that patriotism is something to be ashamed of, Democrat as I am, I would favor a general embargo law, to keep them at home. And when in spite of every precaution the citizens of the United States have become so cosmopolitan, by travel, as to deem it necessary to rail at their own country, as a proof of freedom from "provincial prejudices," I hope there may be some newly discovered California to which I may peacefully emigrate.

I mentioned above the earlier symptoms a fearfully spreading disease, which can only be cured I fear by cauterizing. In the more advanced stages of this epidemic, brought among us from foreign parts, we find its victims affecting the society of transient Englishmen, who, coming to America arrayed in the cast-off airs of their superiors at home, always laugh at their too eager hosts, and make butts of their over-zealous admirers. These cockneys are right in their treatment of such despicable sycophants. Well aware that they are prompted by none of the higher impulses of hospitality, but actuated by the mean ambition of borrowing importance from their servility to them, these Englishmen have my applause, at least, for making them feel their degradation. Alas! that an American freeman should submit to be kicked by an upstart Briton, with the silly hope that there were people around him, silly enough to envy him the supposed honor of his aristocratic associations. The operation of kicking certainly does imply very intimate relations of position, at least, and the American flunkeys may be partially right in their expectations, for there are a few among us, who will persist in estimating an Englishman's real rank by his pretensions, and who will not give up the superstition, that every thing English must necessarily be superior. These transient English do but obey their instincts in kicking all Americans who will allow them. The thing becomes a duty, no less than a recreation, when they happen to encounter those, who consider such a proceeding on their part, not only a great condescension, but an honor to themselves, and will apologize to the kicker, accordingly, for giving him the trouble to confer it. In such instances I always feel tempted to assist John Bull, though to do him justice, the infliction is generally made, I believe, with a very good will. It must be a great luxury for the poor Britishers, to meet with an opportunity of treating other people as they have always been accustomed to being treated themselves. Having all their lives submitted to being kicked at home, they are eminently qualified to appreciate the privilege of kicking, and enjoy it accordingly. What flunkey would not? An Englishman is somewhat excusable after all for his snobbish propensities. Born in the land of flunkeydom, breathing the atmosphere, and reared amidst the prejudices of flunkeys, it would be unnatural, indeed, if he did not himself become a veritable flunkey. But what can be said of Americans, who, without any such apology, knowingly and wilfully become the flunkeys of flunkeys, and toadyize toadies? I am not a harsh man by nature, but I would have such renegades stretched upon the rack of public opinion. Traitors to themselves, their country, and her institutions—I would take keen delight in seeing them so tortured, that their sufferings might prove a warning to all, sufficiently destitute of manhood, to follow their example.

I mean not to intimate in the remotest manner, that every citizen of England who visits our country, belongs to the class I have alluded to, nor do I wish to be understood as insinuating, that every American who extends to an Englishman the ordinary civilities of society, must necessarily be a flunkey. I have myself known several English gentlemen, and I have no doubt there are many coming to America, whose social qualities would make them the welcome guests of every family circle. But I regard it as an excess of absurdity, unworthy of us, warmly to seize every straggler by the hand, simply because he happens to be an Englishman. While our present social relations with Englishmen at home, continue to exist, the mere fact of a man's being from England, so far from becoming a passport into the bosoms of our family circles, should be considered just cause for scrutinizing inquiries, as to his position and real character. For though we occasionally meet with a gentleman from that country, yet past experience should have long since convinced us that we cannot be too skeptical as to a Britisher's claims to our hospitality, till we have some indistinct idea as to what he is. A London cit, accustomed all his days to the degrading consciousness of inferiority, is so intoxicated by the unexpected attentions with which he is generally received in this country, that he ought scarcely to be considered responsible for the sneers, with which, in his drunken elevation, he always repays the kindness our citizens have extended to him. I am a great believer in reciprocity, and I would have it made as difficult for an Englishman to gain access to the better houses of America, as they have made it for an American to enter the higher classes of society in Great Britain. So prevalent is the opinion that Americans are improper inmates of the fashionable houses of England, that I once heard a boastful English Banker giving as an evidence of his superior influence, his having actually been able to introduce a wealthy American, who had for nearly twenty years been a resident of London, into one of their clubs. If an American will consent temporarily to make a penny-postman of himself, and carry a small mail-bag of introductory letters, he may reasonably hope to enjoy the honor of receiving a diminutive bit of glazed pasteboard, with some aristocratic inscription; or if his recommendations are unusually strong, he may be inflicted with the oppressive distinction of a dinner. But as he enjoys no titular rank, he must submit to the mortification of going in at the tail end of all the guests, and being seated at the foot of the table—when positions at table are regarded as matters of import. Who but an Englishman would invite a man to his house to insult him? But such is the custom in England. If the rights of hospitality are not considered superior to mere conventional usages of the country, strangers should not be compelled to suffer on account of the absurd ignorance of their hosts. If a man is worthy of an invitation to another's house, he certainly has a right to expect the treatment due to a gentleman.

There are some of our citizens, who seem to be troubled with a mawkishly tender regard for the sensibilities of the "dear old Mother Country." The truth must not even be told, for fear of giving offence to the burly inhabitants of the sweet land of our ancestors. What have we ever received from that country but injustice? She oppressed us as colonies—she twice attempted to crush us by war—and yet, according to these puling lovers of "the Old Country," we must be humbly grateful, now, because she magnanimously permits us to advance in power and prosperity, when she could not possibly restrain us. When has she ever omitted an opportunity of injuring us, when she could do so with impunity? She has always interfered with our commercial relations, when she dared. She has invariably attempted to shackle our progress, whilst professing to protect the rights of weaker nations. She has assailed us through her press; slandered us in her books; struggled to excite the animosity of other countries against us—and yet we must raise no murmur of retort, because, forsooth, she happens to be "the Old Country." What, I beg to be informed, is this "Old Country" to us that we should truckle to her? Out upon those who preach this miserably servile doctrine. My contempt is scarcely surpassed by what the English must feel for them.

There are many more of us, who, at heart love America, as she deserves to be loved, but have not the moral courage to speak out like men: the English might laugh at our extravagant admiration of our own country. Let them first prove that she does not deserve our most enthusiastic opinions, and I too will become as silent as the most Anglicized. Britain would be delighted to shame us out of our patriotism, for it might, some day, give dangerous animation to our strength. No eulogy of England could be too extravagant, but 'tis absurd to praise America. It seems to me a hard case, indeed, that Americans are to be restrained from a free expression of what they think of America, by the apprehension of English disapprobation. Who appointed her censor of our opinions? What do we owe her that we should so meekly bow to her mandates? Not even the doubtful boon of our birth. The royal miser Henry VII. refused to assist Columbus in his voyage of discovery, and after it was accomplished without him, what English monarch ever essayed to people the new-found world? To the enterprise of Raleigh, aided by English tyranny towards our forefathers, we are indebted for our appearance among nations. Uncared for, and despised, we remained, until our growth made us important to the support of our *tender* parent, whose earliest solicitude for the long-neglected foundling, was manifested by oppression. She first attempted to rob us by means of venal laws. She then tried to crush us in an unequal contest—and finally yielded to force, the rights she had meanly refused to supplication. Does such a course deserve gratitude, or contempt? We should treat her now, as we treated her then: command her respect by our boldness, not beg her toleration by obsequious complaisance. She must feel our power before she will acknowledge it. So long as we attempt to conciliate her by meek submission to her judgment, she will continue to despise us. Our gentle forbearance will be considered weakness—and our friendly advances she will mistake for servility. The Bible, 'tis true, commands us to "forgive our enemies," but the English, influenced by the old adage of judging others by themselves, will attribute our complying with this Christian precept, to a want of spirit to resent her insults. The Quaker doctrine of "turning the other cheek" she cannot understand. Her people cannot appreciate the retiring nature of true gentility, either in nations or individuals. They cannot conceive of a gentleman's being modest in his demeanor, unless from the consciousness of inferiority. Nor can they realize how a nation could fail to be blustering, except from cowardice.

The English are eager to impress upon us the fact that undivided devotion to our country is "provincial." They kindly warn us of the danger of "narrow-minded prejudices," and descant, with tumid eloquence, upon the liberality of enlarged understandings, and cultivated minds. They condescendingly inform us that a man, who could continue to think "there is no place like home," would be very justly suspected of never having wandered beyond the limits of his native country. If he desires to be appreciated, as a traveller, and man of the world, he must give up such old-fashioned notions. He must take England as his model, and sneer at the deficiencies of America, or else he will incur the danger of being considered an individual of limited understanding, and "narrow-minded prejudices." Should he feel any curiosity as to what constitutes this particular genus of "prejudices," which is so industriously harped upon by Englishmen, he will discover that their ideas of "narrow-minded prejudices" consist in doing justice to the two countries. To be "*provincial*" is to adhere to America—to display a cultivated taste, admire England.

The English may be, in some measure, excusable for their own preposterous vanity, and glaring illiberality to other people, from the fact of their having so rarely received the lesson, of seeing themselves as others see them. Most

Americans who have written upon England, have been either flattered or bullied into drawing the most glowing pictures of English comfort—of English freedom—English society—and English every thing. One very naturally supposes them discoursing of a model nation, with model government, model manners, and model dispositions, and feels but little curiosity to test the depth of the gloss with which they have so tastefully varnished every thing in the country. It is not surprising, however, that England should wield a vast influence over men, ambitious of literary fame. When it is remembered how submissively the American public have been wont to abide by the decision of English critics, it ought no longer to appear strange, that aspiring authors should attempt to curry favor of those, in whose hands has been placed the power of awarding the honors of literary distinction. This is all wrong. America, to enjoy that independence, of which she may be so justly proud, should have her own critics, as well as her own manufacturers of cotton and iron.

There have been statesmen in our country strenuously to advocate the protection of home industry. Oppressive tariffs have been supported, in order to assist our domestic manufactures to compete with the foreign. But is it not strange, that it has never occurred to the sages of our Republic, that mills and foundries do not embrace the entire field of American industry? Is it not extraordinary that it has never occurred to them, that cotton and iron are not the only commodities which American genius might work up to advantage if properly fostered? There is a raw material, ordinarily known as *brains*, that we have already employed with success, notwithstanding the difficulties against which we have contended. We have already accomplished much, and may do more, with proper encouragement. Bryant, Halleck, Longfellow and Willis, Sparks,

Prescott and Bancroft, Cooper, Irving and Mitchel, are master workmen, whom we may proudly compare with the world's best living artisans. But this industrial establishment, like all our others, is still young, and requires fostering.

I here declare myself a protectionist—I am an advocate of a high tariff too in favor of *mind*. American intellect as well as American labor deserves to be protected. Discovering our own merits, let us support them. Let us cultivate a national taste, as we have established a national character. We have too long ago asserted our independence of English rulers, to continue dependent of English critics. We have strong native judgment; let us exercise it as fearlessly with regard to literature, as to every thing else. I mean not to favor a cavilling spirit, that would habitually condemn what England praised, and praise what England condemned. I merely insist upon the exercise of that discriminating power, which we possess in a sufficiently eminent degree, to make us certain that the expression of our national opinion will never call a blush into the cheek of one of our citizens abroad. Let us not wait "with bated breath" for what England shall say of a work of art, before we answer with a servile echo from this side the Atlantic. We may be sometimes wrong, most people are, but we can at least be independent.

The attempt is vain to shut our eyes to the fact, that England has hitherto been the model, on which we have dressed ourselves. No native merit, however distinguished, could pass current till stamped by English approbation. An author must be favorably noticed by English critics, before he can hope to be extensively read at home. An actor must cross the seas in search of a reputation, and most of our wiseacres tremble to express an opinion, which is not a close-cut pattern, of what has been said on the other side of the Atlantic. From England we borrowed our notions of etiquette—and from the same notable birthplace of absurdities, we have imported our ideas of gentility. We ran after Englishmen, and affected their opinions of rank. Indeed, England has been our oracle, whose responses were reverenced, like Delphi's of yore; and few have there been, who, like Demosthenes, when he declared that the priestess "Philipized," have dared to express a doubt of their infallibility. But a revolution is commenced—this sort of thing is rapidly passing away; indeed in many portions of our country it has wholly disappeared. There are fortunately many strong intellects among us, who think and speak for themselves of literature, and the arts, as boldly as of politics. I cannot but hope that a reform is at hand in the fashionable world; and I predict that Americans in all parts of the country will soon use silver forks, for some more sensible reason than that Englishmen have pronounced it vulgar to eat with a knife.

There are those among us, who regard the attacks of the English with good-natured contempt, who feel amused, not incensed by their jealousy, and consider it unbecoming Americans to notice their slanders. They very properly regard personalities as low bred, and believe it as ungentlemanly in us to retort, as it is in the English to assail. For the opinions of such persons, I entertain so high a respect, that I most willingly make to them an explanation of my course, in the following pages. I agree with them entirely, that personal attacks are vulgar, and that the indulgence in them, by our assailants, does not justify us in their use. But in any warfare, we must adapt our weapons to the enemy with whom we are engaged, and hard blows are the only logic the English understand. To affect their understandings, we must punch their heads. We have acted on the defensive principle long enough, and if we are not ambitious of always continuing the butts for newspaper jokes, and tourists' slanders, we must ourselves make the attack. To procure peace, we must "carry the war into Africa." If we do not ourselves maintain our dignity, the English will scarcely do so for us. Towards them, we must be as stiff and unbending as themselves. We must demand, not beg their attention. We know what is due us; we must insist upon receiving it. To sum the matter up, it is time we should "set up" for ourselves; we must fulfil our destiny, without stopping to inquire what people in England will say. We have too long been in the leading strings of Great Britain; for even if we were still an infant among the nations of the earth, we should never walk alone, if we did not try. But we are no longer a child. Young as we are we have the strength, and let us show the independence of a man. We have a nationality of our own—it is our duty to support it. To borrow the words of the immortal Washington,—"I want an *American* character, that the powers of Europe may be convinced we act for *ourselves*, and not for others."

CHAPTER II.

SIXPENNY MIRACLES IN ENGLAND.

SOME erudite Englishman, Mr. Leigh Hunt, perhaps, has made the facetious discovery that one vast counter lines the American seaboard, from Maine to Florida. Every American should glory in the commercial enterprise of our country. In defence of our commercial rights we obtained our freedom. Commerce gave us the power to achieve our independence, and by our commerce we have so gloriously maintained it. But in reply to the palpable sneer of the funny gentleman, I will incur the danger of startling my readers by the novelty of an expression, for the sake of its force: "people who live in glass houses ought not to throw stones." Even supposing that Americans are somewhat more addicted to money-making, than is altogether consistent with a philosophic contempt for gold, yet the English would do well to "cast out the beam out of" their own eye, before seeking for "the mote" in ours. We do exert ourselves sturdily in the acquisition of wealth, 'tis true, but 'tis a secondary consideration, it is sought for only as a means of power, and enjoyment. But with an Englishman, money is preëminent; he loves it for its own substantial sake. And if I can show that those ostentatiously paraded qualities of which Englishmen are most proud, are subservient to their thirst for lucre, it seems to me that the most skeptical should be convinced that money is adorable in their eyes, for its own shining charms.

The English are a cold, selfish nation, with few emotions, and a limited number of sentiments. Patriotism, with them, never assumes that rarefied enthusiasm, experienced by other nations. But still an Englishman loves England; he is proud of England, not that he discovers about her any extraordinary charms, but because she can claim the honor of having given *him* birth. Loyalty and religion are affected by an Englishman, like a high shirt-collar, and sleek hat, as the indispensable attributes of a gentleman. Indeed, regarding gentility as impossible without them, he cultivates these desirable qualities with the coaxing assiduity, with which enthusiastic florists, in bleak climes, force tropical plants in hot houses. In accordance with the routine of proprieties, which he has prescribed for himself, the king and the church are the pet objects of his veneration. But when kings and churches cease to be regarded, what can be deemed sacred in England? When both loyalty and religion are traded off, for a paltry consideration, who can doubt the grovelling propensities of the English? *The Government of Great Britain demands sixpence of every visitor to Westminster Abbey.*

The most careless worldling must feel impressed on entering a venerable Cathedral. There is something awful, even to the bravest, about death. There is something sacred, even to the most brutal, in the tomb. Yet the English, professing to be distinguished for their loyalty, and pretending piously to venerate every thing connected with the church, have degraded this hoary pile, among whose crumbling arches a half-dozen centuries are perched, and in whose silent aisles repose the most illustrious heroes of English history, into a show-room, to pocket such pitiful earnings, as the owner of an organ and monkey might scorn to grind for. They take advantage of the desire, shared alike by strangers and Englishmen, to visit the tombs of Britain's

Kings, to charge them sixpence for their admittance. How deep rooted must be the love of gain, when they will invade the sacred precincts of the grave, to levy this black mail on the curiosity of strangers! How lost to all sense of shame to speculate on the loyalty of the nation! How omnipotent must be the reign of gold in the hearts of the nobles, composing the government, when they would coin pennies from the dust of their dead ancestors! What opinion must we entertain of the dignity and liberality of a government that annually devotes millions to the support of its pension list, and will yet drag forth the shades of her heroes to make a spectacle for the gaping multitude. What an exalted estimate they must place upon the services of these dead monarchs, when they exhibit them to spectators at sixpence a head, but demand a shilling for a sight of the live monkeys at the Zoological Gardens. This sordid policy which, in order to put a few pounds into the treasury, compels these ancient worthies, who have all played their parts in history, to play the catchpenny characters before a mob, makes even a stranger, who never loved the English, blush for their baseness. Even I would have them spare themselves this last mark of ignominy.

Their apology is worthy of the nation—*it only costs sixpence!* Price, not principle, is ever uppermost in their minds. It is the amount a man pays, and not the outrage to his feelings, that they think it possible might distress him. But in this instance, the minuteness of the charge is happily apportioned to the motive which prompted it. What could be more contemptible than either?

These sceptred monarchs, who once swayed the wills of millions—formerly the proud possessors of manors and forests, are not now permitted to occupy in peace their poor body's length. The people of Great Britain have grown too eager to reap its profits, and the soil has recently become too valuable to the living, to be consecrated as the resting-place of the dead. These buried kings, in ceasing to be feared, are no longer respected; England has served them, it is now their turn to serve England. It is the duty of a good sovereign to be useful to his people. He must not be a burden to the state, and must therefore issue forth, to dance a melancholy jig for the entertainment of the populace, each one of whom has paid his sixpence to witness the exhibition. A happy commentary truly upon the ancient glory, and modern degeneracy of England;—a heroic monarch reduced to the level of a street exhibitor of Punch and Judy! Who can doubt that the English love money when their loyalty and religion are bartered for pence, and their kings and churches transformed into the base means of disreputable gain?

There is something so venerable about the Gothic arches of Westminster Abbey,—something so solemn in the silent array of its discolored tombs, that it continues to be imposing even in the dirty hands of its showmen. Here reposes all that is greatest and best of England's proud past. Here the most eminent poets and sculptors of the world, have rendered themselves immortal, in paying the last tribute to expired genius. Undying renown not only hangs round the names recorded, but rests on the hands that recorded them. An atmosphere of holiest impulses breathes over these illustrious monuments, and I would have no one drink it in who was not inspired by the genius of the place. A man, who could stand in the presence of these honored dead, without experiencing the most elevated emotions, I would banish as an intruder from the sacred fane. I would have a visit here prompted by the feelings, with which devout palmers make pilgrimages to the holy places of the East. I would fain protect this solemn niche of historical associations from the approach of idle curiosity. But the English seem anxious to destroy its consecrated character. They lower the exalted reputation of the place in offering it to the public as an ordinary spectacle; they assail its sanctity, when they make it a cheap exhibition.

The illiterate have always possessed a strong natural propensity for shows, which becomes especially animated, when it can be indulged at a trifling expense. There is something strangely fascinating in the dignity of spending one's own money, and very comfortable in the idea of getting the worth of it. And it is only necessary to announce a cheap exhibition, of no matter what, to insure crowds of ignorant spectators flocking to see it. In the first place, the name of the thing is attraction, for it is arranged under the head of "Amusements;" then they have the luxury of spending money, without the inconvenience attending a larger outlay, and besides people have a passion for seeing and doing what they have to pay for, whatever is "free" possessing no attractions. Who can doubt that this sixpenny charge proves a bait to swarms of such ignoramuses, who would, otherwise, never dream of entering the Abbey? And what right have the English government to suppose that they would feel greater veneration here, than at any other "show," when they had paid sixpence to get in? They come to see, not to reflect. They tramp through the resounding aisles in search of something they do not find. Lost amidst a labyrinth of names they never heard of, and stumbling among works of art they do not understand, 'tis not surprising that they should indulge their grumbling dissatisfaction. The diminutiveness of the entrance fee becomes a source of complaint, and these Englishmen, who estimate every thing by what they pay for it, wonder at their own folly in not foreseeing the character of the exhibition, from the cheapness of the price of admittance. They have paid their sixpence, however, and feel at liberty to criticise the performance, and it is from the jeering comments, and senseless gibes of a disappointed rabble like this, that I would fain protect the hallowed recesses of Westminster.

Those who attempt to defend this unworthy practice, declare that the inconsiderable charge, which nobody can feel, is made merely to defray the expenses of the necessary guardians of the church against the mutilations of visitors. But would it not be more becoming the position of a government, which generously gives the Queen $300,000 as *pin money*, and can afford to reward her majesty's ex-master of the dance with a pension of five hundred dollars a year—to devote a few hundred to the preservation of a relic, so venerated as Westminster Abbey? Or if the public finances would not permit so inconsiderable an outlay, would it not be more dignified to curtail the perquisites of the dashing noble who now receives as master of the queen's stag hounds, $10,000 a year for occasionally amusing himself by going hunting with a good pack of dogs, rather than subject the poor old abbey to its present ignominy? Or, if this will not do, and the queen's household must remain intact in spite of the abbey, why not leave it to protect itself? It would be safer in its solitary majesty guarded only by the glorious recollections of the past than it could be when watched by this hired train of insolent menials. Its very helplessness would become unto it a wall of strength; its silent appeal for mercy would protect it from the rudest hands; and its monuments, that time and history have united to render illustrious, would be safe, when a regiment of soldiers might fail to preserve them. Englishmen, do this;—do what you will, but spare—oh spare the guiltless shades of your buried ancestors the shame of such an exposure!

But if, in defiance of the sanctity of the place, and the veneration you profess to feel for your forefathers, you will continue to make a show-house of your ancient cathedral, why in the name of all that is decent, do you not make the price of admission worthy of the celebrity of the object? or at least charge enough, to insure the proper conduct of the showmen?

The government having closed the lofty public entrance, either on the economical principle that prompts a man to lock up his parlor, except on Sunday, or because they are ashamed of the business they are engaged in, the visitor to Westminster is compelled to sneak round the back way, through an alley, which is not especially calculated to heighten his preconceived impressions of the Abbey. But he enters, and forgets all else. Standing beneath the vaulted arches of Westminster, he so loses all sense in the delightful mazes of reverie, as seriously to interrupt the business of the day, did not an official in sable softly demand his cane, and thereby wake him up to a recollection of what he came to do. By the by, even if you happen to be a cripple, or a dandy, instantly discard your cane upon arriving at the other side of the Atlantic. I care not how lame you may happen to be; limp, crawl, do what you can, but be not afflicted by this supernumerary nuisance. For if you, as of course you will, visit all the galleries and lions of England, your cane will subject you to a greater expenditure of time, patience, and money, than most people are willing to submit to.

But the cane is deposited, and a new rush of emotions occurs. The accumulated expectations pent up since his boyhood, become oppressive by delay, and the visitor grows warm and fidgety in his anxiety to be admitted to the holier places of the church. This intensely vivified excitement never becomes dangerous, however, as by a charitably considerate arrangement of the English government, it is always allowed ample time to cool. The numerous gentlemen in black, whom the government compels the old church to pay, for so shabbily doing its honors, being of sedentary habits, and a literary turn of mind, are unwilling to be interrupted to convey a single visitor through the interior chapels. It requires a party of seven curious individuals, each one provided with a talisman in the shape of a sixpence, to interrupt the comfortable repose of a pompous official. And as most people have ceased to consider a show, composed of mouldy monuments and tattered flags, a very lively one, even when it happens to be a *great bargain*—a stranger will usually incur the risk of remaining some time in the antechamber. During the painful period of his probation, he is subjected to the impositions of another class of hucksters. Watching with the liveliest interest the various stages of his impatience, they rapidly advance upon him, from every nook and corner, the instant they perceive him arrived at the extreme point of desperation. With unblushing assurance, they poke at the bewildered gentleman descriptions of the Abbey, plans of the building, pictures of the monuments, and armsfull of other plausible stuff, which they feel very confident he has not the courage, in his exhausted condition, to refuse. Of course he buys every thing, without much examining the contents, for in his melancholy frame of mind the advertisements of the "Times," a week old, would prove a refreshing literary treat. At length, however, the mystical number of seven is made up. The stately keeper slowly rises—unlocks the door—passes us in one by one, that being the most convenient mode of collecting the sixpences—enters himself, and again turns the key. An extraordinary metamorphosis instantly occurs. Our guide assumes an alacrity quite startling, when contrasted with his former torpidity. The man appears to be worked by steam. In his mumbled routine of names, dates, and nonsense, the only distinguishable feature is its haste. He rushes us through chapels, over monuments, and along aisles, without ever pausing for breath, till he has put us out at a gate on the other side, with the satisfied sigh of a man who has just accomplished a very irksome task. This is a visit to Westminster! This it is to hold communion with the illustrious dead! This is the intellectual enjoyment which the English government have considered too delicious to be offered to the public *gratis*.

In the inextricable confusion of ages, persons, and events, in which his guide has succeeded in involving him, the visitor feels stunned in attempting to recollect what he has seen: few men would be rash enough to attempt remembering what they had heard. A vague vision of antique tombs, Gothic chapels, and curious sanctuaries is all he has to show for his visit to the Abbey. What time has been allowed to the historian, to connect the chain of events, recorded by these monuments? Has the antiquary had an opportunity of examining the inscriptions? Has the philosopher been permitted to reflect upon the extraordinary changes which these tombs are calculated to call up in his mind? Or what opportunity has the ordinary visitor enjoyed, of either thought or reflection, whilst composing one of the express train, which our locomotive guide has succeded in "putting through," in such extraordinarily fast time? The chief enjoyment in the Abbey arises from association; time must be granted for its indulgence. What educated stranger, in paying his sixpence, would not be delighted to give twenty times the sum, to be allowed to enjoy his visit in his own way, without the hateful domination of the fast guide? But the English government, although too avaricious to surrender so important a branch of the public revenue, are too timid to demand a higher price; their only apology for making the Abbey a paying exhibition, being, that the charge is an extremely "*moderate*" one. Too mean to resist the temptation to make a petty charge, they are destitute of the moral courage to profit by a larger one.

I would love to muse among these gray old tombs. I should delight to study the quaint epitaphs in which the partial friends of ancient times have recorded the imaginary virtues of the dead. I would take strange pleasure in wandering through these lofty corridors and echoing aisles with the spirit inhabitants of the place. I could find exquisite enjoyment in passing with them through the history of the past, some of whose stirring events each one of them has helped to contribute. The food for memory, and the pleasures of association, in a spot like this, seem endless. But for such enjoyment a man must be allowed to linger long and often in these hidden recesses. He must not be interrupted, or hurried by impertinent guides; he must be permitted to fly even from himself, and live only in the past. But such permission would be considered most reprehensible extravagance, in the management of the public funds; it would be giving too much "show" for sixpence.

I have too long lost sight of our visitor. Hurried, and heated, he is ejected from that other gate by the grim janitor, who slams the door in his face when he attempts somewhat to enlighten himself by a civil question, and unceremoniously leaves him to get out as he best can. Thoroughly disgusted with the whole proceeding, he experiences even greater anxiety to make his exit than he had previously done his *entrée.* Proceeding forthwith to the nearest outlet, he demands with sarcastic politeness his cane, which the bland gentleman in black hands him, with a brief, but emphatic, "*Tuppence*, Sir, please." In a fume, he searches all his pockets, which had been previously exhausted of their small change, in the purchase of bad descriptions, and worse pictures of the Abbey, without being able to corner a stray sixpence, or even shilling. He is at length forced to hand a half-sovereign to the bland man, who, smiling his regret that he has nothing *but* small change, industriously proceeds to freight the pockets of the exasperated visitor with pennies, which would all have been unceremoniously thrown into his face, had not the unfortunate sight-seer retained coolness enough to be aware that he would pick them all quietly up again, and be extremely obliged to him for his profusion. Becoming hopelessly conscious of the utter helplessness of his position, he says not a word, but with a slight groan, starts off, packing copper as naturally as the mules in the mines of Peru. Such is the pitch of intellectual enjoyment, to which the enlightened policy of Great Britain has succeeded in elevating a visit to Westminster Abbey.

The sanctity of St. Paul's is invaded by the same mercenary policy, which has degraded Westminster. A stranger, whether actuated by curiosity or piety, cannot cross its sacred threshold, without first depositing a sixpence, which seems the general passport to all the holy places of England. Its being demanded at the door of every public building, worth visiting, has conferred on the paltry price a sort of nationality. From the frequency of its payment, we naturally associate it with the people and the government. Really this perseverance in making this trivial charge, in all public places, evinces a determination on the part of the government to make the minutest of silver coins the standard of British honor. But whether they will succeed in elevating the sixpence to the dignity of the nation, or debasing the dignity of the nation to the value of the sixpence, is a question future historians must determine.

Montesquieu says that *honor* is the safeguard of monarchies, as patriotism is that of republics. Does it not look ominous for the future glory of England, that she herself values her honor so lightly?

If there be in England an object of which all classes may be justly proud, it is St. Paul's Church. It combines all that is stately and beautiful in architecture—every thing that is grand and imposing in religion. Piety and patriotism have thrown about it their powerful influences, though it had no need of either to make it impressive. The magnificent result of one nation's wealth, and one man's genius, it confers honor on Wren, and glory on England. Though the largest Protestant church in the world, and among the brightest triumphs that architecture has achieved,—though it required forty-seven years for its completion, it is remarkable that the unassisted genius of Sir Christopher Wren planned and executed this stupendous work. He laid the corner-stone, and he superintended the erection of the crowning cross.

There is a solemn repose about the looming dome of St. Paul's, an elegance about its graceful towers, and chaste beauty about the supporting columns, that must awe into silent admiration the most careless passer-by. What an effect, then, must it produce upon the stranger, who views it for the first time. Excited, delighted, and amazed by the splendor of its exterior, the visitor hastens to lose himself amidst the glories within—but is rudely stopped at the door to pay his admission-fee. What a fell blow to his noble aspirations! What violence to all sense of propriety, and every feeling of religion! A church, however lowly, should be kept holy as the memory of a mother's name; it should be guarded from pollution like the sanctity of her tomb. To convert the humblest fane to worldly purposes is sacrilege. But what shall we call the act that degrades a temple like St. Paul's to the common custom of a tavern, where everybody may enter by paying—nobody without. To disturb the holy silence of the house of God by the angry chaffering of a doorkeeper about the price of admission, is a deed without a name—a sin without a parallel.

But, once within the doors—once under the influence of the sublime beauty of all above and around him, it is no difficult matter for the visitor again to become wrapped in admiration, and lost in thought. Beneath the vast expanse of that mighty dome, his thoughts soar heavenwards, his soul expands into that almost boundless space,—he hears nothing—he sees nothing—he knows nothing but the marble wonders about him. Little does he dream, all this while, that he has himself been the object of solicitous and unceasing attention. There is a suspicious-looking individual, in shabby black, intensely eyeing him, whom instinct would have told him to avoid, had he been aware of his presence. At length, seeming to despair of any other mode of attracting our wrapped visitor's attention, this gloomy-looking functionary, with the gliding movements and haggard visage of a ghost, delicately touches his elbow, and wishes to know, in the softest possible tones, "Whether the gentleman wouldn't like to visit the whispering gallery?" Stupefied, as if suddenly awakened from a dream, he stares for a moment in silence at the intruder, finds his voice briefly to answer "No!" and takes refuge behind one of the many elegant groups of pillars that adorn the church. His privacy is soon invaded by another hungry official, who insinuatingly suggests to him the propriety of "taking a look at the library." Once more he flies—this time to a remote niche, where his contemplation of the heroes' statue, enshrined within, is again interrupted by a third officious individual, who condescendingly informs him that "the old tower clock is a great wonder of its kind." Justly concluding the plan of persecution to be systematic, and finding it impossible to be alone, or to think, our visitor resolves to be resigned, and yields himself unmurmuring to the guides. With a vast parade of ceremony, he is conducted to the whispering gallery, where, of course, he drops a sixpence; he then sees the library for the same amount, and he is escorted to the grand tower clock, where another sixpence is invested. Thus is he coaxed from object to object, and story to story of the building, till he finds himself at the top of the dome, out of breath and small change, with nothing to compensate him for this double exhaustion, except dense clouds of smoke, with the black tops of tall chimneys occasionally peering through them. He consoles himself with the unsatisfactory reflection that his lofty situation is, at least, an uncommonly airy one. Suffering has made him philosophical; and, with panting sides and aching knees, he counts on his fingers the number of bores through which he has been dragged against his will; and for what? to enable the English government, and its mercenary creatures, legally to empty his pockets of all the sixpences they happened to contain. Not satisfied with interrupting him, whilst attempting to enjoy his visit to the church in his own way, these active allies of petty extortion must subject him to the excruciating infliction of "tower bells," "whispering galleries," and "libraries," which a man would wonder how they could ever consider worthy of being shown till he remembered how essential they were to the extraction of the prescribed quantity of small coin from unsuspecting strangers. In this instance, the sixpence must have been a joint-stock operation,—Government must have quickened the zeal of its minions, by allowing them a small additional commission upon the amount collected. The perseverance with which they adhered to every visitor to St. Paul's, till they had run him through their entire routine, was too unwearying, not to have been quickened by some pecuniary inducement of the sort. But how could a reasonable man complain after having been so highly edified by the extremely interesting objects he had just visited, and when, too, he must have felt so inexpressibly indebted to the polite attentions of his various guides in pointing them out? The view from the summit of the dome of St. Paul's was somewhat on the mysteriously indistinct order, 'tis true, but he could not hold his accommodating guides responsible for the London fog, more especially as they had afforded him such intense gratification in the bell tower and whispering gallery.

Superlatively disgusted, our visitor hurries the next day for consolation to the Tower. The same delays, the same annoyances, and the same petty extortions await him, which had assailed him at the Abbey and St. Paul's. He sadly yielded to the conviction that the English government had, with the wand of power, thrown up a small circumvallation of sixpences around him, from which it was as vain to attempt an escape, as from the magical circle of an enchanter. Destitute of the energy to rail at such interrupted persecution, he surrendered himself into the hands of his tormentors, withont a hope, or even a wish to escape.

There is perhaps no object on the other side of the Atlantic, about which clusters deeper, or more varied interest for the stranger, than the Tower of London. Its fortunes have been so eventful, and of such startling contrast, that its simple annals possess the thrilling interest of romance. The curiosity with regard to it, is not confined to a single class of persons. It possesses a charm for all ages and conditions. The brilliant and bloody pageants which have been enacted within its walls and its fatal green, are strangely fascinating to the raw-head and bloody-bones period of youthful imagination, whilst its long and intimate connection with remarkable events during the most glorious epochs of English history, give it an importance in the eyes of maturer years. Whether we study it whilst flashing with splendor as the residence of a great monarch, or penetrate its gloom when given up to the uses of a prison, the same intense interest pervades the story of its fortunes. Whilst its lofty halls have been ringing with merriment of the masques and mummeries of a court ball, the sigh of some lone martyr to liberty was smothered in the damps of its dungeons. In its mysterious cabinets ambition was born, and conquest planned; in its sombre chambers of strong bolts and grated windows, pined the royal prisoners that victory gave. What strangely mingled tales its old walls might tell of splendor and misery, glory and shame, mirth and sorrow. Its lofty turrets and towers may be justly considered the archives of Britain. On its mildewed walls and creaking portcullis is written the social history of the English people. Yet this hoary pyramid of pride, which the Conqueror reared, and his successors rendered memorable by their presence, and their deeds, has been converted to purposes that an old barn might answer equally as well. The munificent policy by which the English government have been latterly distinguished, has changed this ancient stronghold, so replete with records of which England might boast, into a common warehouse for the lumber and rubbish of the ordnance department. To subject the gloomy old pile to such vile uses, is like baiting a chained lion with lapdogs—the sport is as unworthy those engaged in it as the unfortunate victim.

Light is now excluded from those elegant apartments, which once blazed with all the magnificence of a court, for powder has usurped the place of kings, and the gay courtiers have been banished by lead. Those luxurious chambers, where many an antique dandy has capered "to the lascivious pleasings of a lute," are now stowed with the bales and barrels of government. The spider weaves his web where floated the gorgeous tapestry of other days. And the silence of those lofty corridors, which once echoed the busy hum of a royal residence, is now interrupted only by the gambols of rats that have taken advantage of the solitude.

In a country where they profess to respect every thing old, and where any thing would be idolized that dates back to William the Conqueror; among a nation who estimate the merits of men and wine only by the date of their family and the time of its vintage, its antiquity alone should have protected the Tower. But money is stronger than time among them. Nothing can be so ennobled by the latter that the former cannot purchase its honor. No national monument is respected when money is either to be made or saved by its desecration. To avoid the investment of a few thousand pounds in proper arsenals and storehouses, the stately palace of England's best kings has been subjected to its present degradation. Economy is as honorable in the administration of governments, as it is desirable in the management of domestic affairs. But are such petty savings becoming the wealth and dignity of a great nation? Does not such extreme frugality sink into parsimony? Is it not more sordid than prudent? disgraceful rather than honorable?

The strength of these massive walls and frowning towers—the hoary survivors of eight centuries—are only admirable in their eyes as a safe means of protection to the public stores. The airy turrets, and picturesque beauty of the White Tower—rich in the lore that Englishmen should love to cherish—only appear interesting in their eyes when they calculate the probable amount they may make by their exhibition. Having found that the White Tower could be made more profitable as a showroom than as a warehouse, they have gotten up an exhibition, very similar, in the manner of conducting it, to that of the Abbey. They charge sixpence—only admit visitors in parties—and leave them at the mercy of rude guides, just as they do at the Westminster. The only difference is that the parties must consist of *fourteen* persons, instead of seven, and that the guides dress in red, instead of black.

A stranger, on entering the lowering gateway, is stopped at the ticket-office. "Sixpence, sir," remarks the doorkeeper, as he hands him his ticket. The gentleman pays his sixpence, and is moving off, when he is stopped by "Perhaps you would like to see the Crown Jewels and Regalia?" "Yes, of course; I wish to see every thing that is shown." "Oh, very well; sixpence more, please," as he hands out another ticket. The visitor makes a new application to his pocket, and again moves on, when the doorkeeper once more shouts after him, "We have excellent descriptions of the Tower, will you take one?" The visitor stalks solemnly back, and is greeted with, "*Only* sixpence, sir," as he receives his book, and pays the required amount. "First door on the right," observes the ticket-seller, as he turns to a new applicant. This sharp individual, presiding over the financial department of the Tower, appears to practice on the homœopathic principle of making his charges in infinitesimally broken doses, to adapt them, no doubt, to the constitutional peculiarities of his nation, which would revolt at the enormous charge of a whole shilling, unless artfully divided into sixpences. After entering "the first door on the right," our visitor has nothing more to amuse him, until the fourteen are assembled, except to criticise the somewhat theatrical costume of the guides, who are here dignified by the title of "Warders," and to ruminate upon the very honorable uses the English people make of the advantages their ancestors have conferred upon them: Westminster and the Tower for instance. How can he entertain very exalted notions of England's honor, when he here sees it bartered for so trifling a consideration? How can he respect Englishmen, when they have ceased to respect themselves?

In paying sixpence to see the Tower, is a man not apt, in spite of himself, to estimate the national character at the same cheap rate?

But to the dress of the warders. It consists of a surcoat of red merino, elaborately dashed with black velvet, and set off by a low-crowned black hat, of outlandish appearance, which is said to complete the identical uniform of yeomen of the guard, under Henry VIII. Their honorable employers certainly displayed rare discrimination in rigging out the warders in the livery of the tyrant, when they placed them on their present dirty duty. The arbitrary power, which compels the nation and her guests to pay a paltry sum for visiting public property, like the Tower, possesses all the meanness, though destitute of the boldness, which characterized Henry's outrages against the people. The surcoats of the gentlemen warders are rather scant, but certain I am that the same quantity of merino never covered an equal amount of ignorance and insolence as is stowed away beneath each blushing uniform.

English officials however, are invariably impertinent, from the policeman at the corner to the minister in Downing-street. They all appear so impressed by the importance of their positions, that they look down with a sort of lofty scorn upon the rest of creation, and appearing really deluded into the belief that they confer a favor on the people by accepting their offices, they pocket their money, and treat them as inferiors, with the coolest possible condescension imaginable. They seem strangely to mistake their functions, when, in becoming the servants of the public, they consider it incumbent on them to play its tyrants. A stranger might suppose them paid to insult rather than oblige those whom necessity brings into contact with them. Englishmen themselves avoid them, and urgent indeed must be the occasion which could induce them to brave the unbearable presumption of these insolent servitors. Clothed in a little brief authority, it is really amazing what an amount of arrogance and rudeness a lowborn Englishman manages suddenly to get up. In entering upon the duties of an office, however contemptible, they appear to imagine that they have become integral portions of a haughty government, and must be feared and fawned upon accordingly. In donning the badge of office, they always assume the mysterious official air, which, with bent brows and abstracted gaze, is intended to intimate to the uninitiated how deeply they are immersed in the affairs of the nation. Even when his sole duty is to give such information to the public as may be required, the meanest official will reply to a civil question with monosyllabic tartness, as if his private meditations had been unwarrantably intruded upon. Indeed, none of them ever condescend to attend to the business of their offices, without a supercilious air of doing a favor instead of duty, which they are well paid to perform. From the clerk at the railway dépôt to the secretary of the office where a man is compelled to go about passports, the same laconic rudeness is observable. I conceive it to be the duty of a government, which so frequently demands attendance at its public offices, so to regulate them as to protect not only its own subjects, but strangers, from the insults of these impertinent hirelings.

The party of fourteen have been assembled. We are drawn up in a line, and undergo a brief inspection as to tickets, &c., when our fat leader, in red, places himself at the head of the column, and we immediately take up the line of march, double-quick time, for the White Tower. We make no halts on the way to admire the gloomy portal—the massive walls, fourteen feet thick, and the deep fosse, which is now dry; we pause not to wonder at the ponderous oak doors, and rusty portcullis of the Traitor's Gate, but are hurried on more like a file of prisoners for the dungeons of the Tower, than a party of interesting tourists, each one of whom had paid his sixpence, and was consequently curious to examine all that presented itself. We enter the White Tower when the real animation of the proceedings seems but just commenced. Our guide becomes marvellously lively in his movements, and, considering the tower-like rotundity of his solid person, he performed feats almost miraculous. How he managed to keep in him the requisite quantity of wind for his brisk trot, and unceasing flow of the flat jokes and stale information with which he regaled us, really seemed to me one of the most curious things I witnessed in the Tower. Ours was a breath-taking speed. In fact, if each one of us, on entering, had been mounted on one of the plethoric-looking horses composing the line of equestrian figures in the armory, we could not have galloped through faster, or seen less, than under the direction of our corpulent guide. In our helter-skelter, pell-mell, devil-take-the-hindmost sort of race, there was a prolonged flash of armor, swords, and lances—a hideous vision of instruments of torture, and droll implements for rendering war more terrible, by mangling its victims,—and indistinct phantoms of blocks and axes,—all dancing about Sir Walter Raleigh's prison apartment in inexplicable confusion, when we were suddenly put out, as having seen a sixpence worth of the Tower.

Why is it, I demand again, if government will persist in charging visitors to public places of celebrity, that they will not charge enough to render the style of getting up the exhibition more in accordance with the interest of the objects, and in a way altogether to dispense with these nuisances of guides who at present infest them? Or if it is essential to their own comfort to have some official about the premises, why not make the price of admission sufficiently great to command the services of men of intelligence, who might materially assist and enliven the visitor's examination of the objects of curiosity? Station these persons in the armory of the White Tower, for instance, and allow the intelligent visitor some opportunity of pausing amidst so many ancient and curious things which he finds worthy of study. What time has he during the peripatetic discourse of nonsense with which he is now inflicted, to examine with attention a single object, or indulge, however cursorily, his natural curiosity? Our warder seemed equally put out in his rigmarole by pauses and questions; so he paid no sort of attention to either. He never stopped or even caught his breath till he had gotten through with us and his story together. How remarkably instructive, as well as interesting, he succeeded in making himself, one might judge from the following example: "Ladies and gentlemen, this is a suit of *h*armor worn by 'Enry the *H*eighth." Both pieces of information happened to be equally superfluous, as the name of Henry VIII. was written above the figure in fair Roman characters, and the streaks of gold were very plainly visible at different points of the harness. Yet he delivered himself with all the pompous volubility with which he incidentally made the startling announcement to the company, "That the 'orse of King 'Enry was *h*actually much given to *h*eating *h*oats to *h*excess."

But so long as the English government is directed by the present catchpenny policy, it will be too greedy to abolish charges altogether at Westminster, St. Paul's and the Tower, and too timid to make any alterations in the manner of exhibiting them. The guides, at all the places, are indispensable allies in the present system. By abolishing these irresistible propellers, pauses would inevitably occur, which, by allowing a visitor some opportunity of gratifying his curiosity, might rob the exchequer of an additional sixpence, by lessening the probability of his returning for a second visit. No such danger must be incurred, and the guides are conseqeuntly kept in active requisition. It is now an important part of their duty, like the donkey-boys of Egypt, to keep the party at top speed, to prevent the possibility of a visitor's seeing any thing with sufficient distinctness to make him feel satisfied with a single visit. His introductory rush is merely intended to increase his desire for future inspections. As much as I disliked to become a victim of so miserable a conspiracy, I was compelled to yield, and as fast as I was ejected, I went back, paid another sixpence, and waited the assembling of a new fourteen, till I was able to form some conception of the White Tower. It was my only chance, and by examining a little each time, I at last became somewhat familiar with the intensely interesting objects in the horse armory, and the apartment occupied by Sir Walter Raleigh, during his long imprisonment. But what an insufferable bore a man is forced to submit to, because the English government have not the liberality to throw open these celebrated places to the public free of charge, and yet are wanting in the moral courage to charge as much for one long visit, as a half-dozen short ones cost.

Englishmen universally object to the haste with which an American takes his meals; a dinner, according to their authority, is something to be lingered over with toying fondness; but they dispatch the refined mental enjoyment of Westminster, St. Paul's, and the Tower, with a celerity astounding even to us go-ahead Americans. Their extreme deliberation at the dinner-table, and the excessive rapidity with which they hurry through the intellectual feasts spread at these celebrated places, decisively indicate how vastly more important they consider the gratification of the belly than the mind. It is, however, a happy illustration of the character of the people. The leopard cannot change his spots, nor the Ethiopian his skin. Their innocent ignorance, that a man could derive any sort of pleasure from mere thought and association, would be perhaps a much better apology for their unseemly manner of exhibiting sacred spots, than the *cheapness* of the price of admission. They find it difficult to realize that a man can ever require less substantial food than roast-beef, or that he could long for more ethereal inspiration than a bottle of porter. They appear to think that the mind need possess no higher cultivation, than to appreciate an artistically cooked dish; and that it requires no more intensive knowledge than to find the way to market. Between the dinner-table and the market-house, an Englishman's highest aspirations continually wander; he has no hope, and knows no fear beyond them. All other scenes and plans are mere accessories to these, which may be safely pronounced the *faci* of the ellipse in which rolls his existence.

Better would it be for the honor of the English Nation, if they had been born in the degradation, as they are endued with the propensities, of the modern Egyptians. Brighter far would be their reputation if they had been reared to cry "backsheesh" to each passing stranger, rather than degrade those monuments of glory, received from their ancestors, into lasting memorials of their own shame. A people that have grown up in rags and ignorance, are pardonable for the grovelling instincts of wretchedness. But what palliation can be offered of the conduct of Great Britain? To a nation, whose ostentatious piety sends missionaries into the remotest quarters of the globe, even charity refuses an apology, for the habitual desecration of her churches.

The very advantages which wealth and power have conferred upon her, are witnesses, trumpet-tongued, against her baseness. Is such an example to the rest of the world worthy the enlightened head of civilization in the middle of the nineteenth century? Does the golden or the copper age reign in England, where pelf is dearer than honor, and pence are eagerly received in exchange for reputation? The memorials of munificence, left them by their fathers, have, in their hands, become the testimony which convicts them of meanness.

Want often reduces pride to lowliness, and necessity will sometimes drive the noblest natures to the unworthiest practices. It would be lucky for England if she had been unfortunate; poverty might have proved her salvation. But with wealth, far surpassing that of every other country in the universe, and with all the education and refinement which that wealth could bestow, she disgraces the high position which circumstances have conferred upon her, in mere wantonness of corruption. Their besotted nature would excuse the Hottentots, even in the eyes of the most censorious, for bartering away the priceless mementoes of the past glories of their country. We do but pity the ignorance of the boor, who sold for a few florins the almost invaluable diamond lost by Charles the Bold at the battle of Granson; but what feeling of sympathy can we reserve for a civilized nation, anxious to sell that "immediate jewel of their souls," their own good name? What anathemas do we not feel tempted to heap on the heads of those daily engaged in the traffic of that "purest treasure mortal times afford"—"spotless reputation."

No collection of curiosities in the world better deserves its name, than the Zoological Gardens of London. In the number and variety of animals, they greatly surpass the far-famed *Jardin des Plantes* of Paris. No more extensive or curious field, could be presented to the study of the naturalist. Every zone has been made to contribute some of the rarest denizens of its savage forests. Every species of animal, from the white bear of the polar regions, to the giraffe of the tropics, is so arranged in the same extensive inclosures, as to develope more of their native peculiarities than in any other menagerie in the world. Here we find the seal diving for his fishy meal, the hippopotamus lazily lolling in his quagmire, and the elephant as quietly suckling her young, as if none of them had ever ceased to roam in their own particular element. By the exquisitely artistic arrangements, which wealth and science have united to make, the tiger is cheated of his jungle, and the lioness rears her cubs as regularly as if raging in her own native deserts. It would be impossible, by the most elaborate description, to afford a correct idea of the taste and elegance displayed, as well in the arrangement of the beasts, as in the adornment of the gardens themselves. We find cranes slowly wading their ponds, or eagerly watching for the game that lurks at its bottom. Here all the rarer and more exquisite varieties of water-fowl are seen, with their downy broods, gayly swimming in lakes, so naturally wild, and wildly beautiful, as to make them forget the solitary lagoons 'tis their nature to frequent. It would require a man of scientific attainments in natural history, properly to name even the classes of the various beasts, birds, and reptiles, composing this stupendous collection. All the numerous exhibitions I had previously seen, served to give me but a poor idea of the extent and interest of this. The gardens themselves, which are very extensive, are rendered charming by the exquisite arrangement of mingled grass-plots, trees, and flowers, which enhance the beauty of the place, as much as the interest of the exhibition. Every thing is beautiful, every thing grand and munificent, except the ruling spirit of the place. The Zoological Gardens, like Westminster, St. Paul's, and the Tower, are under the control of the English Government, and are subjected to the same degradation. "The trail of the serpent is over them all." The magnificence displayed in the arrangement of the gardens, acts like a microscope upon the meanness of reducing the nation to the condition of a common showman: it serves to expose its deformity in all its hideousness. If the Zoological Gardens really be a national exhibition, the nation certainly possesses the right to their gratuitous enjoyment. But no! the government would then be deprived of their most acceptable occupation. They basely use, without permission, the authority of the people's name, to make them sharers in a disgrace for which they alone are responsible. A stranger in paying his shilling for admission into an exhibition, which has been dubbed "*national*," in contradistinction from another in the Surrey Gardens, very naturally suspects that the people are partners in this contemptible transaction. But he learns with astonishment that they are fellow-sufferers from this degrading imposition. Many countries have failed properly to remunerate their leaders for the blessings they have conferred upon them; but the English people are compelled to pay for the ignominy, with which their despotic rulers have loaded them.

How marked is the contrast existing between the course of England, and the jealous care with which France preserves her national integrity. In Paris every institution of learning and science, all galleries of fine arts, and places of amusement, except the theatres, are thrown generously open to the public. In making them *national*, France has made them free. She justly considers it a stain upon her honor, to degrade her great public institutions into mean sources of gain. She rightly believes it beneath the dignity of a powerful government, to demand pecuniary rewards for services rendered to its subjects. She seems happily aware of the distinction between the munificence of a nation, and the necessities of an individual. She appears to feel that though a citizen may get up an exhibition, without loss of honor, a nation cannot play the showman, without disgrace. There is no branch of science—no description of literature, which a man is desirous of pursuing. that he cannot accomplish, free of charge, in the celebrated institutions of Paris. The enlightened spirit, which erected the colleges, has nobly thrown open their doors to all classes of citizens. The public galleries, enriched by master-pieces of all the celebrated painters and sculptors of the world, are gratuitously opened to the humblest individual, whose taste may incline to the enjoyment of works of art. There is no learned investigation, which a man may have occasion to make, in which he will not be facilitated, without cost, by the intelligent officials, whom the government has stationed in the public libraries. And every grotesque Frenchman is allowed to enjoy, as long as he pleases, the antics of the monkeys in the "*Jardine des Plantes*" without previously paying a franc for admission at the gate.

Would not the English do well to take a few hints from their neighbors, in their management of the Zoological Gardens? If the government of the wealthiest country in the world cannot really afford to lose the trifling revenue, arising from this public promenade, why not farm the gardens out to a company, instead of stooping to play the showman themselves? Such an arrangement would necessarily involve a division of profits, which the sordid nature of Englishmen could not be persuaded to submit to, though they should be allowed to reserve the lion's share of the spoils. But the genius of the English government appears so happily adapted to the routine of a petty showman, it would be a pity not to go through it. They are conscious of excelling in small exhibitions, and consequently delight in them. From the Fire Tower, to the Great Show of all nations, their pre-eminence in this line is truly remarkable. They have the despicable vanity to feel proud of this accomplishment, and are eager for its display. They seem to think, that success in this *very* honorable ambition culls fresh laurels for the wreathes that Shakspeare has woven, and

Milton twined; they seem deluded into the belief that the inimitable skill they display in twopenny exhibitions, adds to the glory of the nation for which Nelson struggled and Wellington fought.

But the apex of national turpitude is the charge of sixpence for the privilege of visiting Chelsea Hospital, for old soldiers. According to the established rules, at Chelsea, the payer of sixpence is shown through the refectories, the dormitories, and smoking-rooms of the veterans—this is all well enough. But when it is remembered, that the payment of this paltry coin confers the right of invading the sick wards; of disturbing the suffering invalids, by impertinent questions, and rude examinations of themselves and their beds, the hardest heart is moved.

Even charity, which should purely shine in the soul, like dew in flowers, becomes in the hands of Englishmen a black-grained spot on their honor. Grudging the pittance of a shilling a month to the weather-beaten remnants of these once sturdy defenders of their country—the government basely make their wounds and their hardships a catchpenny show for the multitude. Any nation of atheists might make the churches, built in the hated days of belief, a source of profit;—sordid barbarians might degrade the wonderful monuments of their more civilized ancestors, by charging visitors to see them,—but to drag from their lowly retreat these maimed and shattered victims of national ambition, to be stared and wondered at, like caged beasts, is an outrage against humanity, that even savages would shrink from. This is a deed kindly reserved, as the crowning glory of the enlightened Britons of the nineteenth century.

Nell Gwin, who suggested, and her Royal Profligate who founded this asylum for old soldiers, would have been shocked by such a proposition, embarrassed as they often were in their circumstances. For "pretty witty Nelly" and the Merry Monarch were not wholly lost to all the kindlier feelings of the human heart, reckless as the careers of both had been. Nell was truly charitable, and Charles was so, after a fashion of his own, great as their faults undoubtedly were; and either one of them would have scorned so revolting a means to raise money, however sadly in want of it hey might have been. It remained for the boastful countrymen of Chaucer and Spenser, Shakspeare and Milton, to commit, under the name of *charity*,—an outrage, which they alone were capable of conceiving. They may at least exult in the consciousness that theirs is no ordinary baseness. If it be their ambition to excel in this quality, they certainly have reason to feel satisfied with their success.

The valor with which these disabled veterans had, in their youth, defended the government, ought surely to have secured to them a quiet refuge for their age. But past services are never remembered by the heartless, 'tis only the hope of future profit that quickens their charity. Coming into the world as proper food for powder, these poor old fellows should have felt only too much delighted to compound with fate, by becoming inmates of the Chelsea Hospital, instead of some ditch on the Continent. Besides, government had given over fifteen millions of dollars to the Duke of Wellington,—and they should have felt more than satisfied in hearing of the rewards of their commander. What more could they expect from their country? The obscurity of their origin had placed them beyond the pale of British charity—cringing to the great—obsequious to the high—the dwarfed souls of Englishmen have no wide-extending sympathy for the humble—no soothing pity for the lowly. In their eyes poverty is crime,—and wretchedness deserves its sufferings for having been guilty of the sin of being poor.

Our be-sixpenced traveller flies in disgust from the Zoological Gardens to Chatsworth. But how suddenly are all his magnificent notions of luxurious profusion, and generous hospitality put to flight, when he is met at the gate by the same significant extension of the hand, which experience has taught him means no polite welcome, but a new demand on his purse. It requires but a few weeks' residence in the country to convince him, that an Englishman rarely ever extends his hand to a stranger, unless it is to put it into his pocket. But this all classes make it a rule to do, as often, and as deeply, as the loosest interpretation of the laws will permit without their incurring the danger of being indicted as pickpockets.

I never was able fully to realize what splendid triumphs wealth was capable of, when directed by taste, till I visited Chatsworth. It must seem wonderful, even to those accustomed to the profusion of monarchical governments, that a subject should dwell in a palace so gorgeous. Chatsworth is worthy of the enterprise which has constructed a branch railroad leading to Rowsley, for the accommodation of the crowds of visitors, eager to see the magnificence of the mansion, and wander amidst the surpassing beauties of the grounds. The showy magnificence of Chatsworth and Blenheim, and the gloomy grandeur of Warwick and Alnwick castles, serve to remind us, like the glittering shell of the tortoise, what worthless and insignificant animals often inhabit the most splendid mansions.

In all my wanderings I have never seen any thing which approached this beautiful seat of the Duke of Devonshire. The rigid avenues, and spruce flower-beds of Versailles—the floral charms of the Italian villas, and even the varied attractions of Windsor and Hampton Court themselves, must yield in beauty to the countless fascinations of Chatsworth. To throw open so superb an estate for the free enjoyment of the public, seems most munificent. But this munificence sinks into meanness, when it is remembered that His Grace receives a fee of admission from his visitors. Such a proceeding on the part of a nobleman, whose income exceeds $5,000 a day, must satisfactorily demonstrate to every mind, that though an Englishman may have the pride to attempt a magnificent scheme, he lacks the generosity to carry it out. Ostentation suggested to the Duke a course as princely as his income, but that cohesive sympathy existing between a Briton's fingers and ha'pence, chafed parsimony into reminding him, that he might *appear* profuse and yet save money by the operation. In his eagerness to adopt the suggestion, he forgot the first principle in moral philosophy, that the intention with which a deed is done, and not the deed itself, determines its degree of virtue. In his course at Chatsworth, he debases the spirit, whilst he retains the form of a noble action. This regal display of hospitality is made a cloak for the low cunning of a showman. For he is well aware, that this flaming announcement of Chatsworth's being thrown open to the public, like the charity of Jenny Lind, is well calculated to increase the general curiosity. He confirms his nationality, by being mean whilst professing to be sumptuous. He pretends to open his gorgeous palace for the amusement of the public, but takes good care to station a doorkeeper to collect the fees of admission to its different departments. And yet he would no doubt be very reluctant frankly to confess to the world, that although he had the vanity to affect liberality, he was too penurious to bear the expense of it. Like the ostrich, he sticks his head in the sand, and imagines himself in the profoundest concealment. He seems deluded by the hope that the basest counterfeit, emanating from a personage of the Duke of Devonshire's rank, must pass current—and that this affected display of public hospitality must inevitably establish his reputation for generosity. Happy in the fancied success of a deception, which he has only been able to practise upon himself, this silly noble struts about with the airs and pretension of the petted favorite of the kingdom. He clearly manifests the opinion he entertains of the intelligence of the English people, in supposing them capable of being imposed on by so shallow an artifice. The melancholy folly of such vanity can only be injurious to himself. People pity him too much to despise him.

I mean not to intimate that any portion of the large amounts collected at the doors of Chatsworth actually goes into the pockets of His Grace. But they are, nevertheless, remarkably convenient in defraying the expense of a large household of servants. The Duke owns besides Chatsworth, Hardwick Hall, Bolton Abbey, Lismore Castle, Devonshire House, and Chiswick, the large establishments of all of which magnificent seats must be maintained in a style becoming his rank and enormous fortune. The opportunity, afforded by the unsurpassed attractions of Chatsworth to get rid of the expense of one of them, was much too tempting to be resisted by a native of His Grace's country—he therefore sullies a noble name to add a few paltry pounds to a fortune which is eventually to be enjoyed by strangers. No foreigner would hesitate at half-a-crown, and not many Englishmen would grumble at sixpence, as a gratuity to the different servants showing them through the house and grounds—so trifling a remuneration only becomes offensive when it is demanded as a right. No one could consider the amount oppressive: on the contrary, all must acknowledge the show to be a remarkably cheap one; but 'tis the sordid principle that so offends every enlightened feeling. The idea of a private gentleman, of wealth and rank, deriving a profit from the exhibition of his grounds, must be equally revolting to all classes. In such a course there is so glaring a violation of propriety, that the meanest cannot fail to discover it.

The highly acquisitive disposition of the Duke appears to be a birthright; the Countess of Shrewsbury, the founder of the family, having turned her great beauty to some account, in marrying four rich husbands, and prevailing on all of them to settle their fine estates on her, and her heirs for ever. In this judicious arrangement, the large fortunes of Robert Barlow of Barlow, Sir William Cavendish, Sir William St. Loe, and the Earl of Shrewsbury, were all, by the fascinations of Miss Elizabeth Hardwick, amalgamated into one overgrown estate, for the future Dukes of Devonshire. She had an heir by Sir William Cavendish, from whom the family are descended. William the fourth Earl of Devonshire was created a Duke by William III., as a reward for his treachery to the reigning sovereign; and the present Duke seems to consider it impossible farther to degrade a title acquired in such a way.

But the unworthiness of its owner cannot mar the unrivalled elegance of Chatsworth. Ogres have often before been known to dwell in enchanted castles of fairy proportions. The exterior of the mansion is rendered impressive by a graceful façade of Ionic columns; its interior is crowded with every thing that luxury could suggest, or wealth supply. Its ceilings are adorned with the brilliant frescoes of Verrio, and Sir James Thornhill; its rooms of state are hung with the finest specimens of Goblin tapestry. The walls of its picture galleries are filled with works by the old masters; and among them is Landseer's famous Bolton Abbey, exhibiting more breathing animation, and fuller of genius than any modern picture I have ever seen. Here, too, are to be met with many exquisite specimens of female loveliness, in the peculiar floating and voluptuous style of Sir Thomas

Lawrence. In the elegant collection of statuary may be numbered pieces by Canova, Thorwaldsen, Westmacott, and Tanerani, the best of living Italian artists. Opening from this exquisite gallery is the orangery, made poetically attractive by the rare exotics, statues, and birds, that divide the attention. Many of the superb apartments are rendered doubly interesting by the extraordinany carvings in wood, by Gibbons. It is wonderful to study the exquisite grace, and lightness, which he has imparted to his fruit and flowers. The turn of a leaf or the delicacy of a flower are as divinely given, as if things cut in wood were not proverbial comparisons for all that is stiff and ungainly. It would be impossible to conceive of the inimitable naturalness which he has succeeded in throwing into the relaxed limbs and drooping wings of dead hares and partridges—even the distended gills of fish are represented, with a delicate success, that painting itself would fail to equal.

But the grounds present the highest claims to beauty. In no country in the world do the trees seem more coolly shady, or does the grass look greener than in England. The humid climate appears peculiarly adapted to the development of all their beauties in these greatest ornaments of nature. A man cannot know the delicious charms of the English greensward—so fresh, so dark, so closely cut and carefully swept that it may, even in prose, be said to look like a green velvet carpet—till he has rolled on it, under the thick shade of the drooping elms. A poet would fail to do it justice in his happiest description. The grassplots of Chatsworth are tastefully broken by lakes, fountains, and flower-gardens, and from these you could wander away down the shady avenues of fine old trees, whose rustling leaves would whisper to you nothing but the poetic legends of the past. The luxurious softness of this portion of the landscape is strongly contrasted with the wild, almost savage nature of the scenery beyond. From a lofty crag in the distance, made picturesque by crowning firs and rocky pinnacles, a waterfall foams and tumbles with the roar and precipitation of some mountain torrent in Switzerland. Still farther off is a small cascade, whose shadowy stream, undulating as it pours down the bare side of the cliff, looks like some delicate veil of silver tissue, gently stirred by the lazy summer winds. The soft realms of beauty, in which greensward and flowers contend for the mastery, cease at the banks of the river, which, on the other side from the waterfall, winds in graceful curves far as the eye can reach through the sunny meadow-land. The farther banks of the silent stream slowly rise into gentle elevations, shaded here and there with clumps of scrubby oaks, beneath whose shadow crouch whole herds of dozing deer. When wearied with this warmly glowing picture, the visitor turns his footsteps towards the famous conservatory, of which everybody has heard so much, and passing beneath some thick trees he suddenly finds himself in the loneliest of wild scenes. Huge masses of rocks, now gray and moss-grown, and often half concealed with flowering mountain shrubs, have been so artfully piled, that one is reluctant to doubt that nature has placed them there. The effect of suddenly issuing from a spot, smiling with the rarest cultivation, into a scene so rugged, was delightful in the extreme. He pauses to watch the merry gambols of a noisy little brook, that comes bounding and pitching towards him as it chafes into foam against the rocks that obstruct its course. As it nears the spot where he stands, it rolls more calmly over its shiny pebble bed, muttering its complaints against the roughness of its recent encounter with the rocks, in a low babble full of melody. It steals on through banks of freshest verdure, gemmed with wild violets, whose perfume fills the air; its murmurs cease, its course is almost stilled, and it lingers as if enamored of so sweet a lurking-place. Then it goes creeping and peering among the tall water-lilies, whose nodding blooms of white seem laughingly to reprove the truant stream. Again dashing away among the projecting rocks, whose mossy points are more than half concealed by the purple clusters of the rhododendrons, and the delicate flowers of the mountain laurel, our brook goes rejoicing on its way, skipping, wheeling, and dodging, as if in a game of hide and seek with the delighted traveller. Once more it calmly glides into the broad open space, silent, as if in the ineffable joy of being so near the end of its varied pilgrimage. Slowly it moves along, and finally sinks upon the bosom of the expectant lake, without disturbing the glassy stillness of its surface, which is only broken by some playful carp, that occasionally bounds into the soft summer air.

The great conservatory is perhaps the greatest wonder of the whole establishment, although the one we are most familiar with. On his way thither the visitor passes innumerable fountains of various designs; among them is the highest jet of water in Europe, and a fantastic weeping willow of bronze, which scatters around the most refreshing showers, from every leaf and twig. He must also pause to admire the grand cascade, which, issuing from a temple-like structure on the hill, rolls down a long succession of marble steps, dashing its spray upon the antique vases and statues with which they are adorned. The conservatory, which previous to the erection of the Crystal Palace was the largest structure of its kind in the world, has a carriage road through its midst, and measures 276 feet one way, and 123 the other. It looks like two vast domes of rounding oblong, rather than circular form, piled one upon the other—has 67 feet of height in its central arched roof and a span of 70 feet, and contains more than 70,000 square feet of glass. In its vast collection are assembled all the rarer and more beautiful plants from the sunny climes of the East and

South. The bristling cocoanut, the clustering banana, and the unsightly date, are the stateliest specimens of these curious representatives of the tropics. Does it not seem strange that a man, residing amidst a scene of surpassing grandeur and beauty, should fail to imbibe some elevation of spirit from surrounding nature? Does it not appear extraordinary that a man, dwelling in a spot of such fairy loveliness, should retain, and indulge the most grovelling instincts of human nature's lowest grade?

Up to as late a date as 1834, the English game laws existed in a form to embody all the rigor and injustice of the Forest Laws, presenting but this solitary difference, that the former were maintained for the amusement of four hundred tyrants, whilst the latter were enacted for the gratification of a single despot. By the extraordinary legislation of these titled lawgivers of England, *game* was rendered more sacred and inviolate than property. These sporting Lycurguses arbitrarily selected certain beasts of the field and fowls of the air, and made it highly criminal in any "base-born person" "to kill them, or eat them, or buy them, or sell them, or carry them, or to have in his possession any engine or instrument, by which they might be slain, maimed, or injured." Nobody but a *qualified* person could amuse himself by a shot at a partridge or hare. A rich merchant or manufacturer might own land, and give employment to thousands of laborers, but his wealth being *base*, he enjoyed no right to interfere with the aristocratic pleasures of his noble betters. Woodcocks, pheasants, partridges, and hares, were delicacies which he was forbidden even to taste. The sages of the King's Bench finally ruled that "a qualified person might take out a tradesman, stock-broker, clothier, attorney, surgeon, or other *inferior* person, to beat the bushes, and see a hare killed, without being liable to to penalty." But woe to the unlucky wight who took a private shot on his own account, but could not attach some noble title to his name. Nobility was a qualification absolutely essential to a man's becoming a shooter. All unqualified persons were not only denied the amusement of killing game, but they were not allowed the privilege of buying of those who were. The "game" flavor of partridges and hares was not to be tainted, by passing through the *unqualified* hands of chapmen and higglers. Their aristocratic qualities were not to be destroyed by being retailed, like ale and dipped candles, by tradespeople. "Victuallers, poulterers, pastry cooks, and other mean persons should not carry game nor have it in possession." If an unqualified person were suspected of having game, or any dog, gun, or snare for killing or wounding it, his house might be searched, and if any net, or snare, pheasant, partridge, fish, fowl, or other game were found, the offender might be forthwith carried before a justice, and fined, or sent to the House of Correction, and there whipped, and kept to hard labor." "If a man only happened to spoil or tread on an egg of a partridge, pheasant, mallard, teal, bittern, or heron, he was fined or imprisoned." "But if he went forth in the night for the third time, with the full intent of catching an aristocrat bird, coney, or other game, he was transported beyond the seas for seven years." Notwithstanding these absurd restrictions, and severe enactments against the disturbance of privileged birds, by unqualified persons, it was discovered by a committee of the House of Lords in 1828, that game was as regular an article for sale in all the markets of London, as any other commodity. One salesman alone sold 500 head of game in a week. It was impossible for their Lordships longer to pretend ignorance of a fact they had long been aware of. They therefore found it necessary to make the astounding discovery, that the noble Lords themselves must be the principal offenders in this illicit but profitable traffic in game.

Game had been up to this period like the national honor —something for whose preservation every idle upstart felt himself personally responsible. All classes of society united in regarding with becoming horror the unpardonable sin of poaching; and the antipathy to poachers was as universal, among the descendants of Mother Eve by the English line, as the hatred of snakes is supposed to be natural to her posterity generally. Not even the example of the illustrious Bard of Avon could elevate the nocturnal forages of the poacher, into being placed in the same category with the dashing exploits of Captain McHeath, or bold Dick Turpin. Faithful serving-men, in expectancy of pensions, ingratiated themselves with their masters, by midnight prowlings after poachers. Ignorant country magistrates displayed their zealous inefficiency in committing all suspected persons for trial. Rollicking Squires, the Sir Rotgut Wildfires of the country, won easy reputations as public-spirited individuals, by their blustering protection of "game;" and the county assizes never considered their docket complete, unless some unfortunate vagabond had been transported for poaching. The genius of the English nation was emphatically opposed to the crime,—and the solitary poacher was pursued with that sort of vindictive enthusiasm which centuries before had characterized the wolf-hunt. Is it possible to suppose, under such circumstances, that the large quantities of game, daily sold in the markets of London, could have been supplied by the stray poachers, whom keen-eyed prosecution had allowed to escape transportation? It was an absurdity that occurred to the obtuse understandings of their Lordships themselves. They stood convicted of the violation of the laws they had passed, expressly to break, in order to secure the privilege of the exclusive sale of game.

These noble outlaws, who professed to regard a tradesman as a more honest, but much less reputable personage than a highwayman, and would have shrunk from an imputation of trade, as from an accusation of picking a pocket—were yet detected in this peddling traffic under circumstances which should have caused most of them to make voyages to Botany Bay, if the laws had been as strictly enforced against rich offenders, as ordinary poachers. Game was found to constitute a surreptitious branch of huckstering, much too profitable to their Lordships to be shared with plebeian rivals, so long as the monopoly could be enjoyed by stealth. But when their felonious practices were exposed, each noble hypocrite rolled his eyes in horror at the extent to which poaching had been carried, and began to fear that the Game Laws, like Draco's bloody code, defeated themselves by their own severity. Notwithstanding their well-assumed surprise, that daring outlaws enough existed in England habitually to violate laws so stringent, they were overwhelmed by the consciousness that every Briton, though silent, was convinced that they themselves were the violators of these laws. All England was aware that, in order to secure their dirty gains, they endangered the liberty of unsuspecting victuallers, and inoffensive poulterers—whose position did not place them above the laws—by making them accomplices in their petty-larceny villany. The profits were enticing, but the odium was oppressive: they therefore became willing to share the first to shuffle off a portion of the last. Though endued with all the worst propensities of the common poacher, without that apology which want and misery afforded him for breaking the laws, to prevent starvation, they showed themselves destitute of that intrepidity of action, which inspires an involuntary sort of respect, even for an outlaw. Base enough to profit by unlawful practices, they became yet more despicable, when they timidly thrust innocent people between themselves and responsibility. I feel an increased contempt for a poltroon, mean enough to commit a dishonest deed, without the hardihood to brave the consequences of his own roguery. They were arrant knaves, without one mitigating circumstance to plead in their favor. Their fortunes, in placing them so far above want, should have removed them from those temptations to evil, which, when heightened by hunger, the poor must find it so difficult to resist. Nobody but an Englishman could fail justly to discriminate between the guilt of two persons, one of whom, though rich, commits theft in the mere wantonness of depravity, and the other, who steals a loaf of bread to relieve a starving family. Equity leans towards recommending the impoverished wretch to mercy, but English ethics favors the rich criminal, whose wealth should only be a stronger reason for his condemnation. Such is the mystic inviolability of money in England. Even the heinous crime of poaching, which, in a plebeian, is punished with such inexorable severity, becomes, in a Lord, "justifiable" petty larceny. One poacher is transported to a colony of felons, but the other remains comfortably at home, *to protect the game*, and deplore the proneness of the lower orders to depravity.

Detected in the violation of those laws which they themselves had passed, and for whose strict execution they pretended to be eager, the nobility could no longer pretend to maintain the ancient game code. A law was accordingly passed in 1834, allowing all owners of land to kill game themselves, and permitting them to extend the permission to other persons. When it is remembered how money is worshipped in England, and how highly prized is the privilege to shoot, we may be very certain, though the landowners might be sordid enough to rent out their sporting rights, which very many of them do, that the shooting of game was exclusively confined to the wealthier classes of the country There is a vast demand for this still half-interdicted luxury of game to be supplied in all the markets of the United Kingdom. Human nature has apparently inherited from our first parents a decided weakness for forbidden fruits; and this strong inclination is heightened in the numerous class of rich pretenders, by one equally powerful—a desire to ape the aristocracy in their fish dinners and game suppers. When the naturally voracious appetites of the 27,000,000 of Englishmen are increased by two such powerful incentives, we can but wonder how they can ever be gratified by game, though the 30,000 landowners should all take to sporting. If each one of these fortunate 30,000 should shoot, as the most zealous sportsman would, and dispose of his surplus game, it would be utterly impossible to keep up the requisite supply. It is evident that they must assail the doomed pheasants and partridges with some more powerful motive than that which actuates the keenest sportsmen. No one can doubt that, during the Fall months, these privileged landowners and their friends engage in the profitable business of wholesale poulterers, which they pursue with an intensity of ardor only known to Englishmen, when in full cry upon the scent of a sixpence. The nobility, the gentry, and their guests are the hired butchers, who annually contract to slaughter the required quantity of game.

Diana and Apollo came into the world together. The patrons of hunting and the arts are twins; and even in these modern days of degeneracy, the worshippers at the shrine of one are certain to imbibe some of the doctrines of the other. No man can be an enthusiastic sportsman without possessing some of that refinement usually produced by a cultivation of the fine arts. A real hunter, however wild in his habits, or savage in his attire, is certain to have in him some of the elements peculiar to a gentleman. Apollo has kindly imparted some of his native graces to the humblest of his twin sister's votaries.

There is something in the adventurous life of a hunter,

peculiarly adapted to the development of liberal feelings. In the wild woods he has no suspicion, and knows no distrust of his fellow-men. Eternally communing with nature, his soul must, in spite of all his disadvantages, be influenced by the grandeur of the objects around him. The vastness of the forest solitudes leaves room for the growth of all the nobler impulses of man's nature. He may be destitute of the advantages of a cultivated mind, he may have been deprived of all education from books; but he will always display that scorn of a mean action, that unthinking generosity and native courtesy, which constitute the basis of true gentility. What then must we think of these professed followers of Diana, who degrade their goddess and themselves by *selling* the sacrifices avowedly made for her altar? How few of the generous impulses of the real sportsman can actuate the man, who meanly retails the game he kills. If his tastes enabled him truly to enjoy shooting, they would protect the sport from such desecration. Even the least sordid of these Englishmen experience none of the intense excitement and joyful exhilaration of the sportsman,—they hunt, as they patronize the arts, because they consider it *gentlemanly* to do so. Shooting is deemed a peculiar propensity of the gentlemen, as the masses are wholly excluded from its indulgence, and a cockney affects the pea-jacket and hob-nailed shoes of the sportsman, as he frequents the opera with white kids and a *lorgnette*, merely because he is ambitious of appearing *fashionable*. Every gentleman goes down to the country to shoot, and so, of course, must he. But though he throws off his prim city suit, for the free-and-easy costume of the country, he cannot so readily dispose of his sordid inclinations. True to his nature, he makes a profit of his very pastimes. In obedience to the instincts of an Englishman, he degrades the noblest of manly exercises into the dirty means of petty gain. He sells the game, which he professes to shoot for excitement.

Honor is something which the whole world has united in holding sacred even when religion has tottered. It is what man most covets, and woman most admires. Honor is the attribute in which mortals most resemble gods. For honor heroes have fought and minstrels have sung. It is something to which even savages aspire with instinctive adoration. For honor men live, for honor they will die. It is more precious than poetry itself, for poets are eager to embalm it in their verse. Men cling to honor even when hopes of salvation are lost. I can conceive of a man of refined mind becoming so wicked as to sell his own soul, but I cannot imagine a noble being so debased as to part with its honor. The danger which makes the possesion of honor doubtful, makes it precious. The hero's glory has ever been regarded the highest. A soldier's honor like a woman's chastity was wont to be considered above all price. England enjoys the distinction of making it a marketable commodity. It was reserved for her to fix the rate at which it might be bought and sold. She retails the honor of soldiers according to an established tariff, which appropriately adorns all her public places. She speculates in glory as a petty hucksterer does in rancid cheese. But the many who hate, and the few who despise England, cannot exult over her baseness in selling commissions in her own army. There is a degree of degradation, which changes scorn into pity; and makes us sincerly sympathize with those whom we most heartily despise.

I extract a leaf, for the amusement of my readers, from the Army List, which is published every month by authority of the War Office. Among a vast deal of information with regard to the change of quarters, promotions and resignations, deaths and marriages of the officers, it contains the following table for the edification of the curious with regard to the *merit* promotions which have occurred. It is extremely useful to rich young gentlemen in England, who are ambitious of becoming heroes; and will I hope prove not uninteresting to my readers in America. The table is conveniently arranged in pounds, shillings and pence; it is well enough I presume to be particular even to minuteness in so important a transaction as the sale of a reputation.

PRICES OF COMMISSIONS.

RANK.	Full Price of Commissions.		Difference in value between the several Commissions in succession.		Difference in value between Full and Half Pay.		
Life Guards.	*l.*	*s.*	*l.*	*s.*	*l.*	*s.*	*d.*
Lieutenant-Colonel	7250	0	1900	0			
Major	5350	0	1850	0			
Captain	3500	0	1715	0			
Lieutenant	1785	0	525	0			
Cornet	1260	0					
Royal Regiment of Horse Guards.							
Lieutenant-Colonel	7250	0	1900	0			
Major	5350	0	1850	0			
Captain	3500	0	1900	0			
Lieutenant	1600	0	400	0			
Cornet	1200	0					
Dragoon Guards and Dragoons.							
Lieutenant-Colonel	6175	0	1600	0	1583	0	0
Major	4575	0	1350	0	1352	0	0
Captain	3225	0	2035	0	1034	3	4
Lieutenant	1190	0	350	0	632	13	4
Cornet	840	0			300	0	0
Foot Guards.							
Lieutenant-Colonel	9000	0	700	0			
Major, with Rank of Colonel	8300	0	3500	0			
Captain, ——— Lieut.-Col.	4800	0	2750	0			
Lieutenant, ——— Captain	2050	0	850	0			
Ensign, ——— Lieutenant	1200	0					
Regiments of the Line.							
Lieutenant-Colonel	4500	0	1300	0	1314	0	0
Major	3200	0	1400	0	949	0	0
Captain	1800	0	1100	0	511	0	0
Lieutenant	700	0	250	0	365	0	0
Ensign	450	0			150	0	0
Fusilier and Rifle Regiments.							
1st Lieutenant	700	0	200	0	365	0	0
2d Lieutenant	500	0			200	0	0

CHAPTER III.

THE CUSTOM-HOUSE.

THIS chapter shall be a very brief one; for though I rather courted the bores of the custom-house as a good subject for railing at the English, yet they so far surpassed all my preconceived notions of their exaggeration, that I cannot now remember them with sufficient patience to write. But I feel that no description, however glowing, could portray them in their real hideousness. To those who have experienced the annoyance, my description would seem tame and unsatisfactory, and those happy mortals who have never been subjected to the insolence of English custom-house officers, had better remain in blissful ignorance of what may be in store for them. I once attempted to show that Englishmen were instinctively insolent, but I had a very vague idea of what I was describing. I was only familiar with insolence as we read of it, and as we see it under ordinary circumstances in its embryo state. I had never met with it in its perfected development—for I had, at that time, never passed through the English custom-house. One can form some idea of the tyranny concealed amidst the vast ramifications of the English government, when its vulgar fractions in the shape of custom-house officials are so tyrannically insolent.

But as I said before, I shall not dwell upon the weary hours we were compelled to wait, jammed and crowded together in a small pen; our feet trampling on other people's toes, and our elbows in every body else's ribs. I shall not allude to the annoyance of having the little private stores of the passengers subjected to the most scrutinizing inspection. I shall not attempt to describe the provoking deliberation of these impertinent underlings in counting segars; nor the prying curiosity with which they peeped into pots of preserved ginger, and slyly tasted cans of pickled oysters. I shall pass over their manner of turning over and suspiciously snuffing a Bologna sausage, as if apprehensive of its being some infernal machine on a complicated plan, expressly imported for the destruction of the Queen. I shall not dilate upon the minuteness with which they scrutinized soiled linen, and their persevering manner of rummaging through old boots. I shall not even indulge in the solace of a caricature of our chief tormentor, a round-bellied gentleman in black, with more flesh and pomposity than even Englishmen are ordinarily encumbered with. He was very evidently above his business, and was too fat, or too blind, or too ostentatious, or perhaps all three, to read the list of passengers with that fluency desirable to impatient people. But he insisted that every thing should be conducted with formal solemnity, that was positively outrageous. Even after the tedious process of a minute examination had been passed by one happy man, he delayed the rest by clumsily fumbling for the ribbon from which dangled his glass: then he was a long time adjusting his glass to one eye, and a still longer time shutting the other, before he could begin to spell over the entire list till he came to the name below the last. Then it would have puzzled the Delphic Oracle to divine whom he meant when he did call out a name, his sight was so bad or his pronunciation so horrible. All this I shall glide over in comparative silence, but there is one little incident I must beg leave to mention.

I had provided myself with a good many books, to amuse me during the voyage, but being aware that American reprints of English works were confiscated, I had purposely avoided them. I supposed of course that English books, with *London* and my own name staring them in the face from the title-page, would pass unmolested. The books, besides having my name written in them, had been too evidently read for them to suspect me of an unlawful attempt to peddle books without a license. But they emptied my trunk and carpet bag, and proceeded to *weigh* the whole lot as a means of ascertaining their value and determining the amount of duty due on them. An admirable criterion of the English estimate of literature at the present day. I had eight pounds of books, and paid four shillings, which justifies me in concluding that the retail price of knowledge in England is sixpence a pound; somewhat cheaper than damaged herrings. To tax books at all which were evidently intended for personal amusement or instruction was barbarous, in the most extended sense of the term; but the manner of ascertaining their *value* struck me as being peculiarly English. They were piled into a large pair of scales, and weighed as we do live hogs in the West. What degradation to some of the mightiest names that England has produced. But pet copies of Shakspeare and Byron only differed in their eyes from a keg of lard in not being so heavy, and consequently less valuable.

I have an abiding conviction, that the statesman who introduced the law upon tbe introduction of books, was an admiring reader of Knickerbocker; Walter the Doubter must have been his highest judicial authority. His statute bears a startling resemblance to the only decision of that famous Dutch Lawgiver, when he commanded the ledgers of two litigating grocers to be weighed and gave judgment in favor of him whose ledger was heaviest. Their estimate of justice and knowledge were equally extended, and equally worthy of this most enlightened nation of the nineteenth century.

CHAPTER IV.

RURAL SCENERY.

THIS England—the country I mean—the fields, the trees, and the hedges, is truly very, very beautiful. Pleasing at all seasons from its tidy evidences of superior cultivation, it becomes enchanting when seen, as I lately saw it, whilst every leaf and spear of grass shone with the glistening freshness of early spring. I positively believe I should feel enthusiastically in love with the country, if I could for one little half hour forget the nation. But being unfortunately situated like Yankee Doodle, when he complained that "he could not see the town for the houses," I can never admire the country, without being reminded of the people.

The pastoral scenery of England is peculiar, possessing all the polish of art in its highest perfection, without its primness. Soft and shining as a long summer's day, the full-blown charms of the island droop under their fairy loads of poetry and loveliness. Well may it be named the Eden of the universe, but its inhabitants with equal justice may be denominated the "fallen" of creation. The beauties of England being those of a dream, should be as fleeting. To a man whose blood needs no champagne to hurry its coursing, with a fancy as swift as the steam that hurls him along, they never appear so charming as when dashing on after a locomotive at forty miles an hour. Nothing by the way requires study, or demands meditation, and though objects immediately at hand seem tearing wildly by, yet the distant fields and scattered trees, are not so bent on eluding observation, but dwell long enough in the eye to leave their undying impression. Every thing is so quiet, so fresh, so full of home, and destitute of prominent objects to detain the eye, or distract the attention from the charms of the enchanting whole, that I love to dream through these placid beauties, whilst sailing in the air, quick, as if astride a tornado. All things then assume the delicious indistinctness of some bright vision, during an after-dinner doze in an arm-chair. Nothing then appears so palpable as to break the hazy drowsiness of the scene, by its too substantial reality.

Thick-headed tourists, who have no poetry in their souls, may sneer at the idea of enjoying the rural scenery of England from the window of a railroad car. Such mathematical individuals would fain take the dimensions of each fairy landscape, as a mason would measure the proportions of a brick wall. But give me the velocity, the exhilaration, and the panting breezes of the cars; let me enjoy the shadowy charms and softly-creeping fascinations of an English landscape, seen from their windows. There is wild delight in the consciousness of such motion. There is intense excitement in this shadowless velocity. There is glorious independence in the power of bounding to a place, swiftly almost as the conception of the wish to be there. What could be more intoxicating than this tumultuous throb of mingled emotions, felt in this panorama of green fields and flowers, gliding fleetly and softly as the fancies of the opium eater?

"Will you make an excursion with me from Liverpool up to London? Be quick; whilst you hesitate we may both be left. The express train starts at the minute, without delaying for loitering passengers. You will go? Very well; here you are." We are off; already grinding through "utter darkness," where there is no "gnashing of teeth," but a fearful clash of wheels: we are in the tunnel. Suddenly we shoot into open air like a sunbeam piercing a fog, and the boundless beauty of the landscape breaks at once upon us. Liverpool is already a mile behind. Far as the eye can reach, on every side, it is greeted with the same lovely view. We rush through a succession of fresh green fields and greener hedges; of villages embowered in fruit trees, with the tapering spires of country churches modestly overlooking them; of bustling market towns, and smoky manufacturing cities, which do not interrupt the character of the scenery, but serve pleasingly to dot the vast expanse of shining verdure. The fresh-springing crops of grain trembled to the lazy breezes, and sometimes seemed to wave for very gracefulness, when there was no breath to stir them. The scene appeared a wanton waste of loveliness. I could not reconcile myself to the thought that these beauteous meadows, so thickly strewn with flowers that one might imagine them an emerald copy of the starry heavens, were only kept to graze beef cattle. It could not be, that these hedges, trimmed with such exquisite taste, were only intended as ordinary barriers against erratic horses, and trespassing sheep. Every thing was too, too beautiful for this! But just when the eyes reeled, and sense grew drunk, and I was dreaming of the frolics of Puck, and the fairy reign of Titania, plump we came upon a brick-yard, with its prim rows fresh from the moulds, and its pyramidal kilns smoking away, to remind me that this delicious land of verdure and flowers, was not only inhabited by the English, but that they were commonplace enough to shut themselves up in brick walls from all this loveliness. And then, in spite of myself, came gloomy pictures of English ogres in Elysian gardens, flitting across my mind, like the passing shadows of clouds over some sunny landscape. But these unwelcome thoughts are dispelled by the sight of a lowly thatched cot, with a rosy-faced baby hurrying on all fours to the front door, as its chubby little brothers and sisters climb the wicket gate to greet us with their tiny cheers, as we flit gayly by. A blossoming clover field fills the whole atmosphere, as we pass, with its deliciously refreshing odor. And look at those beans, wagging as knowingly their flowery heads, and giving birth to as much poetry and perfume, as if they had not been planted there for horse-feed. Every thing was enchanting except the sky, and that was cold and gray enough. But what of that? It is only the background to an exquisite picture, and nobody ever dreams of regarding it.

Now we rattle through a bustling market town, with its little alehouses, and staring squads of idlers. An ambitious village cur darts furiously out, and vainly tries with us his speed, snapping and yelping as if to frighten our spirited steam-courser. We swiftly pass fields, ready prepared for late crops, so perfectly ploughed and harrowed that they look like huge pieces of brown satin stretched upon the green. See, winding through those lovely meadows, that deep, narrow stream of clearest water, brimming its banks of living verdure, and so placid it scarcely stirs the long moss floating on its edges. No trees fringe its banks; it steals before us with its nude beauties unveiled. In its gentle course it makes a thousand picturesque bends, and wanders about as if seeking to lose itself in these grassy plains. It has no hurrying occupation; no mills to turn, no roaring rivers to feed. It is but an elegant idler in this delightful champaign country. And as it loiters lazily along, it dreams of no more arduous task, than lending new beauties to my Lord's beautiful estate. I am sorry that last idea occurred to me—for my thoughts made a sudden transition to the worthlessness of all lackeys to the rich and great; the lazy-footmen, dozing butlers, insolent grooms, and, I was going to say, placid streams—but I stopped. For there was a rustic bridge, so rude, so crazy, and so picturesque, it must have been thrown across the stream merely to prevent the possibility of the scene's sinking into too much softness. Nobody would ever dream of crossing on it—it seemed only put there to look at, and it may be to interrupt disagreeable trains of thought. A flock of noisy rooks mount high into air, wheeling and cawing around us as if to speed us on our way. A large herd of fine short-horned cattle are browsing in social little knots, and look up and gaze stupidly after us as we roll smoothly by. The whistle sounds: we are approaching some station. Gradually we lessen our speed, and finally stop. The "company's servants," in coarse liveries of black velveteen, with the initials of the particular railroad, and their numbers, marked in white cloth on their collars, rapidly move from car to car, unlocking them, and loudly announcing the name of the station, and its various connections. There is much slamming of doors as people get out, because they have arrived at their journey's end, or merely to stretch their legs. The low hum of the passengers and porters, hurriedly searching for baggage, is mingled with the shrill cries of news-boys, running up and down the platform along the train, with this morning's papers from London. Then comes the warning bell; and then the final order of the conductor. Then there is again great slamming of doors, which are all relocked—the whistle sounds, and off we bound after two minutes' delay in our flying journey.

We rush through a labyrinth of cottages and gardens, full of comfort and cabbages, with their trim hedges appropriately adorned with blue smockfrocks and wet breeches hung out to dry. A large flock of newly-sheared Southdown sheep are quietly grazing in the neighboring field, but, on our approach, hurriedly scamper off with much shaking of short tails and ringing of sheep-bells. Is it not beautiful? that deep brawling brook with its lofty banks, wild, broken, and picturesque, spanned by a single arch of stone, crumbling and moss-grown, through which it foams; it rushes madly into a wooded glen, where it is wholly lost to view, and when again it gladdens the eye, it is warring bravely with the green slimy wheel of a mill—a hoary patriarch, that may have ground flour for Cromwell's troopers. The country beautifully undulating, as if under the agitating influence of its own surpassing charms, now rises into gentle slopes, now runs into wavy irregularities, then sinks into unbroken level. It seemed that some tasteful hand had been at work in its arrangement, to produce the happiest display of its wooded hills and green walled vales. The variety, in size and shape, of these hedge-bound fields is endless. Shady trees, scattered through them all, break into ever-varying effects the vast sheet of shining green. Considerable tracts of woodland meet the eye at every turn; their changing foliage clustering under the magical effects of light and shadow to lend some new fascination to the scene. And when nature did start into abrupter eminences, its savage features were always masked in the russet and gold of flowering broom piled up in undisturbed luxuriance. The hedges on each side the road looked, as we flew along, like two green coursers, of goblin shape, racing furiously with each other; and the daisies and batchelor-buttons in the fields beyond seemed to our swimming eyes to grow into many-tinted ribbons forcibly blown from the mouth of some modern magician. But, in the distance, the scene was a floating sea of loveliness. What a stately mansion is that! looking out from its shady clump of fine old oaks. See that merry little rivulet, skipping along its pebbly bed, with its narrow banks thickly lined with old willows, which have been so hewed and hacked for their pliant shoots, that their gnarled and knotted trunks resemble the venerable olives in the garden of Gethsemane. The ditch of that sunk fence is arbored o'er with blossoming briers and wild creepers. The hedge is no longer a close-built wall of verdure, but it is broken into sweet irregularities by the masses of wild plum and hawthorn in bloom—their snowy flowers beautifully contrasting with the dark, brilliant green of the hedge; and there is a noble old castle, with its Gothic battlements and swelling towers, seemingly based upon a huge mound of leaves, so thickly wooded are the sides of the hill on which it stands. What a pity that all this beauty is created by the aristocracy, even as the pearl hidden in the shell of the oyster is the result of disease.

In contrast with these princely mansions we roll glibly by a modest cottage, with its gable-end hung with a dark mantle of ivy, and its door half-curtained with clambering roses and honey-suckles. On its window-sills are ranged modest pots of heliotrope, and mignonette, breathing their sweet odors upon the happy inmates of the lowly cot. In the little yard of grassplots and flowers a stately cock convoys his numerous hens, which are busily scratching and pecking for worms, regardless of his proffered gallantries. Chanticleer glories in his charge, and loudly crows as he flaps his burnished wings of gold. But courageous as he seems, he lowers his proud crest and utters his cackling note of alarm as we whiz swiftly by. In the stable-yard stands an old white horse, freckled with age, munching his oats beside a rough Shetland pony. Snugly reposing under the shed was the red milch cow, chewing the cud as she dozed unmindful of our momentary presence. A large peacock, with the gorgeous glories of his tail spread to their utmost, strutted stiffly along in solitary grandeur, the gaudy monarch of birds. On the roof-shaped hay-rick, a whole flock of pigeons were dozing in [illegible]ne, with their heads tucked comfortably under their wings, and the noisy Guinea fowls shrieked wildly below. What a snug picture of home comforts to excite all the enthusiasm of romantic young advocates of "love in a village!" It only required Cupid peeping out of the kitchen window in a white apron, with a napkin tucked about his neck, and a piece of dough in his hand, to complete this ideal paradise of dumplings and devotion. More sweet fields and sweeter hedges. A solitary horse, carelessly nipping the short juicy grass, looks up as we smoke and puff towards him—gazes for an instant with bowed neck and raised tail, and then snorting loudly, bounds off, his head half-turned in proud defiance as he gallops slowly away. On a bare eminence a lonely windmill twirls its gigantic arms in creaking agony. How distinctly we can trace the course of that stream through these delicious meadows by the clustering trees that grow along its margin, and hang so tenderly over it with their long drooping boughs, as entirely to conceal the water from the light; and then when it does gleam forth for an instant from its leafy covert into sunshine, it flashes like some rich vein of quicksilver issuing from its rugged native mine. A frightened hare, startled from her grassy form by our steaming uproar, bounds forth, and with her long ears resting upon her back fleetly scours the plain.

And soon there came on a mist. It was no fog,—no drizzle; but thin, shadowy and almost impalpable, it floated between us and the beauteous landscape, lending a softened, but intenser interest to the scene. And then it commenced to rain. At first it was only a few big drops, that rattled through the leaves, and pelted the tops of the cars. And then it poured in right good earnest, beating down the agitated foliage of the waving boughs, and rudely pattering upon the glassy surface of the placid stream. The cattle sought shelter under the nearest trees, the horses drooped, and the sheep huddled close together, with their noses stuck close to the ground to avoid the raging storm. The whole scene becoming very dismal, and very English, I put up the window and soon fell asleep, to dream of the wild forests on the banks of the Mississippi. The whistle startled me, and I looked out upon that huge tinkery of iron pots—hammering Birmingham—where all the world come to buy their soup-ladles. The scattering forest of gaunt, spectral furnace-chimneys, that, Babel-like, kissed the clouds, were all puffing furiously away, as if each one was bent on doing its best to smoke the gloomy piles of dingy houses as black as smoke could make them. Here we had ten minutes for *ennui* and refreshments. People stretched their legs, and some took sandwiches, and others a glass of porter, and after the ten minutes had appeared half an hour, compared with the excitement of the former portion of the journey, the whistle sounded, and off we rattled once more.

The sun came out from shelter, and with him the cows. The horses once more took to grazing, and gradually the sheep scattered over the fields, and the frolicksome lambs frisked round them as if in playful derision of their damp, close-sheared skins. What a pity that these woolly innocents should ever go up to Smithfield, to be made mutton of. The sun shone, or rather did its best to shine brightly, but it was not that fierce, glaring sunshine that appears eager to drink up at once all the moisture that the pitying heavens had shed upon the earth beneath. There was nothing dazzling, nothing parching about it. It was the mellowed, luxurious light of a shaded lamp—a fit illumination for enchanted bowers and submarine grots; it was just the sort of light, in fact, that a fairy or a mermaid would have revelled in, or a romantic traveller would have chosen to see the softly beautiful scenery of England by. The tender crops were still, as if lulled into speechless happiness by the refreshing shower. And every thing looked up and smiled, except the poor beans, which drooped their heavily wreathed beads, weighed down by the glittering moisture. The blithe lark soars high above us, singing as he dries his fluttering wings in the stray sunbeams. And here and there a dripping sparrow hops merrily forth from his protecting hedge, chirping as gayly as if it had never been known to rain in England. All things seemed softer, sweeter, and fresher than before. We rush swiftly by a flourishing field of hops, the creeping plants stuck with straight, branchless hoop-poles, fiercely bristling in their formal rows, like the hundred thousand bayonets of the *Champ de Mars* on review day. We plunge into another tunnel. Amidst the weighty darkness, and the sulphureous smell from the furnace,—the stunning roar of the wheels, and the terrific yells of the locomotive whistle,—one might imagine himself in the depths of a certain brimstone pit, with a whole squadron of devil's imps careering madly through it.

"I'll not march through Coventry with them, that's flat." So said I to myself of my English fellow-passengers, who had already discovered ways of rendering themselves disagreeable before arriving at that ancient city. But unfortunately for me, I was not captain, as the fat Knight was, and so the whistle sounded and off we all rumbled together, furious as so many cats shaken up in a bag. An Englishman is decidedly a muffin, not only in his puffy appearance, but in his quiet endurance of an oven-height temperature. He rather enjoys being gently baked, and shuns draughts of fresh air as he does beggars. If it were his fortune to take a siesta under the equator, he would tenderly insert his head in a woollen nightcap, as a proper precaution against the possibility of getting cold in the head, of which, after indigestion, he lives most in dread[illegible] leaving Birmingham, we had so changed our directio[illegible]o turn *their* faces towards the iron horse, and thereby to give them the control over the windows which we had previously enjoyed. The lively lick at which we moved created an invigorating breeze. An Englishman would have been false to his nature had he quietly exposed himself to such a draught; so each flushed gentleman, with determined composure, proceeded to put up a window, and put on his nightcap, and after wrapping himself up in his India-rubber overcoat, he snugly composed himself to sleep. Stifling hot became the car; our condensed breath ran down the glass in streams, and yet they snoozed on, toasting as comfortably as fellow-muffins, waiting their turn to go into breakfast. Through the combined assistance of his odoriferous overcoat and the sweltering heat, each dozing Englishman soon succeeded in making a scent-bag of himself, which, if crows had noses, would prove invaluable in a corn-field afflicted with those destructive birds. Was it not suffocating? provoking? And then to hear them snore too! It was positively frightful. What social punishment could be deemed too severe to be inflicted on any civilized Christian, who would get into a confined atmosphere in an India-rubber coat?

We dash through more fields and hedges; and there, half-hidden in the deepest shadow, is the picturesque porter's lodge, opening upon the long broad avenue of drooping elms, which leads to some aristocratic dwelling. These venerable elms may be considered the living sign-posts to aristocracy; and really if this aristocracy in its action on men resembled its influence on nature, it would be an uncommonly pretty thing to look at. I have since this railroad trip often trotted in a dog-cart along the shady lanes and retired roads of England, pausing by the way to wonder at and admire the exceeding loveliness of many a mansion of aristocracy. A man must see in order to appreciate these secluded hiding-places of wealth. The taste, the care and ingenuity displayed in the style of architecture of the houses, and in the keeping of the grounds and parks, surpasses the most exaggerated fancies of an imaginative mind. But, alas! the careful culture of trees and cattle, as ministers to its luxury, monopolizes all the attention of the aristocracy, whilst thousands of operatives in mines and manufactories, and paupers in cities, are left to starve in ignorance and vice. Trees are pruned, watered and manured, and the unceasing care of countless laborers is devoted to them. The sleek horses and bullocks are considerately blanketed; due regard is had to the air, light and cleanliness of their stables, and every attention is paid to the quantity and quality of their food. But millions of human beings are left by their noble landlords to rot in those dens of "graduated starvation"—the workhouses,—or else to eke out an existence of protracted wretchedness in stifling coalpits, and suffocating factories, or to die unheard of in the cheerless garrets and loathsome cellars of the large cities of the kingdom. The horses and bullocks the aristocracy intend to ride and eat, and they are, for that reason, no scanty recipients of affectionate attentions. But the other class, God having seen fit to forbid by their peculiar conformation, their being subjected to either one of the above-mentioned uses, can hope for no place in the sympathies of their more fortunate fellow-men. The aristocracy then being unable either to ride or to eat them, innocently wonder what on earth they were made for, and so leave them to starve or be miraculously fed by the ravens as may happen. When it is remembered that in the park alone of Chatsworth there are 1600 acres, and that all the four hundred titles, and a vast number of ambitious commoners, own one or more seats with extensive parks attached; some idea may be formed of the immense tracts of the finest land kept idle to bolster up the proud supremacy of these wealthy sluggards, which, if brought into cultivation, would assist in feeding the starving millions of London and the mining and manufacturing districts.

CHAPTER V.

ENGLISH WRITERS ON AMERICA.

A FEW meek, submissive, anglicized Americans are nervously anxious to convince England, and America, that the deepest, most abiding affection subsists between them. They most assiduously labor to prove by facts, and figures, that certain prejudiced travellers, and narrow-minded journalists, do but waste ink in their efforts to disturb the harmony of two nations, allied in origin, and bound by common ties. They blandly assure England, that America still bases her national pride upon the triumphs of "the mother country." They confidently assert, that the American people, proud of their English descent, still insist upon sharing with Great Britain the glories of their common ancestors. They cajole Americans with the soft assurance, that England regards their progress with that sort of interest which the parental heart can only feel; they protest that she is proud of her offspring; and that she glories in their success at home and abroad, as new evidence of the invincibility of the Anglo-Saxon race. They hope, by judiciously tickling the vanity of Johnny Bull, to restrain him from the commission of excesses, to which even Americans would fail to submit. And by dinging into our ears the familiar whine of "the mother country," "our common ancestors," and the glory of being descended from a people "who can claim Shakspeare and Milton as countrymen," they hope to reconcile Americans to the degradation of a tutelage which must prove a stain on our national character. They would fain convince us that we must be servile, in order to be proud; they insult our understanding, by attempting to convince us, that we could maintain our honor at the sacrifice of our independence.

According to the convenient doctrine of these complying sycophants, gratitude for the honor conferred on us by our English relationship, should make us forgive any offence, and submit to any imposition England may be pleased to inflict. We are considerately warned of the danger of offending our parent; her insults must be treated as badinage; her hostility deemed all a joke. If we should resent her outrages, she may declare us to be no longer her heirs; if we excite her ire, she might cut us off from the rich inheritance of her glory. Though her good will could prove valuable, and America could learn to humbly sue for her favors, ought our interest to make us forget that forgiveness may cease to be magnanimous, and that forbearance may, after a while, sink into pusillanimity? But "to crook the pregnant hinges of the knee, when thrift may follow fawning," is something that America has yet to learn. On our own strength, and not on England's favor, we rely for success. We renounce all claim to England's glory, by succession. We scorn to be honored as the reputed descendants even of Great Britain. As American citizens we present to the world our claims to respect; as American citizens we are ready to maintain them. That solitary relic of England's absurdities, that honor could be derived from ancestors, has never been received with favor in our land. Our theory and our practice have ever been, that "true nobility looks to the future, not to the past." If we wear any of England's laurels, we have won them, not borrowed them. And if we are proud of being Americans, it is not because we may as descendants of Englishmen share their national pride, but because as foemen, in equal fight, we have humbled it. 'Tis most true that Britain's triumphs are our glory. But we have appropriated, as she gained them, on the ocean and in the field.

It is our interest, as it has ever been our pleasure, to do justice to England's greatness. In acknowledging her reputation we establish our own. Prowess in the vanquished is the proudest tribute to the victor. She has hitherto been supreme; but her ambition overleaps itself; her pre-eminence is likely to prove her ruin. She so long stood alone among nations, that she can but ill brook the presence of a rival, more especially when that rival appears in a nation whom she has struggled to think of with scorn and treat with derision. In order to convince the world and themselves of the sincerity of their disdain, Englishmen have resorted to the vilest slander and abuse. They indulge their native malevolence in every species of injustice, in every form of attack. There is no crime too flagrant, no outrage too glaring, for Americans to be accused of. But their own fury blinds them. They forget that malignity cannot be mistaken for indifference; that rancor can never be construed into contempt. The bitter pleasure they derive from assailing America, shows that they fear as well as hate her. The very pains they take to convince the world that we are unworthy of all consideration, proves of how much more importance we are in their eyes than they would have it supposed. Such intense hatred lives not without a cause; indifference on any subject produces silence; and if we were so despicable as they pretend to believe, we should much less frequently be the theme of their invective. But it is the privilege of helpless malice to rail, and England too well deserves the right not to be allowed to enjoy it. If, in abusing us, she finds relief from the choking accumulation of her spleen, I can say from my heart let her rail on. Her satire has hitherto proved more harmless, if possible, to America than her arms. Her assaults, of both kinds, have always redounded as much to our honor as her own confusion. But I would have her spite ascribed to its real motive; I should like to see her attacks received in the proper spirit. What could be more humiliating than to behold her "lily-livered" partisans, whilst wincing under her savage calumnies, vainly attempting a grinning approval of their wit? What could be more disgusting than to observe those Anglicised Americans, whilst cowering beneath the fierceness of her rebuke, meanly acknowledging the justice of it? I would not have my countrymen forget the fact, that her malice arises from envy, and that jealousy sustains her bitterness. I would have them amused by what is worthy of being laughed at, at the same time that I would have them despise the vituperation, which has nothing but its Billingsgate coarseness to distinguish it. I can always laugh at a really good thing, even when perpetrated at my own expense; I could enjoy even English sarcasm could it ever fail to sink into scurrility.

It would be cruel to restrain England in her propensity to vilify us, when she displays such remarkable fluency in a slanderous style of speech. When the ability to calumniate is the only power which has survived the gradual encroachment of bowels upon intellect in Great Britain, it would be a pity to rob the English even of this miserable evidence of mind. When vituperation is the solitary approach they are capable of making to any quality which belongs to eloquence, it would be excessive enmity not to leave them to its indulgence. I should be as reluctant to deprive them of the free exercise of their undoubted talent for abuse, as I would be to curry favor with them by submission. But I should like to reserve the privilege of receiving and replying to their invectives, without regarding the flunky dictation of some few Americans, who have shown themselves unworthy of the name. I have no desire to curtail, in the least degree, the ample range of England's vile imagination; but I do not relish being insulted, by being told that she basely slanders because she tenderly loves us.

Mutual enmity is the only feeling which can ever be maintained with sincerity between the two nations; and there is something much more attractive, to me, in the frankness of declared hostility, than the empty professions of a truce which neither pretends to respect. We must be foes; but let us be courteous foes. All that we demand of Englishmen is, that there shall be "a fair fight" and "no hitting under the belt." We expect no gentle consideration for our inexperience on their part; but, on entering "the ring," we defy them to do their worst. We have nothing to fear in this contest. A brave foe, though vanquished, commands the admiration of his adversary. 'Tis true America is young, and not much skilled in "the science of fistiana;" but though we may be conquered after some "hard fought rounds," yet we will much more certainly secure England's respect than we could purchase her forbearance by "going down" without a single blow. But if we will "hit out" vigorously, there is no certainty that the issue of the battle will be against us. Englishmen, though strong, and much practised in the cunning tricks of "the ring," present so many assailable points, that our victory is certain if our determination prove valiant. Let them thoroughly understand "the articles of the fight;" that the contest may hereafter be conducted with the punctilious propriety of "an affair of honor," not the low indecency of a brothel brawl.

We are assured that England regards us with a most parental affection; we are informed that she is proud of her offspring. She has, indeed, been most touchingly affectionate. From the 13th May, 1607, to the 20th December, 1852, her solicitous attentions have been unceasing. From the time of Captain Christopher Newport's landing his fleet of three ships, with the 105 settlers of Jamestown, to the date of our present glorious Republic of thirty-one States, the marks of her sincere regard have been too unmistakable for even "the most prejudiced and narrow-minded of Americans" to deny them. Her devotion has truly been very extraordinary. Nature affords but a single parallel of her maternal affection. She gloats over us with that sort of appetizing tenderness, which might be supposed to have animated a sow "that hath eaten her nine farrow." We are probably indebted to our strength and numbers for not having been subjected to the same practical illustration of her extreme devotion enjoyed by the pigs. Twenty millions of hardy freemen would prove a troublesome meal, even for ogreish England.

But England regards our progress with parental exultation. That she *does* watch our advancing strides with the deepest interest, I am most ready to admit. But hers is a keener anxiety than ever animates even a parent's breast. It is the feverish, all-absorbing interest of an apprehensive rival, whose soul is racked by mingled hate and fear. If she pretends to glory in our success, as her kindred of the Anglo-Saxon race, she has been rather too tardy in discovering the tie of relationship, to make its acknowledgment at all flattering now. The truth is, that even her purblind jealousy at last permits her to feel that some honor might arise from claiming us as of her own family, and she has become wondrously proud of a connection that she has been something less than a hundred years in finding out. In defiance of her persecutions, wars, and slanders, we have assumed such a position, that even she might derive consequence from patronizing us. But she strangely mistakes our relations, when she supposes that the American people would submit to being treated as inferiors. Having shown ourselves her equals in peace, and her superiors in war, we must respectfully decline her patronage, as we have steadily defied her malice. The hope that she could flatter us into bolstering up her tottering empire is eminently worthy of her selfishness, but does not reflect much credit on her judgment. She gave us no assistance in our rise; she must expect none from us in her decline. She must not hope—she must not hope, by playfully claiming us as her "American kinsfolk," that the reflection of our rising glory will illumine her waning power. We disclaim all sympathy with people who can only remember that they are related to us, when it becomes their interest to do so. We should have despised them less had they continued to assail us as enemies, instead of making pusillanimous professions of friendship it is impossible for them to feel. The favors we have received from England will not be troublesome to return. We may be as slow to extend as we have been to receive friendly greetings.

But then we have "common ancestors." We spring from the same origin, and speak the same language, 'tis true. But all this only serves to widen the gulf between us. Common enmity is mild compared with the hatred which springs from friendship outraged and confidence abused. Neglected duties and broken ties do but increase the bitterness of those who have once been united. Like objects negatively electrified, England and America fly farther asunder, from having so closely adhered. The laws governing our sympathies are as unchangeable as those of electricity, and we now mutually repel, because we once mutually attracted each other. Position, the times, and fate unite in making us rivals. It is impossible that we could ever be otherwise whilst England continues powerful, or

America free. The two greatest nations on earth—the occupants of different hemispheres, and the representatives of antagonistic principles of government, necessity would make us rivals in spite of the sincerest inclination to be friends. It is but natural that England should feel most acutely this feeling of jealousy. The weaker rival ever nurses the bitterest hate. And England cannot escape from the consciousness that her strength must wane as ours grows, though she may attempt to deceive others by her boasts and sneers. She already bears about her the evidences of o'er-ripe maturity, whilst every year must develope some new power in America. Decay must soon begin in England, and time, which will prove her ruin, will be our friend. Her successful rivals, we have not time to pause in our career to wonder if England cheers our progress. We are not anxious, because we have nothing to fear. We are less bitter, because we feel secure. Our advance is too rapid to give us time to watch England. We hate her with much less intensity than she has honored us with, because we feel no apprehension of her power. As she cannot obstruct our path, we naturally forget her presence. But we must be eternally in her thoughts, because we are gradually eclipsing her greatness. The spectre of some dreaded object haunts the apprehensive mind with much more constancy, than the loved one's image lives in a devoted heart.

England's distrust commenced at our birth, and has increased with our strength. The apprehension with which she regarded us, seemed almost instinctive. Whilst we were as yet a sickly settlement, feebly contending in the wilderness against savages and famine, she seemed oppressed by the consciousness that there was danger to her in our success. With unnatural barbarity she turned from us, with the vain hope that we must perish amidst the privations of the desolate spot, in which our lot was cast. But the God of nations, who sent ravens to feed Elijah in the desert, succored us. And from a handful of men, whose hopes of existence were reduced to a few grains of corn, we have been raised up into a powerful protector to the rest of the world against the encroachments of the English system. England's deadly enmity, originally shown in neglect, was afterwards manifested in a series of persecutions, which finally drove us into open resistance. In her attempt to coerce us by arms she lost her colonies, and we gained our independence. Her hatred, increased by the bitter mortification of defeat, was not long in again bursting into unrestrained fury. She resolved to cripple our growing commerce by exercising the arrogated right of search. Once more she struggled to annihilate our power in war. Her baffled hate received another terrible rebuke, and our brilliant success by sea and land, which added a long list to our heroic names of the Revolution, first taught her to fear as much as she hated America. She no longer dared assail us openly, and her national rivalry sunk into personal spite. Destitute of the power to injure us as a nation, she condescended to assail individual peculiarities, and by the ridicule of our manners by her tourists, and attacks on our social and political institutions, by her periodicals and daily press, she hoped to accomplish by cavilling at us, what she had failed to do by her arms. Her jealous disposition has been evident to all those familiar with the newspaper literature of the country; but it is so happily displayed in the following petty attack from the London Times on the American contributions to the world's fair, that I cannot resist the temptation to quote it. It is a fair specimen of the tone of the London press generally:—

If the Americans do excite a smile, it is by their pretensions. Whenever they come out of their own province of rugged utility, and enter into competition with European elegance, they certainly do make themselves ridiculous. Their furniture is grotesque; their carriages and harness are gingerbread; their carpets are tawdry; their patchwork quilts surpass even the invariable ugliness of this fabric; their cut glass is clumsy; their pianos sound of nothing but iron and wood; their bookbinding is that of a journeyman working on his own account in an English market town; their daguerreotypes are the sternest and gloomiest of all daguerreotypes; their printed calicoes are such as our housemaids would not think it respectable to wear. Even their ingenuity, great as it is, becomes ridiculous when it attempts competition with Europe. Double pianos, a combination of a piano and a violin, a chair with a cigar-case in its back, and other mongrel constructions, belong to a people that would be centaurs and mermen if they could, and are always rebelling against the trammels of unity.

The displays of her mean disposition to detract from our merits are not confined to the absurd scurrility of her newspapers or the stale slanders of her books. In her blustering course with regard to the McLeod difficulty, the Northwestern boundary, and the recent fishery question, her malevolence almost got the better of her prudence; she plainly showed that she still possessed the will, though destitute of the courage to attack us. England should be careful of these outbursts of fury. She should remember, that, like the bee, which in leaving its envenomed sting with its foe, sickens and dies, the enraged rival may become the victim of his own wiles. The means to which Great Britain resorts to overthrow America, may prove her own ruin.

It is true that a cowardly policy during the uncertainty of the late dispute about the Newfoundland fisheries, dictated a great change of tone in the press of England since the period when its head, the *London Times*, denounced America as a Republic of scoundrels, with a few honest men intermixed. But their unconquerable aversion to America embitters the soothing cup of flattery they commend to our lips; and they lose the advantage of their attempt to conciliate, by allowing their miserable jealousy to shine through their labored efforts at praise. The *Times*, about the period when many thought the two countries might be involved in war, contained this somewhat remarkable article, in which it lauds our power and progress, but insinuates that we are pirates and villains, who, regarding the laws neither of God nor man, are yet destitute of the courage to avenge the murder of our citizens, which resulted from our unscrupulous ambition. It is useless to comment on the subtle injustice of the article. It speaks for itself:

THE LEAP OF THE UNITED STATES TO THE FIRST RANK OF NATIONS—THE CONQUEST OF CUBA.

[From the London Times of September 6, 1852.]

It has ever been the delight of historians and philosophers to trace and work out an analogy between the peculiarities of climate and scenery, and the character and disposition of nations. There is something singularly wild and extreme in the physical phenomena of the American continent. The mountains literally pierce the clouds, and pour down from their snow-capped summits rivers that sweep their uncontrollable course for thousands of miles, and bear with them, as trophies of their might, trees of a girth and growth unknown to the European observer. The seasons are as strongly marked. A summer of raging and almost intolerable heat is succeeded by a winter of little less than Arctic severity. All things there tend to represent the course of nature as the result of a series of violent and uncontrollable impulses, and to conceal those silent and unvarying laws which regulate alike the fall of a drop of rain and the course of the mighty Father of Waters.

There never probably was, since the beginning of the world, an instance of such solid, sudden, and dazzling prosperity as has been achieved within the last fifty years by the United States of America. By peaceful industry and bold but well-weighed enterprise, they have advanced to a degree of material well-being which, to those who only know the world from books, must appear almost incredible. They have but to persevere in the same course, and there is no limit to the triumphs that lie before them. They have still a boundless territory to occupy and improve, in the possession of which they are without a neighbor, and a mission of civilization and consolidation to execute as noble as ever devolved upon the sons of men. But the previous triumphs of their industry and their enterprise have been so rapid and portentous that they would seem to have a tendency to turn aside the nation from its steady onward course, and to enlist it in more brilliant but far less certain schemes of aggrandizement. A nation of hard-headed traders and speculators, struggling day by day with praiseworthy perseverance and intensity for the possession of the "almighty dollar," this people, so shrewd and calculating in its private transactions, becomes, when it touches on public affairs, wild and extravagant, boundless in its aspirations and insatiable in its cupidity. It possesses a will as uncontrollable as the powers of nature which surround it, and spurns the control of law to which these mighty agencies so humbly submit themselves.

There are at present two courses of policy open to the United States—the policy of commerce and the policy of conquest. It is open to them to throw down commercial restrictions, to stimulate the spirit of traffic, to give up aspirations of military glory, and found a power like that of their mother country, relying rather on arts than arms; or they may substitute the military for the commercial spirit, seek to establish within themselves a world of their own, and to enlarge a territory already too vast for unity, by the forcible annexation of lands too weak to resist the onset of the mighty confederation. Never had a people good or evil set so fairly before them, and never was the choice more doubtful or momentous.

It is now just a year since the piratical expedition to Cuba, resulting in the sanguinary execution of fifty American citizens and the ignominious death of the "unprincipled adventurer" by whom the descent was planned. We had hoped that this severe lesson—a single reverse amid so much prosperity and progress—would have taught the United States the folly and wickedness of such unwarrantable enterprises, and finally decided the balance in favor of the policy of justice and moderation. There is much reason to fear we are mistaken. A sort of "guild" or "order" has been formed in the South, consisting, we suppose we must say, not of unprincipled adventurers, but of many of the most "worthy and influential merchants, lawyers and politicians of the country." The object is the extension of American influence over the Western hemisphere and the islands of the Atlantic and Pacific. The first booty on which they have cast their eyes is Cuba, and from that island they propese to sweep away every vestige of Spanish authority before two suns have risen and set on the invaders. "Enlightened public opinion in the United States," it is said, will sanction this measure, seeing that there are many reasons why Americans require the possession of the island. In the first place, they wish to substitute for the iron rule of Spain, the republican system of government; next, they anticipate assistance from the discontented Creoles—a fallacious hope, if we may judge by the experience of Lopez. Thirdly, they see in the acquisition of this island a guarantee for the permanency of the institution of slavery. Fourthly, such a conquest would extend their commerce. Fifthly, the rich and luxurious covet this gem of the Antilles, as an agreeable and accessible retreat from the severities of a New-York winter, and long to exchange the frozen breezes of the North for enchanting visions of orange trees and sherry cobblers. The sum and substance of all these reasons is that, without pretending a shadow of right to this possession of the crown of Spain, the Americans desire it, and therefore will have it. Whatever the Americans can take belongs to them, according to this new school of ethics; and come peace or come war, they will not permit the intervention of any European power between them and any friendly ally whom they are determined to plunder.

It is no little question that is raised by these avowed intentions—nothing less than whether one of the first-rate powers of the world shall declare itself exempt from the provisions of the law of nations—shall deny the existence of any right except that of the stronger, and claim to set no bounds to its aggressions, except the limits assigned by its boundless cupidity and lust of dominion. Shall there arise in the middle of the nineteenth century, a piratical State, bound by no laws, recognizing no rights, and avowedly basing its policy on principles which in the case of individuals this very same society would visit with the penitentiary or the gibbet? There was a time when, intoxicated like the United States with its enormous prosperity, ancient Athens laid down for itself the same rule of conduct, and boldly professed that while justice might regulate claims between equals, the stronger had a right to impose every thing to which the weaker might be compelled to submit. After a few years the vicissitudes of events placed this arrogant State in the very position it had described, and rendered it dependent on the contemptuous clemency of a conqueror for that very existence to which, upon its own principles, it had lost all right when it became unable to defend it. Suppose we were to apply a similar reason to the island of Madeira. Nothing would be easier than to take it from the feeble power to whom it belongs. It is not too well governed by the Portuguese, it is a commanding commercial position, and its climate is regarded as a specific for the national disease of consumption. We have, therefore, many reasons to desire it. Why, then, do we not make it our own? For two reasons, which our American friends will do well to consider. *We will not violate the principles of eternal justice, tarnish the lustre of our arms, and disgrace our character for fairness and moderation, by wresting his property from our ally because he is unable to keep it.* And if we wish to do this we dare not. We dread the retribution which follows on such acts, and have learnt that, sooner or later, the force of public opinion will put down any power which claims to emancipate itself from the control of conscience and the practice of justice. We commend these considerations in no unfriendly spirit to our friends across the Atlantic, and trust that they will see, on calmer reflection, that in this case, as in all others, their duty is identical with their interest, and that enlightened public opinion in the States, instead of supporting "worthy and influential" men who form themselves into secret societies for the purposes of piracy and buccaneering, will declare that such objects are unworthy, and that their promoters ought not to be influential.

But the ingenious gentlemen, alluded to in the commencement of this chapter, insist that the people of England are devotedly attached to us, and pretend that the ribald assaults so frequently made upon us through all the literary channels of the country, are but the unheeded ravings of rabid editors, and the frothy emanations of tourists' brains. This absurd declaration requires no refutation among those who have been in England, who have encountered Englishmen in travelling in the older continents, or who have been much associated with them in our own; but those who have been so fortunate as entirely to escape the annoyance of intercourse with them, need require no better evidence of their hostility, than the tone of their books and newspapers. The peculiar opinions of any people may be best judged of by the style of the books written for their amusement. It is the labor of every author so to adapt his style and sentiments to the tastes of his readers, as most probably to secure their approbation. Whether he writes for fame or money, selfishness prompts him to pursue this course ; and the opinions he advances will inevitably be colored by the prejudices of the community in which he lives. The consciousness that his success is so wholly dependent on their ap-approval will make him, without his being aware of it, adapt his ideas to theirs, even whilst he imagines himself a bold and independent writer. No book was ever yet written without an expectation on the part of the author of its finding readers. 'Tis ridiculous to suppose that any man would submit to the labor of book-making merely for the fun of composition. The preface to a mediocre volume often declares the consciousness of the author, that the tenets of his work must prevent its ever being read. But the pains he takes to make the announcement shows its absurdity. The preface which contains the modest declaration betrays its insincerity. He may pretend that he has resorted to writing to while away leisure hours, or to alleviate mental suffering; and I can very readily conceive of his wishing his lucubrations printed for his own convenience, as a permanent record of his feelings at the time. But surely the preface is altogether superfluous, unless he hopes that other eyes than his own will peruse his thoughts. And the man who unblushingly declares in one of those necessary attachments prefixed to every printed volume, that he has written a book which he believes nobody will read, convicts himself of something very like lying.

Even authors, purely actuated by the higher impulses of ambition, will in spite of themselves study the feelings of their probable readers. How preposterous then is it to declare, that writers in a country like England, where every thing is undertaken with the hope of gain, would crowd their books with sentiments notoriously unpopular. In

England an author's popularity is not estimated by the number of editions issued, but by the *price* paid for his work by the publisher. He is not so much celebrated for the reputation he has established, as the money he has amassed. He writes not for fame but gold. And he endeavors not so much to give utterance to sentiments which will give immortality to his name, as to express opinions which will secure the most favorable terms from his publishers. Nothing is better calculated to produce servility, than a base love of gold. And so long as Englishmen continue to write for money, they will not only studiously avoid shocking the prejudices of their countrymen, but will take particular pains to minister to them. Every prejudice is weighed—every passion consulted by these mercenary bookwrights, in order, by inflaming them, to create a greater demand for their works. They would be the last men in the world to assail America, if they were not assured that scurrilous abuse of that country was the most saleable commodity of their trade.

The press may be justly considered the best thermometer for ascertaining the true state of public opinion, on any subject, in any country, where even the forms of freedom are observed. Editors, in addition to many other manifestations of talent, evince an extraordinarily quick perception of the inclinations of the majority, and generally manage to use them to their advantage. It is a well-approved saying even in America, where a greater independence of spirit and more freedom animates the press than any country in the world, that on all questions of taste or national utility, the press follows public opinion so closely, as to appear to direct it. How much more applicable is this proverb to England, where the acceptance of money for advocating any man or measure is not deemed a prostitution of the press. In the universal scramble for gold which convulses the country, editors of periodicals and newspapers are not ashamed openly to avow their ministering to the most bigoted prejudices, and exciting the worst passions of the people, as a source of profit to themselves. That policy is advocated, that government praised, and those opinions encouraged which it is supposed will pay best. And when this most sordid principle animates the social and political system of England, Americans must not be surprised that Quarterlies—Monthlies, Weeklies and Daylies, should unite in heaping contumely on America, whilst the morbid tastes of Englishmen continue to relish such abuse. As the stereotyped slang, in which they habitually assail us, requires but a small investment of talent, and yields a very handsome profit, an attack on America has become a favorite speculation with the penny-a-liner tradesmen of Great Britain. It is a branch of the business, in which the vilest scribblers may set up, as a large stock in trade is not requisite to make an imposing show. The basest tinsel appears gold, and the lowest Billingsgate is thought to be gay trimming, when they adorn the doublet of slanders, in which these catchpenny speculators in second-hand clothes attempt to array America.

When I can show that both tourists and editors indulge in the coarsest invective against America, I think my readers will agree with me that Englishmen are not quite so ardent in their affection for America as some of our anglicized countrymen would have us suppose. In presenting the following extracts, I have no expectation of informing my readers of what they have not for a long time been aware of. I merely desire to refresh their memories as to the very many outrageous things which have been said of us. Both as to authors and quotations, I have been influenced by convenience; a sufficient number will be given, I hope, to convince even those who may not be familiar with the style of English writers on America, that I have not been unjust in my conclusions with regard to the sentiments of Englishmen towards us.

Mr. Featherstonhaugh has well deserved the honor of being placed in the front rank of those I shall mention, by the freest indulgence of those euphonic epithets which appear most acceptable in the refined circles of England. From Washington to New Orleans this highly tasteful gentleman has adorned his crowning wreath of slanders with the choicest flowers from Billingsgate. The *F. R. S.* ostentatiously tacked to his name, might be very naturally translated by the ignorant into First Royal Scavenger, he appears so perfectly at home in the handling of filth. But though he has so copiously bespattered us with his foul language, I am certain he has caused us no greater uneasiness than the annoyance we should feel in being defiled by any other dirt-cart which happened to pass. But the distinguished gentleman and scholar shall speak for himself. His opening sentence is worthy of the author and his book.

> Any one who has endured for many days the filth and discomfort of that caravansary called *Gadsby's Hotel* at Washington, the city of "magnificent distances," will feel exceedingly rejoiced when, after a short interval of two or three hours, he finds himself transferred by the railroad to Barnum's at Baltimore.

Hear him on the White Sulphur Springs of Virginia:

> Language cannot do justice to the scenes we witnessed, and through which we had to pass at the White Sulphur Springs. It must appear incredible to those who have heard so much of the celebrity of this watering-place, but who have never been here, to be told that this, the most filthy, disorderly place in the United States, with less method and cleanliness about it than belongs to the common jails of the country, and where it is quite impossible to be comfortable, should from year to year be flocked to by great numbers of polite and well-bred people, who have comfortable homes of their own, and who continue to remain

amidst all this discomfort, which, from the nature of things, they know is unchangeable. This requires some explanation.

As a specimen of the "polite and well-bred people," the lucky Mr. Featherstonhaugh encountered at the "Springs," I beg leave to call the attention of my readers to the following conversation between three newly arrived gentlemen from Virginia, Kentucky and Mississippi. The citizens of those States will, of course, recognize the accuracy with which the learned author has given their respective dialects as existing in "polite and well-bred" circles:

One of them maintained that in "the hull woorld there was no sich bacon as Virginia bacon." Another, who was a Kentuckian, felt himself hurt by this observation, and put in an immediate rejoinder; saying, "I allow the Virginians do flog all mankind at praising themselves, and their bacon might be pretty good, but it war'nt to be compared, no not for a beginning of a thing, to the bacon of the western country, where the land was an almighty sight finer, produced better corn, and, of course, made better hogs." The Virginian now became nettled, and swore they had "more *reel* luxuries in old Virginia than they had in the *hull woorld*," and asked the Kentuckian if they had "oysters in Kentucky, and clams, and sich-like;" finishing with a declaration that the finest land in the "hull woorld" was in Southampton County. These oysters silenced the Kentuckian, who, living far in the interior, had never seen any; but a resident of the State of "*Massa*sippi," who could not stand this boast of fine land, put it to the Virginian whether they could grow sugar in Southampton County, and added that he had "always heer'n that the hawysters of New-Orl*ee*ns had sich a *on*accountable fine flavour, that they would knock the hawysters of Old Virginny into their ninety-ninth year any day." "I reckon they get that from the yellow fever," rejoined the Virginian.

He gives a truthful and graphic description of the style of accommodation prevailing at the Springs:

The mattress was full of knots, and what was in the thing that was intended to be my pillow I never ascertained; but a gentleman informed me that he and his wife having, after the usual vexatious delays, got into some room resembling ours, as soon as they laid down for the night, found their pillow not only very disagreeable from a sickening odour that came from it, but gifted with some curious hard knobs in it that were moveable. As it was out of the question to sleep upon it, he threw it on one side, and had the curiosity to examine it in the morning, when he discovered that they had not only bountifully put a handful or two of dirty live feathers into it, but the necks, with the heads to them, of two chickens and a duck. I have not the least doubt of the truth of this, for the slaves who attend to such matters have entirely their own way, and there is no one to examine their conduct.

The fossil gatherer is thrown into a helpless state of wondering bewilderment by the "grand bolting operation." The astonishment is truly incomprehensible which could deprive an Englishman of his dinner:

But who can describe the noise, the confusion incident to a grand bolting operation, conducted by three hundred American performers, and a hundred and fifty black slaves to help them? It seemed to me that almost every man at table considered himself at job-work against time, stuffing sausages and whatever else he could cram into his throat. But the dinner-scene presented a spectacle still more extraordinary than the breakfast. And, first, as to the cooking, which was after this mode. Bacon, venison, beef, and mutton, were all boiled together in the same vessel; then those pieces that were to represent roast meat were taken out and put into an oven for awhile; after which a sort of dirty gravy was poured from a huge pitcher indiscriminately upon roast and boiled. What with this strange banquet, and the clinking of knives and forks, the rattling of plates, the confused running about of troops of dirty slaves, the numerous cries for this, that, and the other, the exclamations of the new-comers, "Oh, my gracious! I reckon I never did see sich a dirty table-cloth," the nasty appearance of the incomprehensible dishes, the badness of the water brought from the creek where the clothes were washed, and the universal feculence of everything around, the scene was perfectly astounding. Twice I tried to dine there, but it was impossible. I could do nothing but stare, and before my wonder was over everything was gone, people and all, except a few slow eaters. I never could become reconciled to the universal filth, as some told me they had got to be, and my wife would literally have got nothing to eat if I had not given a douceur to the cook, and another to one of the black servants, to provide her every day a small dish of fried venison or mutton, for which we waited until it was placed before her; this, with very good bread—and it always was good—was her only resource. Much squeezed as we were at first, there was a sensible relaxation and more elbow-room in a very few minutes, in consequence of the great numbers who had the talent of bolting their "feed" in five minutes. A gentleman drew my attention to one of these quick feeders, who had been timed by himself and others, and who had been observed to bolt the most extraordinary quantities of angular pieces of bacon, beef, and mutton, in the short period of two minutes and a half. This was a strange, meagre, sallow-looking man, with black hair and white whiskers and beard, as if his jaws had done more work than his brains. All the bolters went at it just as quick feeders do in a kennel of hounds, helping themselves to a whole dish without ceremony, cutting off immense long morsels, and then presenting them with a dexterous turn of the tongue to the anxious œsophagus, would launch them down by the small end foremost, with all the confidence that an alligator swallows a young nigger, into that friendly asylum where roast and boiled, baked and stewed, pudding and pie, all that is good, and too often what is not very good, meet for all sorts of noble and ignoble purposes. These quick feeders, with scarce an exception, were gaunt, sallow, uncomely-looking persons, incapable of inspiring much interest out of their coffins, always excepting, however, the performer with the white whiskers, whose unrivalled talent in the present state of the drama, might, perhaps, be turned to great account in some of the enlightened capitals of Europe.

Our friends in St. Louis have reason to feel indebted for the subjoined glowing description of their principal hotel:

At the tavern where I lodged all was dirt, disorder, and want of system. A pack of ragged young negroes performed the service of chambermaids and waiters, and did it about as well as a pack of grown monkeys, caught in the Brazils, would do in three months' teaching. The landlord, who to me was always very obliging, seemed to have no sort of authority either over his servants or his guests. These principally consisted of those impudent, smoking, spitting shopboys, who are dignified in the United States with the appellation of "clerks." I only occasionally dined there; but it was always the same thing. At the ringing of a bell these "clerks" rushed in crowds to the table, just as a pack of hounds or a drove of swine would to their feed. I found it most prudent to wait a short time, for in eight minutes they had gobbled everything up, and had again rushed out to take a glass of swipes, a cigar, and go to their "stores." One of the intolerable evils of practical equality is, the obliging clean people to herd with dirty ones. The landlord, however, seeing my way of doing things, used generally to send me something hot and comfortable to eat at my leisure.

After allowing his mouth to water over the various "good" things of the country, which were spoiled however in the cooking, the rock-cracker indulges in a passing hit at American avarice:

The country, indeed, abounds with what is good, but the majority of the people do not seem to care how they live, provided it does not interfere with the grand exclusive object of their existence, making money. Wherever I go—with the fewest exceptions—this is the all-prevailing passion. The word money seems to stand as the representative of the word "happiness" of other countries. In other lands we see rank, distinction in society, scientific and literary acquirements, with the other elevating objects that embellish and dignify human life, pursued by great numbers with constancy and ardour; but here all other avenues to advancement, except the golden one, seem nearly untrod—the shortest cut, *coute qui coute*, to that which leads to ready money being the favourite one. Where this sordid passion stifles the generous ones, a rapacious selfishness is sure to establish itself; men cease to act for the general welfare, and society at length resolves itself into a community, the great object of every individual of which is to grasp as much as will last as long as himself.

His description of the people of New Orleans is brief, but complimentary:

The population partook strongly of the character of the latitude it was in, a medley of Spaniards, Brazilians, West Indians, French Creoles, and breeds of all these mixed up with the negro stock. I think I never met one person without a cigar in his mouth, and certainly, taking it altogether, I never saw such a piratical-looking population before. Dark, swarthy, thin, whiskered, smoking, dirty, reckless-looking men; and filthy, ragged, screaming negroes and mulattoes, crowded even Rue de Chartres, where our lodgings were, and made it a very unpleasant quarter to be in. Notwithstanding it was Sunday, the market was open, and there I saw green peas (January 1st), salads, bouquets of roses, bananas from Havanna, and various good things that reminded me I was in the 30th degree of N. lat.

He does not appear, however, to entertain a very exalted opinion of the religious principles of the "Crescent City:"

It is evident that the future population of New Orleans is likely to afford a rare specimen of the forms society can be made to take in a semi-tropical climate, where the passions act unrestrainedly, and where money is the established religion of the country.

He is singularly mild when he touches on my adopted State of Arkansas:

This territory of Arkansas was on the confines of the United States and of Mexico, and, as I had long known, was the occasional residence of many timid and nervous persons, against whom the laws of these respective countries had a grudge. *Gentlemen*, who had taken the liberty to imitate the signatures of other persons; *bankrupts*, who were not disposed to be plundered by their creditors; *homicides, horse-stealers*, and *gamblers*, all admired Arkansas on account of the very gentle and tolerant state of public opinion which prevailed there in regard to such fundamental points as religion, morals and property. Here, flying from a stormy world of chicane and trouble, they found repose from the terrors it inspired, and looked back upon it somewhat as Dante's storm-tossed mariner did upon the devouring ocean.

Here is another pleasant allusion to "Jonathan and the Dollar":

Such is the plastic nature of Jonathan, his indomitable affection for the almighty dollar, and his enterprise in the pursuit of it, that it is far from being impossible that there are lots of his brethren at this time in the interior of China, with their heads shaved and long pig-tails behind them, peddling cuckoo clocks and selling wooden nutmegs.

I give an agreeable little sketch of the delights of boat-travelling in the Southwest. What opinion must we form of this scientific traveller when he introduces the name of a private gentleman into his vile pages, in connection with such epithets as Mr. Rector is coupled with. Persons in distant parts of the country will be surprised to learn that this blackguard, as described by Mr. Featherstonhaugh, is a man of position and intelligence; I know him personally, and his manners and appearance are those of a man of refinement and good breeding. Few citizens are more respected among those who know him than this much slandered Mr. Rector. How can Mr. Featherstonhaugh expect to be believed in other respects when he perpetrates such base calumnies, and allows his opinions to be so warped by prejudice:

Upon embarking on board of this steamer I was certainly pleased with the prospect that presented itself of enjoying some repose and comfort after the privations and fatigues I had endured; but never was traveller more mistaken in his anticipations! The vexatious conduct of the drunken youth had made a serious innovation upon the slight degree of personal comfort to be obtained in such a place, but I had not the slightest conception that that incident would be entirely thrown into the shade by others a thousand times more offensive, and that, from the moment of our departure from the post of Arkansas until our arrival at New Orleans, I was destined to a series of brutal annoyances that extinguished every hope of repose, or a chance of preserving even the decencies of existence.

I had been told at the post of Arkansas that ten passengers were waiting to come on board, and that several of them were notorious swindlers and gamblers, who, whilst in Arkansas, lived by the most desperate cheating and bullying, and who skulked about alternately betwixt Little Rock, Natchez, and New Orleans, in search of any plunder that violent and base means could bring into their hands. Some of their names were familiar to me, having heard them frequently spoken of at Little Rock as scoundrels of the worst class. From the moment I heard they were coming on board as passengers I predicted to Mr. T******** that every hope of comfort was at an end. But I had also been told that two American officers, a Captain D***** and a Lieutenant C******—the latter a gentleman entrusted with the construction of the military road in Arkansas—were also coming on board; and I counted upon them as persons who would be, by the force of education and a consciousness of what was due to their rank as officers, on the side of decency at least, if not of correct manners; and if those persons had passed through the national military academy at West Point, or had served under the respectable chief* of the Topographical Bureau at Washington, I should not have been as grievously disappointed as it was my fate to be. It was true I had heard that these officers had been passing ten days with these scoundrels at a low tavern in this place, in the unrestrained indulgence of every vicious extravagance, night and day, and that they were the familiar intimates of these notorious swindlers. Nevertheless, believing that there must be some exaggeration in this, I continued to look forward with satisfaction to having them for fellow-passengers, confident that they would be our allies against any gross encroachments of the others.

Very soon after I had retired to the steamer at sunset, the whole clique came on board, and the effect produced on us was something like that which would be made upon passengers in a peaceful vessel forcibly boarded by pirates of the most desperate character, whose manners seemed to be what they aspired to imitate. Rushing into the cabin, all but red-hot with whiskey, they crowded round the stove and excluded all the old passengers from it as much as if they had no right whatever to be in the cabin. Putting on a determined bullying air of doing what they pleased because they were the majority, and armed with pistols and knives, expressly made for cutting and stabbing, eight inches long and an inch and a half broad; noise, confusion, spitting, smoking, cursing and swearing, drawn from the most remorseless pages of blasphemy, commenced and prevailed from the moment of this invasion. I was satisfied at once that all resistance would be vain, and that even remonstrance might lead to murder; for a sickly old man in the cabin happening to say to one of them there was so much smoke he could hardly breathe, the fellow immediately said, "If any man tells me he don't like my smoking I'll put a knife into him."

* Colonel Abert.

As soon as supper was over they all went to gambling, during which, at every turn of the cards, imprecations and blasphemies of the most revolting kind were loudly vociferated. Observing them from a distance where Mr..T******** and myself were seated, I perceived that one of them was the wretched looking fellow I had seen at Hignite's, on my way to Texas, who went by the name of Smith, and that his keeper Mr. Tunstall was with him. The most blasphemous fellows amongst them were two men of the names of Rector and Wilson. This Rector at that time held a commission under the national government as Marshal for the territory of Arkansas, who was a man of mean stature, low and sottish in his manners, and as corrupt and reckless as it was possible for a human being to be. The man named Wilson was a suttler from cantonment Gibson, a military post about 250 miles up the Arkansas: he had a remarkable depression at the bottom of his forehead; and from this sinus his nose rising with a sudden spring, gave a fural expression to his face that exactly resembled the portrait of the wicked apprentice in Hogarth. The rubric on his countenance too was a faithful register of the numerous journeys the whiskey bottle had made to his proboscis.

We have in the following extract another specimen of this impartial author's delicacy in introducing private persons by name into such a work as his. It seems the chief crime of these "Mississippi gentlemen" was gambling. I wonder if he ever heard of the notorious "hells" of London? Have *gentlemen* never gamed in England?

Vicksburg is a modern settlement situated on the side of a hill very much abraded and cut up into gullies by the rains. The land rises about 200 feet above the Mississippi, but sinks again very soon to the east, forming a sort of ridge which appears at intervals as far as Baton Rouge. On returning to the steamer we were informed that eight or ten *gentlemen*, some of whom were planters of great respectability, and amongst the rest, a Mr. Vick, after whom the place was called, were coming on board with the intention of going to New Orleans. This determined us to continue on with the boat, conceiving that we should be too many for the ruffians in the cabin, and that the captain—who was anxious to keep up a good understanding with the planters—would now interfere to keep some order there. But supper being over, and the faro-table spread as usual, what was my horror and astonishment at seeing these Mississippi *gentlemen*, with the *respectable* Mr. Vick, sitting down to faro with these swindlers, and in the course of a very short time gambling, drinking, smoking, and blaspheming just as desperately as the worst of them! The cabin became so full of tobacco smoke that it was impossible for me to remain in it.

I shall dismiss Mr. Featherstonhaugh with the following extract, from which there seems to be an inclination towards prejudice against America in England:

It is not to be concealed, nevertheless, that this frequent expression of aversion to the mother country, added to the late notorious violations of the most solemn engagements from the same quarter, have raised a strong and a deep-rooted prejudice on this side of the Atlantic, which, although natural, is to a certain extent unjust, because there is little or no discrimination observed in it.

Mrs. Trollope is in every respect the worthy companion of Mr. Featherstonhaugh. Her name is so peculiarly illustrative of the style of her book, that one feels half inclined to suspect that it was assumed for the occasion. I regret that I shall be unable to draw copiously from her highly variegated pages. I shall begin with the two general observations on American character, which follow:

It was not till I had leisure for more minute observation, that I felt aware of the influence of slavery upon the owners of slaves; when I did, I confess I could not but think that the citizens of the United States had contrived, by their political alchemy, to extract all that was most noxious both in democracy and in slavery, and had poured the strange mixture through every vein of the moral organization of their country.

How often did our homely adage recur to me, "All work, and no play, would make Jack a dull boy;" Jonathan is a very dull boy. We are by no means so gay as our lively neighbors on the other side of the Channel; but, compared with the Americans, we are whirligigs and tetotums; every day is a holiday, and every night a festival.

For fear that our northern friends should be mortified by supposing that the attention of such talented writers had been exclusivelv devoted to the South, I beg leave to direct their attention to what Mrs. Trollope politely says of them:

Nothing can exceed their activity and perseverance in all kinds of speculation, handicraft and enterprise, which promises a profitable pecuniary result. I heard an Englishman, who had been long resident in America, declare that in following, in meeting, or in overtaking, in the street, on the road, or in the field, at the theatre, the coffee-house, or at home, he had never overheard Americans conversing without the word DOLLAR being pronounced between them. Such unity of purpose, such sympathy of feeling, can, I believe, be found nowhere else, except, perhaps, in an ant's nest. The result is exactly what might be anticipated. This sordid object, for ever before their eyes, must inevitably produce a sordid tone of mind, and, worse still, it produces a seared and blunted conscience on all questions of probity. I know not a more striking evidence of the low tone of morality which is generated by this universal pursuit of money, than the manner in which the New England States are described by Americans. All agree in saying that they present a spectacle of industry and prosperity delightful to behold, and this is the district and the population most constantly quoted as the finest specimen of their admirable country; yet I never met a single individual in any part of the Union who did not paint these New Englanders as sly, grinding, selfish, and tricking. The Yankees (as the New Englanders are called) will avow these qualities themselves with a complacent smile, and boast that no people on the earth can match them at overreaching in a bargain. I have heard them unblushingly relate stories of their cronies and friends, which, if believed among us, would banish the heroes from the fellowship of honest men for ever; and all this is uttered with a simplicity which sometimes led me to doubt if the speakers knew what honor and honesty meant. Yet the Americans declare that "they are the most moral people upon earth." Again and again I have heard this asserted, not only in conversation, and by their writings, but even from the pulpit. Such broad assumption of superior virtue demands examination, and after four years of attentive and earnest observation and inquiry, my honest conviction is, that the standard of moral character in the United States is very greatly lower than in Europe. Of their religion, as it appears outwardly, I have had occasion to speak frequently; I pretend not to judge the heart, but, without any uncharitable presumption, I must take permission to say, that both Protestant England and Catholic France show an infinitely superior religious and moral aspect to mortal observation, both as to reverend decency of external observance, and as to the inward fruit of honest dealing between man and man.

Mrs. Trollope being a native of England, descants of course upon our style of dinners and parties, and being a woman, she very good-naturedly introduces the ladies. The gossiping female was ugly as well as fat, and should, therefore, be excused for what she says of her own sex. Human nature is very weak, and envy overwhelmingly predominant in the female heart:

They seldom indulge in second courses, with all their ingenious temptations to the eating a second dinner; but almost every table has its dessert (invariably pronounced desart), which is placed on the table before the cloth is removed, and consists of pastry, preserved fruits, and creams. They are "extravagantly fond," to use their own phrase, of puddings, pies, and all kinds of "sweets," particularly the ladies; but are by no means such connoisseurs in soups and ragoûts as the gastronomes of Europe. Almost every one drinks water at table; and by a strange contradiction, in the country where hard drinking is more prevalent than in any other, there is less wine taken at dinner; ladies rarely exceed one glass, and the great majority of females never take any. In fact, the hard drinking, so universally acknowledged, does not take place at jovial dinners, but, to speak plain English, in solitary dram-drinking. Coffee is not served immediately after dinner, but makes part of the serious matter of tea-drinking, which comes some hours later. Mixed dinner parties of ladies and gentlemen are very rare, and unless several foreigners are present, but little conversation passes at table. It certainly does not, in my opinion, add to the well ordering a dinner table, to set the gentlemen at one end of it, and the ladies at the other; but it is very rarely that you find it otherwise.

There large evening parties are supremely dull; the men sometimes play cards by themselves, but if a lady plays, it must not be for money; no ecarté, no chess; very little music, and that little lamentably bad. Among the blacks I heard some good voices singing in tune; but I scarcely ever heard a white American, male or female, go through an air without being out of tune before the end of it; nor did I ever meet any trace of science in the singing I heard in society. To eat inconceivable quantities of cake, ice, and pickled oysters—and to show half their revenue in silks and satins, seem to be the chief object they have in these parties.

The most agreeable meetings, I was assured by all the young people, were those to which no married women are admitted; of the truth of this statement I have not the least doubt. These exclusive meetings occur frequently, and often last to a late hour; on these occasions, I believe, they generally dance. At regular balls married ladies are admitted, but seldom take much part in the amusement. The refreshments are always profuse and costly, but taken in a most uncomfortable manner. I have known many private balls, where every thing was on the most liberal scale of expense, where the gentlemen sat down to supper in one room, while the ladies took theirs, standing, in another.

What we call pic-nics are very rare, and when attempted, do not often succeed well. The two sexes can hardly mix for the greater part of a day without great restraint and ennui; it is quite contrary to their general habits; the favorite indulgences of the gentlemen (smoking cigars and drinking spirits) can neither be indulged in with decency, nor resigned with complacency.

The ladies have strange ways of adding to their charms. They powder themselves immoderately, face, neck, and arms, with pulverized starch; the effect is indescribably disagreeable by daylight, and not very favorable at any time. They are also most unhappily partial to false hair, which they wear in surprising quantities; this is the more to be lamented, as they generally have very fine hair of their own. I suspect this fashion to arise from an indolent mode of making their toilet, and from accomplished ladies' maids not being very abundant; it is less trouble to append a bunch of waving curls here, there, and every where, than to keep their native tresses in perfect order.

Though the expense of the ladies' dress greatly exceeds, in proportion to their general style of living, that of the ladies of Europe, it is very far (excepting in Philadelphia) from being in good taste. They do not consult the seasons in the colors or in the style of their costume; I have often shivered at seeing a young beauty picking her way through the snow with a pale rose-colored bonnet set on the very top of her head.

She evidently does not admire the dancing of our American ladies, and regrets that there are not a greater number of French dancing-masters among them. Our men are good looking, but, like the ladies, do not understand the mysteries of "carrying themselves" to Mrs. Trollope's satisfaction. I am especially sorry for this, as "comeliness" of our people is about the only thing which Mrs. T. was pleased to think passable.

I fancied I could often trace a mixture of affectation and of shyness in their little mincing unsteady step, and the ever-changing position of the hands. They do not dance well: perhaps I should rather say they do not look well when dancing; lovely as their faces are, they cannot, in a position that exhibits the whole person, atone for the want of *tournure*, and for the universal defect in the formation of the bust, which is rarely full or gracefully formed.

I never saw an American man walk or stand well; notwithstanding their frequent militia drillings, they are nearly all hollow-chested and round-shouldered: perhaps this is occasioned by no officer daring to say to a brother free-born "hold up your head;" whatever the cause, the effect is very remarkable to a stranger. In stature, and in physiognomy, a great majority of the population, both male and female, are strikingly handsome, but they do not know how to do their own honors; half as much comeliness elsewhere would produce ten times as much effect.

I regret exceedingly that circumstances should prevent my enjoying the pleasure of presenting to my readers a few extracts from Capt. Hall and Mr. Dickens, for although they may be familiar with these authors, yet they probably would not have objected to perusing them a second time, as they have well deserved a place beside Mr. Feathersonhaugh and Mrs. Trollope. But the extracts I have made will be sufficient, with some that I shall add from the Quarterly Review, for my purpose of illustrating the spirit of the literary world towards us.

In the following extracts from "Men and Manners in

America," by the author of "Cyril Thornton" and "The Stranger in America," by Charles William Janson, the same tone is observable, though my readers are, perhaps, less familiar with them than the preceding distinguished commentators on our country:

Men and Manners in America, by the author of "Cyril Thornton."

Page 29:

My curiosity was somewhat excited by the high reputation which an actor, named Forrest, has acquired in this country. I have since seen this rara avis, and, I confess, the praise so profusely lavished on him does appear to me somewhat gratuitous. He is a coarse, vulgar actor, without grace, without dignity, with little flexibility of feature, and entirely common-place in his conception of character.

Page 30:

Bunker's Hotel, New-York.

Around I beheld the same scene of gulping and swallowing as if for a wager, which my observations at breakfast had prepared me to expect; each individual seemed to pitchfork his food down his gullet.

Page 116:

A traveller has no sooner time to look about him in Boston than he receives the conviction, that he is thrown among a population of a character differing in much from that of any other city of the Union.

Observe him in every different situation,—at the funeral and the marriage feast, at the theatre and the conventicle, in the ball-room and on the exchange, and you will set him down as of God's creatures the least liable to be influenced by circumstances appealing to the heart or the imagination.

Page 126:

There is nothing of local attachment about the New Englander. * * The whole Union is full of stories of his cunning frauds and the impositions he delights to perpetrate on his more simple neighbors. Whenever his love of money comes in competition with his zeal for religion, the latter is sure to give way. He will insist on the scrupulous observance of the Sabbath, and cheat his customer Monday morning. * * * The New Englanders are not an amiable people. One meets in them much to approve, little to admire, and nothing to love. * * * Nature in framing a Yankee seems to have given him double brains and half a heart.

Page 169:

In truth every year must increase the perils of the Federal Constitution; like other bubbles, it is liable to burst at any time, and the world will then discover that its external glitter covered nothing but wind.

Page 173:

The leader who gave the first powerful impulse to the democratic tendencies of the Constitution. His countrymen call him great, but, in truth, he was only great when compared with those by whom he was surrounded. * * * We seek in vain in the writings of Jefferson for indication of original or profound thought. * * * He has been truly called a good-hater. His resentments were not vehement and fiery ebullitions of passion burning fiercely for a time, and then subsiding into indifference or dislike. They were cool, fiendlike, and ferocious; unsparing, undying, unappeasable. The enmities of most men terminate with the death of their object. It was the delight of Jefferson to trample on the graves of his political opponents.

Page 174:

The moral character of Jefferson was repulsive. Continually puling about liberty, equality, and the degrading curse of slavery, he brought his own children to the hammer, and made money by his debaucheries. Even at his death he did not manumit his numerous offspring, but left them, soul and body, to degradation and the cart-whip. A daughter of Jefferson's was sold some years ago by public auction at New-Orleans, and purchased by a society of gentlemen, who wished to testify, by her liberation, their admiration of the statesman, "who dreamt of freedom in a slave's embrace." This single line gives more insight to the character of the man than whole volumes of panegyric. It will outlive his epitaph, write it who may.

Page 195:

In the present generation of Americans I can detect no symptom of improving taste or increasing elevation of intellect.

Page 196:

There is at this moment nothing in the United States deserving the name of library. At present an American might study every book in the limits of the Union, and still be regarded in many parts of Europe, especially Germany, as a man comparatively ignorant.

Page 224:

I have already described the hall of the Representatives. I would now say something of the members (of Congress). Their aspect, as a body, was certainly somewhat different from any idea I had formed of a legislative body. Many were well-dressed, and of appearance sufficiently senatorial to satisfy the utmost demands even of a severer critic in such matters than I pretend to be; but a large proportion undoubtedly struck me as vulgar and uncouth, in a degree which nothing in my previous experience had prepared me to expect. It is impossible to look at these men without at once receiving the conviction that they are not gentlemen by habit or education, and assuredly in no society in Europe could they be received as such.

Page 260:

Mr. Burgess's Speech in Congress.—Were it possible to give any valuable report of the speech, which of itself would fill a volume, I would willingly appeal to it as exemplifying the justice of every blunder, both of taste and judgment, which I have attributed to American eloquence. There were scraps of Latin and Shakspeare. There were words without meaning, and meanings not worth the trouble of embodying in words. There were bad jokes, and bad logic, and arguments without logic of any kind. There were abundance of exotic graces and homebred vulgarities; of elaborate illustration, of established truths, and vehement invective, and prosy declamation; of conclusions without premises, and premises that led to no conclusions; and yet this very speech was the object of an eight days' wonder to the whole Union. The amount of praise bestowed on it in the public journals would have been condemned as hyperbolical if applied to an oration of Demosthenes. Mr. Burgess, at the termination of the session, was feted at New-York; and Rhode Island exulted in the verbal prowess of the most gifted of her sons.

Page 294:

I had never heard of Mrs. Trollope; but at New-York I had afterwards the pleasure of becoming acquainted with her, and can bear testimony to her conversation being imbued with all the grace, spirit, and vivacity which have since delighted the world in her writings. How far Mrs. Trollope's volumes present a just picture of American society it is not for me to decide, though I can offer willing testimony to the general fidelity of her descriptions. * * * But her claims to the gratitude of the Cincinnatians are undoubtedly very great. Her architectural talent has beautified the city, and her literary powers have given it celebrity. For nearly thirty years Cincinnati had gradually been increasing in opulence, and enjoying a vulgar and obscure prosperity; corn had grown, and hogs had fattened; men had built houses, and women borne children; but in all the higher senses of urbane existence Cincinnati was a nonentity. "It was unknown, unhonored, and unsung." Ears polite had never heard of it. There was not the glimmering of hope that it would be mentioned twice in a twelvemonth on the Liverpool exchange. But Mrs. Trollope came, and a zone of light has ever since encircled Cincinnati. Its inhabitants are no longer a race unknown to fame. Their manners, habits, virtues, tastes, vices and pursuits are known to all the world; but, strange to say, the market-place of Cincinnati is yet unadorned by the statue of the great benefactress of the city.

Page 296:

In regard to the passengers (on the steamboat) truth compels me to say that any thing so disgusting in human shape I had never seen. Their morals and their manners were alike detestable—a cold and callous selfishness, a disregard of all the decencies of society, were so apparent in feature, word, and action, that I found it impossible not to wish that their catalogue of sins had been enlarged by one more—hypocrisy. Of hypocrisy, however, they were not guilty. The conversation in the cabin was interlarded with the vilest blasphemy, not uttered in a state of mental excitement, but with a coolness and deliberation truly fiendlike. There was a Baptist clergyman on board, but his presence did not operate as a restraint. The scene of drinking and gambling had no intermission; it continued day and night. The captain of the vessel, so far from discouraging either vice, was one of the most flagrant offenders in both. He was decidedly the greatest gambler on board, and was often so drunk as to be utterly incapable of taking command of the vessel. * * * One circumstance may be mentioned, which is tolerably illustrative of the general habits of the people; in every steamboat there is a *public comb* and hairbrush, suspended by a string from the ceiling of the cabin. These utensils are used by the whole body of the passengers, and their condition the pen of Swift alone could describe. There is no tooth-brush; simply, I believe, because the article is entirely unknown to the American toilet.

Page 266:

On the following evening I attended the President's (General Jackson's) levee. Three—I am not sure four—large saloons were thrown open on the occasion, and were literally crammed with the most singular and miscellaneous assemblage I had ever seen. * * * The numerical majority of the company seemed of the class of tradesmen and farmers, respectable men, fresh from the plough or the counter, who, accompanied by their wives and daughters, came forth to greet their President and enjoy the splendors of the gala. There were also generals, and commodores, and public officers of every grade, and foreign ministers, and members of Congress, and ladies of all ages and degrees of beauty, from the fair and laughing girl of fifteen to the haggard dowager of seventy. * * * There were mayors in broadcloth and corduroys, redolent of gin and tobacco, and mayors' ladies in chintz or russet, with huge Paris ear-rings and tawny necks, profusely decorated with beads of colored glass. There were tailors from the board, and judges from the bench; lawyers, who opened their mouths at one bar, and tapsters who closed them at another; in short, every trade, calling, craft, and profession, appeared to have sent delegates to this extraordinary convention.* * * For myself, I had seen too much of the United States to expect any thing different, and certainly anticipated that the mixture would contain all the ingredients I have ventured to describe. Yet, after all, I was taken by surprise. * * * There were present at this levee men begrimed with all the sweat and filth accumulated in their day's—perhaps their week's labor. There were sooty artificers fresh from the forge or the workshop; and one individual I remember, either a miller or baker, who, wherever he passed, left marks of contact on the garments of the company. The most prominent group, however, in the assemblage was a party of Irish laborers, employed on some neighboring canal, who had evidently been apt scholars in the doctrine of liberty and equality, and were determined on the present occasion to assert the full privileges of the great "unwashed." I remarked these men pushing aside the more respectable portion of the company with a certain jocular audacity which put one in mind of the humors of Donnybrook fair.

Page 279:

During the time I was engaged at the levee, my servant remained in the hall, through which lay the entrance to the apartments occupied by the company, and the day following gave me a few details of a scene somewhat extraordinary but sufficiently characteristic to merit record. * * * It appeared that the refreshments intended for the company, consisting of punch and lemonade, were brought by the servants, with the intention of reaching the interior saloons. No sooner, however, were these ministers of Bacchus descried to be approaching, than a rush was made from within, and the whole contents of the trays were seized *in transitu* by a sort of *coup-de-main;* and the bearers, having thus rapidly achieved the distribution of their refreshments, had nothing for it but to return for a fresh supply. This was brought, and quite as compendiously dispatched; and it at length became apparent that, without resorting to some extraordinary measures, it would be impossible to accomplish the intended voyage, and the more respectable portion of the audience would be suffered to depart with dry palates, and in utter ignorance of the extent of the hospitality to which they were indebted. The butler, however, was an Irishman, and, in order to baffle further attempts at intercepting the supplies, had recourse to an expedient marked by all the ingenuity of his countrymen. * * * He procured an escort, armed them with sticks, and, on his next advance, these men kept flourishing their *shillelahs* around the trays with such alarming vehemence that the *predatory horde*, who anticipated a repetition of their plunder, were scared from their prey, and, amid a scene of execration and laughter, the refreshments, thus guarded, accomplished their journey to the saloon in safety.

Page 346:

The inhabitants (of Georgia) bear a bad character in other parts of the Union. They are, perhaps, a little savage and ferocious, and, in regard to morals, one is tempted occasionally to regret that the gibbet is not abroad as well as the schoolmaster. From Fort Mitchell, I travelled with three attorneys, two storekeepers, two cotton planters and a slave dealer. My notions of the sort of conversation prevalent in Newgate may not be very accurate, but I much doubt whether it would be found to indicate such debasement, both of thought and principle, as that to which I was condemned to listen during this journey. Georgia receives large accessions of population in the off-scourings of other slave States. The restraints of law are little felt, and it is the only State where I heard it publicly asserted that justice is not purely administered.

The Stranger in America, by Charles William Janson.

Page 9:

While at our first meal on board, a specimen of American effrontery was given us by Bob, the cook-boy, a sprig of a true-born Yankee, who, reaching his dirty arm across the table, took a tumbler and deliberately filled it with equal parts of rum and water. He looked round, and familiarly nodding his head, said, "Good folks, here's to you."

Page 29:

At Boston they distil large quantities of that detestable spirit called New England Rum. It is made of damaged molasses, and its baleful effects are severely felt in every part of the Union. In Virginia, the Carolinas, and Georgia, it foments quarrels, which produce combats, like bears and wolves, gouging, biting, kicking, and tearing each other's flesh, of which I shall make particular mention when I speak of those States.

Page 309:

On a branch of this river (the Alligator, in North Carolina), in the year I have already named, lived a wealthy planter, by name John Foster. With this man I remained several days, and in him learned something of a Southern Planter. * * * Mine host had led me over the plantation, and we arrived, almost exhausted from the effects of a scorching sun, at the dinner hour. Our meal consisted of venison and a variety of vegetables, which we diluted with apple brandy and water. This is a most detestable beverage. * * * I had no choice of spirits, and to drink water undiluted is often of dangerous tendency. * * * Thus is an Alligator tavern provided with liquors, and, in fact, it was as well supplied as any other place of public resort in the district.* * * A different circumstance produced on me, while at dinner, more disgust than even the fumes of the deleterious drink. This was the officious attendance of two wenches, three-parts grown, without even the covering our first mother made for herself after her expulsion from Paradise. * * * The effluvia arising from the body of a negro in the month of July are by no means odoriferous; hence I could have dispensed with one of these placed, in compliment, behind my chair. To complete the scene, Mr. Foster's daughter, a fine girl of sixteen, dined at our table, and gave orders to the naked creatures of her own sex with the most perfect *sang froid.*

What I shall give from the Foreign Quarterly Review, of January, 1844, is merely an example of the tone of the periodical and daily press towards us for years past, as those will admit who have been familiar with that branch of English literature. The article referred to, is on the Poets of America, and commences as follows: "AMERICAN POETRY always reminds us of the advertisement headed, 'the best substitute for silver;' if it be not the genuine thing it 'looks just as handsome, and is miles out of sight cheaper.'"

We are far from regarding it as a just ground of reproach to the Americans, that their poetry is little better than a far-off echo of the father-land; but we think it *is* a reproach to them that they should be eternally thrusting their pretensions to the poetical character in the face of educated nations. In this particular, as in most others, what they want in the integrity of their assumption, they make up in swagger and impudence. To believe themselves, they are the finest poets in the whole world: before we close this article we hope to satisfy the reader that, with two or three exceptions, there is not a poet of mark in the whole Union.

A very original notion of our moral and physical nature is advanced in the following:

They have felled forests, drained marshes, cleared wildernesses, built cities, cut canals, laid down railroads (too much of this too with other people's money), and worked out a great practical exemplification, in an amazingly short space of time, of the political immoralities and social vices of which a democracy may be rendered capable.

There must be a national heart, and national sympathies, and an intellectual atmosphere for poetry. There must be the material to work upon as well as to work with. The ground must be prepared before the seed is cast into it, and tended and well-ordered, or it will become choked with weeds, as American literature, such as it is, is now choked in every one of its multifarious manifestations. As yet the American is horn-handed and pig-headed, hard, persevering, unscrupulous, carnivorous, ready for all weathers, with an incredible genius for lying, a vanity elastic beyond comprehension, the hide of a buffalo, and the shriek of a steam-engine; 'a real nine-foot breast of a fellow, steel twisted and made of horse-shoe nails, the rest of him being cast iron with steel springs.'

The subjoined picture of American society is highly interesting, as it emanates from the leading British Periodical. It is often gratifying to know what our neighbors think of us. The English have been always *very* candid:

Peopled originally by adventurers of all classes and casts, America has been consistently replenished ever since by the dregs and outcasts of all other countries. Spaniards, Portuguese, French and English, Irish, Welsh, and Scotch, have from time to time poured upon her coasts like wolves in search of the means of life, living from hand to mouth, and struggling outward upon the free Indians whom they hunted, cheated, demoralized, and extirpated in the sheer fury of hungry and fraudulent aggrandizement. Catholics, Unitarians, Calvinists and Infidels were indiscriminately mixed up in this work of violent seizure and riotous colonization, settling down at last into sectional democracies, bound together by a common interest, and a common distrust, and evolving an ultimate form of self-government and federal centralization to keep the whole in check.

This brigand confederation grew larger and larger every day, with a rapidity unexampled in the history of mankind, by continual accessions from all parts of the habitable world. All it required to strengthen itself was human muscles; it lacked nothing but workmen, craftsmen, blood, bones, and sinews. Brains were little or nothing to the purpose—character, morality, still less. "A long pull, a strong pull, and a pull altogether," was the one thing needful. Every new hand was a help, no matter what brand was upon its palm. The needy and dissolute, tempted by the prospect of gain—the debased, glad to escape from the old society which had flung them off—the criminal, flying from the laws they had outraged—all flocked to America as an open haven of refuge for the Pariahs of the wide earth. Thus her population was augmented and is daily augmenting; thus her republics are armed; thus her polite assemblies and select circles are constantly enlivened by fresh draughts of kindred spirits and foreign celebrities—the Sheriff Parkinses, the General Holts, the town-treasurer Flinns, the chartist secretary Campbells, and the numerous worthies who, having successfully swindled their own countrymen, seek an elegant retirement in the free States of the Union to enjoy the fruits of their plunder. The best blood America boasts of was injected into her at the time of the Irish rebellion, and she looks up with a justifiable pride, taking into consideration the peculiar quality of her other family and heraldic honors, to such names as those of Emmet and M'Nevin.

Can poetry spring out of an amalgam so monstrous and revolting? Can its pure spirit breathe an air so fetid and stifling? You might as reasonably expect the vegetation of the tropics on the wintry heights of Lapland. The whole state of American society, from first to last, presents insuperable obstacles to the cultivation of letters, the expansion of intellect, the formation of great and original minds. There is an instinctive tendency in it to keep down the spiritual to the level of the material. The progress is not upwards but onwards. There must be no "vulgar great" in America, lifted on wings of intellectual power above the level of the community.

Our orators and editors appear to enjoy no brighter reputation with them than the mass of society—

The orator is compelled to address himself to the low standard of the populace; he must strew his speech with flowers of Billingsgate with hyperbolical expletives, and a garnish of falsehoods, to make it effective, and rescue it from the chance of being serious or refined. The preacher must preach down to the fashion of his congregation, or look elsewhere for bread and devotion. The newspaper editor must make his journal infamous and obscene if he would have it popular; for let it never be supposed that the degradation of the American press is the work of the writers in it, but of the frightful eagerness of the public appetite for grossness and indecency.

How conveniently oblivious the learned reviewer appears to be of those passages in our history, in which England so conspicuously figured. He may possibly though never have heard of the Revolution, or the war of 1812; and may be ignorant that such battles as Yorktown and New Orleans have ever been fought:—

One grand element is wanted for the nurture of the poetical character in America:—she has no traditions. She started at once into life, rude, rugged, savage, self-confident. She has nothing to fall back upon in her history—no age of gold—no fabulous antiquity—no fairy-land. The want of historical elements is supplied by the intensity of the glorification. The two great subjects are Liberty and the Indians.

They don't admire the subject of "Liberty and the Indians."

Two more unfortunate topics could not have been hit upon. All men are born equal, says the declaration of independence; we are the freest of the free, says the poet; and so the slave-owner illustrates the proposition by trafficking in his own sons and daughters, and enlarging his seraglio to increase his live stock. He is his own lusty breeder of equal-born men. A curious instance of American liberty is cited by a traveller, who informs us that he knows a lady residing near Washington, who is in the habit of letting out her own natural brother! As to the Indians, nothing can exceed the interest these writers take in their picturesque heads and flowing limbs—except the interest they take in their lands. Nobody could ever suspect, while reading these fine effusions upon the dignity and beauty of the Indians, that they were written by people, through whose cupidity, falsehood and cruelty, the Indians have been stripped of their possessions, and left to starve and rot; that while they were thus evincing the tenderest regard for the Indian nations in octosyllabic verse, Congress was engaged, through its servants, in suborning Indian chiefs, and making them drunk, to entrap them into deeds of sale of their hunting grounds; and, as if these and similar atrocities were not enough to mark the difference between the poetry and the policy of the States, importing bloodhounds from Cuba to hunt the Indians of Florida! It is quite impossible to account for the incredible folly which tempts them to indulge in such themes, unless we refer it to the same infatuation which makes them boast of their morality in the face of their filthy newspaper press, and of their honesty in the teeth of pocket-picking Pennsylvania.

Speaking of some of our national songs, he says:

This standing invitation to go to war, although there be no foe to fight withal, hits off with felicity the empty bluster of the national character. The call upon the "immortal patriots" to "rise once more" is sung at all hours in every corner of the Union by men, women, and children; and it is very likely that every day the "heaven-born band" get up out of their beds they believe they are actually rising once more to defend their rights and their shore. This is the key to the popularity of "Hail, Columbia." It flatters the heroic qualities of the people, without making any further requisition upon their valor than that they shall implicitly believe in it themselves. "The Star-spangled Banner" is constructed on the same principle, and blows the "heaven-born" bubble with equal enthusiasm; closing with the vivacity of a cock that knows when to crow on the summit of its odoriferous hill.

Here is another condensed commentary on our society and manners:

These are genuine samples of the cock-a-doodle-doo style of warlike ballads. But the most remarkable writer of this class was Robert Paine, a heaven-born genius, who is said to have ruined himself by his love of the "wine-cup"—which is American for mint-julep and gin-sling. He was so depraved in his tastes, and so insensible to the elegant aspirations of his family, as to marry an actress! It is amusing and instructive to learn from the American editor that this monstrous union between two professors of two kindred arts was regarded with such genteel horror in the republican circles, as to lead to poor Paine's "exclusion from *fashionable society*, and to a disagreement with his father, which lasted till his death!" The false nature of all this is as striking as its *pseudo* fine breeding; and it shows how much bigotry and intolerance may be packed under the surface of a large pretension to liberality and social justice. Certainly, there is nothing so vulgar and base as American refinement—nothing so coarse as American delicacy—nothing so tyrannical as American freedom.

Read his summing-up on American literature:

Stepping out of the literature of England into that of America, is like going back twenty years into a sort of high-life-below-stairs resuscitation of the style of that period.

The following occurs in his closing paragraph:

Literature is, consequently, the least tempting of all conceivable pursuits; and men must float with the stream, and live as they can with the society in which they have been educated. Even were the moral materials by which this vast deposit of human dregs is supplied, other than they are—purer, wiser, and more refined,—still America could not originate or support a literature of her own, so long as English productions can be imported free of cost, and circulated through the Union at a cheaper rate than the best productions of the country.

And yet there areAmericans, who, in order to extenuate their senseless devotion to England, will obstinately close their eyes to the fact that such things have been written of us in the "fatherland." But when they are compelled to remember that an article, rich in such extracts as the preceding, has appeared at the head of the leading Quarterly of Great Britain, they will scarcely dare contend that Englishmen tenderly love us. The simple statement of so absurd a proposition must at once become its refutation.

When the learned and elegant "Foreign Quarterly" can descend to such epithets as are so profusely applied to us in the above extracts, it is unnecessary to cull "Flowers of Billingsgate" from the more licentious daily press. When

Featherstonhaugh, Trollope, and Hall, have made their reputations, and Dickens increased his, by such slanderous attacks on America, it is natural that they should have crowds of humble imitators in their calumnious slang. But I shall dismiss English writers, and turn to some of their specified accusations.

If spitting be, as the English fain would have it, a nationality, let us boldly spit it into respectability. Our own timorous apologies for this heinous sin of expectoration, only encourages our rivals to lecture us upon it. I am no advocate of the habit, but at war as I consider it to be with good taste, I am willing to see it carried to excess, if but to set at defiance the impertinent criticism of Englishmen. I often feel heartily inclined to become a tobacco-chewer myself, in order to show my individual contempt for these officious meddlers. Who appointed them moral regulators of our domestic economy? or what right have they to interfere with our practices, whatever they may be? Their presumption is founded on our condescending to deprecate their attacks.

In what does it concern John Bull, if each Western farmer, and Southern planter, should be pleased to fill with tobacco juice a pool, that would float a whole hogshead of the weed? He might not approve of it, he might even be disgusted by it, but I would have him taught better manners than to sneer at it. I am willing that our spitting should be a source of annoyance to him, but not of contempt. When we have taught him to entertain a proper respect for us, he will discuss with considerate caution even what we ourselves may be willing to confess a fault. When he is convinced that we have attained such a position in the world, as to enable us even to spit with impunity, he may still attack the habit, but will no longer attempt to ridicule it.

Although I am a strong believer in every individual's

being permitted to do what happens to be most in accordance with his own fancy, provided he does not interfere with the rights of his neighbors, yet, as I said before, I am no advocate of the peculiarly free-and-easy habit of tobacco-chewing. I regard it as being inconsistent with that scrupulous neatness in household arrangements, which is the basis of true elegance. I believe it is often most inconvenient to him who indulges in it; but for the life of me, I cannot discover any thing about it so especially offensive. I contend that it is superlatively disgusting to the English, merely because it is an American habit. Hating us with an intensity that helpless rage can only know, it is their chiefest delight to cavil at us. And finding nothing more serious to object to, our earlier traducers seized upon this, and each hireling caterer to the morbid feeling against America in England, attempts a facetious improvement on the stereotyped jokes of his predecessors. By constant exaggeration, a simple habit has grown into a great bugbear, whose terrors no Englishman, who crosses the Atlantic, ever omits to enlarge upon. What after all is there so unbearably revolting about spittle? Our Saviour in one of his earlier miracles "spat on the ground, made clay of the spittle, and anointed the eyes of the blind man with the clay." "And he said unto him, go wash in the pool of Siloam. He went his way therefore, and washed, and came seeing." I have with a crowd of pilgrims gone down to drink from this very pool, for the water had borrowed new virtue from the miracle.

A spittoon is certainly rather an unsightly sort of an article, but I have no recollection of ever being seriously affected, by witnessing the ejection of the amber colored juice, by the most inveterate devotee to the weed. But admitting that the leniency with which I regard tobacco chewing, is the result of prejudice, and that the habit is as stomach-turning as the English profess to consider it, I still contend that its terrors are heightened by being most prevalent in America. Other nations have peculiarities; infinitely more trying to mawkishly delicate sensibilities than the chewing of tobacco, which are not only passed over without condemnation, but English travellers pride themselves upon the ease with which they conform to them. The English at home are guilty of things positively nauseating, yet the stoutest among them, who would pretend great indifference to a whizzing cannon ball, professes to be faintishly affected by the sight of a tobacco quid.

What could be better calculated, under ordinary circumstances, to destroy an appetite, though as vigorous as an Englishman's, than to see some awkward lout groping with his thumb for the stuffing of a turkey, or dabbling in the gravy with his fingers? Yet what upstart islander has ever preached a crusade against the Turks, because they did not introduce knives and forks at their tables, but primitively preferred their "pickers and stealers." In this instance, his railing would have a dash of patriotism and common sense about it; for if successful, he might materially increase the trade of Sheffield by his efforts. But so far from his objecting to the Oriental style of feeding, a chapter in almost every English book of travels in the East, is devoted to the infinite grace with which the author sat cross-legged, and took his food with his fingers.

In Paris, at the end of a dinner, a small cup of perfumed water is placed before each guest, with which he is expected thoroughly to rinse his mouth, and then spirt, deposit, or let fall the water—whichever term you prefer—in a silver basin which accompanies it. So far from an Englishman's discovering any thing objectionable about this habit, he highly approves it, and is rapidly introducing it into England. Next to the delight enjoyed during his dinner, nothing appears to afford him so high a degree of satis-

6*

faction, as this rather too French operation after it. Although I have reason to suspect—from the fact of water being scarce in Paris, and the contents of the little cups always being highly unctuous to the touch—that the perfumed water furnished at the cafés washes more than one mouth during the day; yet an Englishman rejoices in its use, and still professes, like the Turks, to make cleanliness a part of their religion. If spitting be objectionable on general principles, it seems to me that, as little fastidious as I am, I might be excused for considering it disgusting at table. But although the femininely frail nerves of an Englishman instantly become relaxed in the presence of a spittoon *on the floor* in America, yet he deems the same article an appropriate ornament of a dinner table in France. This seeming contradiction is perfectly accountable. One custom is American, the other French. France assumes, and maintains the privilege of setting the fashions for the politer portion of the world, and of course what she does, however absurd or disgusting, is necessarily in accordance with good taste. But America being, even according to her own confession, but the modest imitator of England, must expect to be laughed at by her distinguished model.

It has often afforded me great amusement in the cafés of Paris, to watch the movements of a newly-arrived John Bull, eager to assume the deliberate air of a man of travel and observation. His extraordinary attempts at the names of the French dishes—his frequent calls for the *gascon*, as he usually pronounces the name—his multitudinous wants, and his sputtering rage when every thing was not done to his satisfaction, were all ludicrous in the extreme. But it was the climax of the funny to see him, at the end of his ample repast, seize his little cup of water, and gaze profoundly into it. With a sigh of secret satisfaction, he would swig three-fourths of its contents at a gulp, roll it in his mouth with frightful contortions of feature, and a gurgling sound of semi-suffocation, and then squirt into his basin, or rather spittoon, a cascade worthy of a sea-sick toper. It was very —very rich. The simply disgusting became, in his hands, laughable. One forgot his loathing in his merriment. But this same cockney coxcomb, who seemed to pride himself on the size and force of the stream he could throw at the dinner-table, would have instant recourse to his vial of aromatic vinegar upon the most unobtrusive getting-rid of superfluous saliva, by an American in the street. As I said before, the former habit is *French*, and *so* conducive to cleanliness. To rinse one's mouth before leaving table is certainly not a comely habit to look upon, though it is, without doubt, very French, and very clean. Using the same argument, it might be declared that the vulgar habit of a man's blowing his nose with his fingers was, in the abstract, much cleaner than using a handkerchief, and carefully stowing it away in his pocket. But I scarcely think that even the most adventurous of Frenchmen would, on this account, advocate the introduction of the custom into refined circles. In theory it may be clean to do, but it is decidedly not pleasant to see. And so I think of the Parisian habit of rinsing the mouth at table—British advocacy to the contrary, notwithstanding.

Nature has wisely placed the nose as a sentinel to the stomach, and whatever is offensive to one, we may be sure is not proper for the other. And yet the elegant gourmands of England contend that venison is not fit to be served till the very waiter must hold his nose at it, as he places it on the table. The daintiest epicures will greedily devour pheasants and partridges which have picked themselves, merely because the flesh has become too "short" to retain the feathers. Yet these bold Britons, who have from their infancy, in violation of nature's laws, loaded their stomachs with such loathsome crammings, profess that their insatiate maws are endued with sensibilities so delicate, that they are painfully affected by the sight of a little tobacco-juice. Could affectation be more absurd, or contradiction more ridiculous? I would as soon think of a brick's being dissolved by the sight of mortar, as an Englishman's stomach being turned by the sight of any thing. It's much the firmest part about him.

But in conclusion of this not very interesting subject, if we in America *must* spit, let us spit out courageously before the whole world. There is nothing to be ashamed of in it, and even if there was, our attemping to spit by stealth would only invite new attacks from our enemy, by this implied confession of a fault.

Many things are judged of in this world, by the manner in which people do them. Nothing can be more opposed to the loosest notions of morality, and chivalry, than stealing. Yet what Christian, or modern hero professes to despise the Spartans, as a nation of thieves? And why do they not do so, as they ought, in accordance with their moral professions? Simply because the Spartans gloried in theft. A scared dog with a tin pan to his tail will always have the whole pack of village curs at his heels, but if he turns upon them his assailants pause ere they attack him.

So I beseech again, let us spit fearlessly and profusely. Spitting, on ordinary occasions, may be regarded by a portion of my countrymen as a luxury: it becomes a duty in the presence of an Englishman. Let us spit around him—above him—and beneath him—every where but on him, that he may become perfectly familiar with the habit in all of its phases. I would make it the first law of hospitality to an Englishman, that every tobacco twist should be called into requisition, and every spittoon be flooded, in order thoroughly to initiate him into the mysteries of "chewing." Leave no room for his imagination to work. Only spit him once into a state of friendly familiarity with the barbarous custom, and he will be but too happy to maintain a profound silence on the subject for the rest of his life. I would give each hurrying tourist, who lands on our shores, inflated by preconceived opinions for an abusive book on America, his fill of spitting as an infallible remedy for his windiness. Let the dose be copious, and the cure will be complete. If no more desirable end be attained by the prescription, we shall at least be allowed to spit in peace.

After the notable habit of salivarizing, there is nothing about Americans so constantly harped upon by Englishmen, as their precipitate rush to the table, and even greater hurry to leave it. The general stampede for the table, which I acknowledge sometimes occurs on steamboats, and in interior towns, but never in our cities, I most emphatically disapprove of. Such haste is too indicative of the carnivorous propensities of the English themselves, to be at all in accordance with my rigidly American notions. But what reasonable objection could be urged to a gentleman's quietly leaving a public dinner-table, when his wants were satisfied, it would, without English assistance, be somewhat difficult to divine. An Englishman objects to the haste with which we dispatch so important an affair as dinner. Being himself endowed with the voracity of a shark, the gizzard of an ostrich, and "the dilating powers of the anaconda," he imagines that every one must, from necessity, gorge his food as he does himself. To any man who has ever taken the dimensions of an Englishman's appetite, it can no longer be a matter of surprise, that with him feeding becomes a very serious sort of undertaking. It is one of those things which, like the "cooling" of a steamer, necessarily requires time, and which, not even the hurry of coal-heavers could decidedly facilitate.

The process of "bolting food," so minutely elaborated on

by Englishmen, I have never seen in any portion of our country, though these six-week travellers, more fortunate than myself, appear to have met with it everywhere. But in England I have witnessed this bolting operation, which I immediately recognized as the original of pictures of imaginary scenes in America drawn by Englishmen. And yet I never knew an Anglo-Dane-Saxon-Norman to make a hasty meal. Shovel his food as he may, it is nevertheless a slow operation—so is levelling a mountain.

Although the dinner-table is the scene of an Englishman's most extraordinary exploits, he has the bad taste not to be proud of them, though Heliogabalus himself might justly have been so. Although a glutton by nature, yet strangely enough he is sensitive on the subject of his gluttony. He cannot endure that the moderate appetites and simple wants of another nation should render his own greediness so conspicuous. He has attempted therefore to force them into at least an affectation of his peculiar habits, by railing at the haste with which they take their meals.

It seems to me that the time allowed for dinner in our principal towns and cities, ought to be ample for the satisfaction even of a British appetite. But it appears that this is not so. Every book of travels which is given to the world after twenty days' close study and minute observation of a country, nearly equal in extent to the whole of Europe, teems with piteous complaints of the hurry with which the author was compelled to take his dinner. He apparently demands even a longer time for his meals in America than is required in his own country—this may be accounted for by the fact, that in England a man pays for each article he orders—which is measured out with mathematical exactitude. An Englishman's economy, under such circumstances, neutralizes his voracity. But in America, where a sumptuous display of viands is made, to which he has never been accustomed, and where he enjoys the privilege of stuffing himself to his utmost capacity, without an increase of expense, he very naturally feels inclined to improve his opportunities, and lingers at the table accordingly. His expressions of grief are so earnest, and his lamentations so touching, that from my heart I pity him. I cannot resist the temptation of suggesting, that an English dining-room be furnished in our principal hotels, where hungry Islanders may sociably spend the day in a manner most in accordance with their feelings.

Americans really eat with no more haste than Englishmen,—the difference in the time, demanded for dinner by the two nations, arising altogether from the difference in the quantity of food consumed. As an Englishman eats three times as much as an American, it is evident from calculation, that even with the assistance of the English habit of "bolting," he must remain a considerably longer time at table. The travelled fox lost his tail, and earnestly advised his fellow-foxes to follow the newly imported fashion. An Englishman dwells on his dinner, like an enraptured lover on a kiss, and wishes to force all the world into acknowledging the same ecstatic bliss in its enjoyment. Because he himself is transported by the excitement of eating, he would have every body else experience the same table enthusiasm.

A common charge against Americans is their "excessive love of money," and "inordinate greediness for gain." We sometimes "talk of dollars" in America, and are actually guilty of exerting ourselves to make them. What presumption in Republicans! Trying to attain that which constitutes the power of the English aristocracy. If making money had been a crime, the present nobility of England would have all been residents of New South Wales—as their ancestors would undoubtedly have been transported thither. What was it that made most of their progenitors worthy of being ennobled? What is it that sustains the importance of the present nobility—but *money?* And how was this vital spark of aristocracy originally acquired unless it was worked for? A few noble families, 'tis true, owe their wealth to what in England is considered the rare good fortune of having the illegimate sons of a king for ancestors. A still smaller number are indebted for their importance to the plunder of Saxon churls by Norman invaders. But the large majority of the founders of the present titled families of Great Britain must have toiled most manfully for the fortunes, which formed the basis of their earliest distinction. The 430 noble personages of England give tone to public sentiment,—they think—they speak—they act for the nation. The great mass of the people have no opinion—no voice of their own. And when the nobility inveigh against those attempting to make fortunes, the entire people echo the sage sentiment—but none so noisily as the merchants and tradesmen, who have already, by dint of struggling and hoarding, become rich enough to retire from business, and entertain vague hopes of being ennobled some day themselves.

These 430 drones, hiving on the wealth which the labor of others has amassed, never omit an opportunity of sneering at those engaged in the acquisition of riches. Enjoying incomes themselves of from fifty thousand to three millions of dollars, they can well afford to condemn money-making as unworthy. And all the rich citizens and popular journals cry "hear! hear!" as if an oracle had spoken. No pursuit is dishonorable, unless the object pursued be base. And if money-making, in some honorable occupation, be so shamefully unworthy, then the nobility must be the quintessence of baseness, for money, as I said before, gives vital power to their order. What would they be without it? What is a title, without a fortune to maintain it? A mockery, which the very mob hoots at. But notwithstanding their ostentatious professions of contempt for lucre, the aristocracy know the real value of money, and are jealous that people beyond their own circle should possess it. Hence their zeal to convince the world, that any active pursuit, in which money is to be made, is dishonorable. To rival them in fortune is to share their power,—to surpass them, would be to destroy their present monopoly of influence. Is it surprising then, that they should constantly cause crusades to be preached against money-making? What could be more absurd, than this pretended indifference to money, and contempt for its seekers?

When money-making is confined to the sordid passion of accumulation, when the wretched miser pinches himself and grinds every body else to enjoy the mean gratification of gloating over heaps of shining metal, I cordially assent to the strictures, which in all countries and every age have been passed on avarice. But so far from this most degraded of passions being common in America, our citizens are too often destitute of a becoming sense of economy, and run into the other extreme of extravagance. It is true that almost every one in America is engaged in some active pursuit. In a country yet young, and almost entirely deficient in those convenient haunts for idlers, the parks, the clubs, the drives, the promenades, and all the possible varieties of amusement, even those who could live without it, seek occupation as a source of enjoyment. We cannot escape the original curse that man should earn his bread by the sweat of his brow; exertion of some sort is essential to existence, and no man can be contented, unless he is, or imagines himself to be, employed. I cannot conceive a more dreary sort of existence than a mere idler in most portions of America, deprived as he is of the elegant means of killing time, which are provided for the various aristocracies of Europe. Yet many, with mistaken notions of aristocracy, submit to the penance of idleness, in order to appear genteel. If gentility can present no higher claims to consideration, I fear it will never flourish in America. What could be more ridiculous than a man's boring himself by doing nothing, merely to ape the aristocratic indolence of the nobility of Europe, where the idlest of men can be the most busily engaged in the countless pleasures which surround him? But that Americans are generally so wedded to business as to have no time for the ordinary enjoyments of life, is glaringly untrue. We constantly find them indulging in those more refined pleasures which are only enjoyed by the strictly aristocratic circles of England. Money is only valuable to them on account of the comforts and the enjoyments it procures. Large fortunes by inheritance are comparatively unknown in America, the fathers of our Republic having overthrown the aristocratic law of primogeniture as inimical to our institutions. Almost every man with us must start in life with the manly consciousness that he has his own fortune to make. And any young gentleman who is so verdant as to doubt that "ready money" is "Aladdin's lamp," should be sent to England to complete his education. When he witnesses the miracles it works there, his skepticism will be removed I am very sure. One distinguished bard has declared that "love rules the camp, the court, the grove." But Byron, more familiar with the domestic economy of Great Britain, says, that "*cash* rules love, the ruler," and therefore rules the world.

The young men of most wealthy families in America are reared with tastes that their inheritances cannot support. But those young Americans who are prepared by education and early association for the enjoyment of the luxurious indulgences which fortune only can procure, not being so lucky as the youthful nobles of England, who have their fortunes ready made to their hands, must strike boldly out, and labor for the means of indulging the elegant tastes of educated refinement. And the snob who is so snobbish as to sneer at a young gentleman so engaged, deserves to be crowned chief of the fraternity. But although young Americans exert themselves with laudable energy in the acquisition of fortune, yet they spend it with a liberality altogether unknown in England. I have closely observed my countrymen both at home and abroad, and I have invariably found them living with a profusion far surpassing that of the moneyed circles of Great Britain of ten times their income. So far are they from deserving the oft-repeated charge of sordid meanness, that their liberality in proportion to their resources would be condemned in England as reprehensible extravagance.

But this very objectionable mania for lucre, of which Englishmen so unjustly accuse us, is not only prevalent in their own middle classes, but is found in its most animated perfection among the nobility themselves. Those who have the candor to inquire, will find the commercial circles of Great Britain so inveterately wedded to their business as to be deprived of all those enlightened amusements which even ordinary wealth could procure them. They allow their dreams of riches to be interrupted by no pleasing relaxations, except equally halcyon visions of dinner. They are not satisfied with a competent independence. They persevere in slaving and hoarding, till they have amassed a fortune immensely greater than is ever enjoyed by Americans, except in extremely isolated cases. Buried in the dark lanes of "the city," they are as integral portions of their counting-rooms as the high stools or the iron safe. They hear no news but the rise and fall in stocks, and have no conversation except on the past and probable variations in the price of "stuff." They read no books but the ledger, and feel no interest in any thing but their *cash*. When that "balances," they are as happy as their natures are capable of being.

The interior of a theatre is wholly unknown to them, and an opera is something they have yet to hear. Their ideas of amusement are concentrated in the occult science of "book-keeping by double entry." Their only excitement is counting money—their only grief is its loss. They go to church to carry their wife's prayer book, and sum up long calculations of last week's profits. The disturbances in France are only regarded as active causes of depression of public credit and the price of rich silks. "The summary" by the last steamer from America possesses no charm for them beyond the probable decline of cotton, or a reported advance in pork. Their education consists in writing a round, commercial hand, calculating compound interest, and being able to cipher in "the double rule of three." They never bother their heads by conjectures as to whether the earth is square or oblong; they know nothing, and care less, about the motions of the heavenly bodies, except that the declining sun indicates the hour for going to dinner; they have no intercourse with their fellow-beings beyond the formalities of a business transaction; and were never known to manifest a friendship except for the warehouse cat; they have no time to talk, and never write except on business; all hours are "office hours" to them, except those they devote to dinner and to sleep; they know nothing, they love nothing, and hope for nothing beyond the four walls of their counting-room; nobody knows them, nobody loves them; they are too mean to make friends, and too silent to make acquaintances; they are as methodical, as uninteresting as their own day-book; their only aim in life is to make money; their only exertion is to avoid spending it; and when, in the decline of a life of privations, they do retire from the harassing toils of business, it is to grumble in monosyllabic spleen at their superiors, and to make ostentatious donations to charitable institutions, for which they are never thanked; they sink into the grave unloved and unmourned, leaving a vast fortune to some selfish son, who has all his life been ashamed of his father, and will use his money to purchase a position from which he may look down with scorn on all merchants and tradespeople. I am not surprised that English exclusives should sneer at the commercial classes of America, if they imagine that our merchants resemble their own.

The same grasping greediness is constantly manifested by the nobility, notwithstanding their enormous fortunes by inheritance. There is no office they will not sue for—no position they will not accept, which gives promise of profit. The ermined robe of a Peer, like the blue gown in Scotland, confers on its lucky wearer the privileges of a licensed beggar. This is no ordinary advantage in a country where common beggars are so severely punished. The sinecure positions under government, and the pension lists, are the poor-house unions, established for the accommodation of noble mendicants. In their applications for "relief," their Lordships unite the whining perseverance of the ordinary pauper, with the sturdy intrepidity of the highwayman. The vile street-beggars may be summarily disposed of, and the white-waistcoated citizen never hesitates to relieve himself and the public from their importunities, by depositing information at the police office. But unfortunately there is no aristocratic house of correction, to which importunate nobles may be consigned, when they become troublesome in their applications. Partly by urgent solicitation, and partly by pertinacious bullying, they generally obtain what they desire from government, however unreasonable and inconvenient their demands may be. Search through the profitable sinecures and the oppressive pensions, and you will find them all monopolized by their noble Lordships themselves. Examine the army and navy lists, and it will be seen that the commissions in the Royal regiments, with high pay and nothing to do, and the prominent commands in the naval service, which justly belong to older and abler sailors, have all been appropriated to the support of their Lordships' sons. They deem it a stain on a noble escutcheon to engage in any active occupation, however respectable, but they seem to be conveniently destitute of scruples about becoming pensioners upon the strained charities of an over-taxed people.

But in searching for examples of the voracity displayed by rich Britons in keeping all they have, and clutching at more, we need not descend lower than the palace. The proud court of England's Queen affords the most startling instances of the national vice. That kingdom is deemed happiest, whose monarch adopts the sentiments, and practises the customs of the people. England should be very happy in her Queen. In her evident appreciation of money, Her Majesty is peculiarly successful in adapting her own taste to that of her subjects.

The English nation, in order to support the dignity of their royal ruler, annually appropriate the very inconsiderable sum of $1,925,000. It is to be hoped that the people are amused by the regal rattle, since they are compelled to pay so dearly for it. After meeting every possible expense she might chance to be subjected to in her domestic arrangements and her public duties, they contribute $300,000 as *pin-money* to the Queen. In addition to this snug little sum, she enjoys $70,000 from the Duchy of Lancaster, and derives $60,000 more from pickings, in various quarters. During the minority of the Prince of Wales, she possesses entire control over his Duchy of Cornwall, and the right to use the $190,000 yielded by the principality, after the deduction of salaries, expenses, and allowances to its numerous officers. Every personal want is considered and every public emergency provided for, when the ministers annually present the budget to Parliament. Every possible public and private expenditure of the Queen is paid from the vast sum of $1,625,000 appropriated by parliament for that purpose. Yet, in addition, she has her *pin-money*, $300,000, which is granted by parliament; she has the $260,-000 produced by the two Duchies, and the $60,000 derived from other sources, making in all the vast sum of $620,000, which the Queen receives annually as her private pocket-money, besides the $1,625,000 devoted to her support. When it is remembered that every article of apparel she wears and every meal she takes—that all the equipages and horses she owns—that her servants, her furniture, her travelling expenses, and her palaces, are all provided for from the immense sums allotted by the government to the support of the different departments of her household, the question naturally arises, what can she do with the $620,000 which she receives independent of all expenses? That this sum *is* exhausted, 'tis our duty to believe, since we shall see that the Queen appropriated a small public fund, which should have been sacred even in the eyes of Royalty, to charities to her own personal favorites. Though her profusion should equal Caligula's, and she should amuse herself by seeing the mob scramble for her largesses, it would yet seem strange that in one year she could squander so immense a sum, in addition to the million and a half of dollars appropriated to her support. But the question is of *money*. Remember that lucre is the subject of surmise, and the mystery is solved. The Queen would be unjust to herself and insulting to her people, should she display a careless indifference to what they so highly prize. She would prove recreant to the duties of her position, did she not carefully hoard what every Englishman guards more tenderly than England's honor or his own.

This wonderful people of England, after having so magnificently provided for their Queen, generously set aside the enormous sum of $6,000, to be distributed among such individuals who have by their talents or scientific attainments deserved "the gratitude of the country." It is an eloquent commentary on the amount of intellect existing at present in England, that all the men of genius and learning in the kingdom are estimated by parliament at one-fiftieth part of the importance of Her Majesty's *pin-money*. If the talents of the nation *must* be rated and are rated so low, is it surprising that the standard of intellect should sink? Ought it to seem strange that the present race of Englishmen are so much more expert with their knives and forks than their pens?—that their tongues are so much more happily employed in mastication than in eloquence?

Even we Republicans are accustomed to associate the highest degree of magnificence and liberality with the title of King. We are familiar from our infancy with "royal munificence" and "princely generosity" as figures of speech conveying ideas of superlative profusion. Queen Victoria seems by no means insensible of the ordinary attributes of royalty, but entertains somewhat original notions of the manner of displaying them. She is *very* charitable, but is rather peculiar in being so at other people's expense. She appears to think, that as her ministers must bear the odium attached to the unpopular acts of the crown, the people ought to sustain the expense of such deeds as might win for it popularity. She being the acknowledged head of the British nation, her munificence must necessarily reflect honor on them, and they should be but too happy to pay for it.

Although I have shown that the Queen is in the yearly receipt of $1,625,000, and has a privy purse of $620,000 per annum, yet when she desired to manifest her substantial gratitude to her seven private teachers, she boldly quartered them on the public, and granted them all pensions of $500 apiece, out of the pitiful fund appropriated for needy authors, "who had deserved the gratitude of the country." The mere fact of these persons having been the instructors of the Queen would, in a country like England, have given them all a far greater number of the wealthiest scholars than they could possibly have attended to, and must have placed them, not only far above want, but in affluent circumstances. But even supposing those worthy people to have been in need of the royal bounty, would it not have been in better taste, to say nothing of regal munificence, to have supplied their wants from her own privy purse, rather than misapply a large portion of a fund, which the people had appropriated for the benefit of such of themselves who had rendered important services to their country?

It is true, that this squad of fortunate foreigners had imparted to the Queen some knowledge of the pretty little accomplishments of their respective countries. But by what ingenious interpretation of the act they could be numbered among those "who had deserved the gratitude of the country," it would be somewhat difficult to determine. If enabling Queen Victoria to strum by rote one of Strauss's waltzes on the piano, or to hop through a polka, with ease to herself and satisfaction to her partner, could be properly placed in the category of eminent services to the state, these whiskerandoes had deserved the gratitude of the country; and by a forced interpretation of the act, might have been pensioned from this fund. But it seems to me that these elegant pastimes being much more amusing to the Queen than useful to her subjects, she should have rewarded her seven faithful teachers from her own ample privy purse of $620,000, and not arbitrarily mounted them on the shoulders of the already overloaded public. If these pensions were intended, as mementoes of affectionate remembrance to her different instructors, would they not have been much more acceptable if generously bestowed by herself, instead of being forced from the public? During this year $3,500 of the magnificent literary fund were consumed by fiddlers and singers, whilst the dazzling sum of $1,500 was left to be divided among all the genius and learning of Great Britain. The grant of these pensions was made 23d July, 1840, Viscount Melbourne being Premier.

As an evidence of the rare discrimination displayed by Her Majesty, in the appreciation of merit, I beg leave to refer to the pension of $500 to Peter Warren Dease, Esq., "chief factor in the service of the Hudson Bay Company; in consideration of the personal danger and fatigue undergone by him, in geographical discoveries on the Northern coast of America." "Granted March 17th, 1841, Viscount Melbourne, Premier." Mr. Dease, for his useful geographical discoveries, is honored by being raised to the level of Her Majesty's dancing-master. Such extraordinary acuteness in determining the degrees in which persons had deserved the gratitude of their country, justly entitles Queen Victoria to the thankful acknowledgments of her subjects, and should reconcile them to the burthen of the seven private teachers.

During another year Her Gracious Majesty made two grants, within five months of each other, from this identical literary fund, of $2,500 each, to Mademoiselle Augusta Emma D'Este, the illegitimate daughter of the Duke of Sussex, "in consideration of her just claims on the Royal beneficence." His Royal Highness of Sussex married Lady Augusta Murray, the daughter of the Earl of Dunmore, at Rome, and afterwards in London, in 1793. The issue of this union were a son and daughter; but the marriage was dissolved as contrary to the Royal Marriage Act, in 1794; thus unfortunately for them bastardizing both of their children. This was the misfortune, not the fault of Mademoiselle. And every voice must have approved the munificence of the sovereign, had she granted a pension to her unfortunate cousin from her enormous privy purse. But Her Gracious Majesty resolved to be generous and unjust, to be charitable and prudent, and boldly appropriated to her own private use, in a pension to Mademoiselle D'Este, $5,000 of the $6,000 intended for poor authors. The reputation for charity, acquired at the expense of justice and honor, would scarcely add to the list of the Queen's reputed virtues. Such profusion could not readily be mistaken for liberality. Upon such terms, any one could afford to appear generous who was unscrupulous enough to appropriate what did not belong to him, as the means of making the display.

This daring proceeding was not only a violation of the rights of the people, whom she professed to govern according to a free constitution, but it was in open opposition to the laws, which it was her sworn duty to see executed. For Mademoiselle D'Este could not advance even the imaginary claims of the Queen's teachers to the gratitude of the country. What had she done, that this sacred fund should be squandered in her behalf? No one can hereafter doubt the properest possible appreciation of the value of money in Her Majesty, when she would so fearlessly disregard public opinion, in order to preserve intact her own darling privy purse. After such indubitable evidence of the Queen's ability to take care of her own funds, it seems somewhat extravagant to pay Col. Phipps $10,000 to take care of them for her. $10,000 to "the keeper of Her Majesty's privy purse!" What a commentary in the very name of the office upon the abuses under the English government! The first pension was granted to Mademoiselle D'Este 5th March, 1845, the second, 28th July, 1845, Sir Robert Peel being Premier. The fact of its being notorious, that she was then engaged to be married to Sir Thomas Wilde, who was annually in receipt of $40,000 as Lord Chief Justice of the Court of Common Pleas, in addition to his enormous private fortune, accumulated in his profession, made the outrage of these pensions the more glaring. And, although she was married within six weeks after the last grant, no intimation of a desire to return the $5,000 a year to the much abused fund has ever been made, notwithstanding the immense revenues of her husband.

A pension of $2,000 to the Baroness Lehzen was granted 24th Sept., 1842, Sir Robert Peel, Premier. The Baroness, for a long period, during the minority of Her Majesty, was her private secretary and confidential attendant. Her faithful services and constant devotion to the Queen may have deserved some lasting mark of her appreciation, but to provide for her from this fund, intended for poor authors, and the useful laborers for the public weal, evinced a wanton contempt of law, whose enormity far surpassed that of the other two instances, given above.

It was but natural that Queen Victoria, having grown up under the eye of Baroness Lehzen, should regard her with the sincerest affection. Their associations were of the most intimate character, and their attachment mutual. As Her Majesty's confidence in her friend was unlimited, it was not extraordinary that she regarded the opinions of the Baroness with deferential respect. But, although there is no evidence that the Baroness ever exerted her great influence for purposes of political intrigue, yet the people, always jealous of foreign interference, became alarmed. It was soon whispered that the Baroness exercised a sway in the Queen's Councils, inconsistent with British interests. The murmurs swelled into clamor, and the three kingdoms resounded with discontent. The universal disapprobation was too boldly expressed, for the power even of the Queen long to protect her favorite. Deeply attached as she undoubtedly was to the Baroness, and wilful as she had ever been in trifles, she lacked the moral courage to resist the common wish of all classes of the nation. The obnoxious favorite was, therefore, gently dismissed from court, and escorted into a sort of honorable exile in Germany. But at parting, she received from the poor mutilated literary fund a nice little token of the Queen's regard and regret, in the shape of a pension of $2,000 a year. A fugitive from the resentment of an indignant people, she was yet permitted to bear off, in triumph, this substanlial evidence of "the gratitude of the country." The people might very cheerfully have given $2,000 a year during her lifetime, to get rid of her; but to quarter her on this fund, so positively provided for those whose talents or services had been useful to the state, required the ingenuity, as well as the power of a sovereign. Hers was not the negative position of Mademoiselle D'Este. She was not simply without claims, but she was notoriously odious to all classes of the people. Yet, in the Queen's anxiety to save her own money, she was rewarded in a way which announced to the world that she had deserved their warmest gratitude. Does it not seem incredible that the Queen's annual income is $2,245,000? By what epithet can impartial historians in times to come characterize such a transaction? The pension to Mademoiselle D'Este was a contemptuous disregard of her subjects' rights; the one to Baroness Lehzen was an insulting mockery of their helplessness. Although I am examining the conduct of the Queen in her official capacity, I cannot forget that she is a woman, and gallantry restrains me from the expression of feelings, which such proceedings naturally excite. These are not isolated examples of outrage, which I have given, as they will find who will take the trouble of examining the pension list for themselves, but are fair illustrations of the strictly impartial manner in which the rewards of *literary merit* are dispensed by Her Majesty.

Prince Albert enjoys a rather comfortable sort of income of $300,000 a year. $150,000 are appropriated by Parliament; the other half he receives as jobbing colonel of regiments he does not command—ranger of parks he never enters—governor of castles he never sees—and fancy-farmer on land for which he pays no rent. Not the least considerable of these profitable sundries is the Flemish farm, which is not only very profitable to His Royal Highness, but is enjoyed rent-free. Possessing an income, more than four times as large as those of all the governors of all the States of our Union together, and being besides one of those rarely lucky fellows, who get their board and washing for nothing, it appears presumable that Prince Albert might gratify "his modest little wants" without the necessity of sordid savings. But such seems from the archives of the country not to be the case. Although his chief items of expense may be enumerated under the heads of bouquets and white kid gloves for levées—cocked hats and top-boots for reviews—and Macassar oil and Lubin's perfumes for "private drawing-rooms;" yet the consumption of these articles must be prodigious, as the Prince seems reluctant to pay the only debt which even the noblest Englishman cannot shirk—his taxes. When called upon by the tax-collector, he meanly skulked behind the petticoats of his wife, to avoid the payment of his taxes for the Flemish farm. He declared that he never occupied the farm without Her Majesty, and that therefore he was exempted from the payment of taxes. On this trivial pretext he was allowed to escape. It is difficult to determine which is worthier of contempt, the Prince who could stoop to so mean an outrage, or the nation who would submit to it. An inexorable government enforces its demands from the neediest freeholder, even to selling the pet pig, or family cow. A Prince is exempted from the payment of his legal taxes, because there is no officer with the moral courage to arraign him. Alas! for the majesty of law in England! How Justice has been shorn of her glories since the days when the madcap hero of Agincourt could so meekly bow to her decrees. The nation could not now exclaim with Henry IV.: "Happy is the King with a Judge bold enough to execute the laws, and a son magnanimous enough to submit to them." England has been prolific in Princes: she has produced but one Sir William Gascoigne. The proud dignity with which the venerable Chief Justice resented the blow received from the mad Prince Hal, by committing him to prison, gave an illustrious precedent to the Judges of England. But the days are passed for such precedents to be remembered. The ermine, which clothes the back, has enervated the soul of British Justice—her heart will soften to maudlin weakness towards any one who sports the spotted fur. What common subject of Britain could with impunity have set at defiance the laws of the land, and escaped the payment of his taxes, upon such absurd pretences? His Royal Highness was not satisfied with the possession of this farm rent-free, to add to his already swollen revenues. Being husband to the Queen, he had the power to avoid the expense of taxes, and he had been too long in England not to do so. He never occupied the farm without the Queen, and he was therefore not subject to be taxed. This was the truth, but not "the whole truth;" for probably neither one of them ever did, or ever would, occupy the premises a night during their lives. But the Prince pocketed the profits of the farm—and as a subject of the realm he was bound, both by honor and law, to pay his taxes. "The True British Farmer," as he affectedly styles himself, forgets the first principle which actuates every honest tiller of the soil. He has but a poor conception of his assumed character of a farmer, when he knowingly sullies his honor. But is such miserable prevarication as Prince Albert's, worthy of a man who should give tone to the most honorable circles of Great Britain? Is it becoming in the first subject of a great kingdom, to set such an example of defiance to the laws, in order to escape this paltry tribute to a government which had shown such munificence towards him? And yet Prince Albert would be foremost among his titled parasites, in railing at all those who were endeavoring by honorable means to make a fortune. One might conclude from this brilliant evidence of financial tact, that His Royal Highness was eminently qualified for the lucrative and highly honorable office of "Keeper of Her Majesty's privy purse." He certainly displays the sordid wisdom of saving in a sufficient degree to draw the purse-strings tightly enough. And as somebody must receive the salary of $10,000, I am somewhat surprised, in remembering the acquisitive propensities of the family, that so fat a sum should be allowed to pass into the hands of strangers. The Royal consort seems troubled for a want of something to do, notwithstanding his extremely important functions at reviews and levées. The supervision of that precious purse might have afforded him some healthier mental occupation, than growing mammoth gooseberries, and inventing bad hats. But I suppose it was considered unworthy of the dignity of His Royal Highness to write the checks, which is the only duty which the keeper of the privy purse is ever called on to perform. The notions of Englishmen on many subjects are peculiar; for instance—resorting to a mean subterfuge in order to save a few paltry pounds of taxes, was not deemed unbecoming in the Royal Drone. But the slightest blot of ink, acquired in so *business* an operation as writing checks, would have polluted the immaculate purity of the Royal digits—and was not therefore to be thought of. Such is the absurd superstition of Aristocracy in England.

After such developments, where is the toady so daringly unscrupulous, as to express a doubt of Prince Albert's keen appreciation of money? An allusion to the Flemish farm must silence the most brawling bigot of them all. Every unprejudiced mind must be convinced that, although the Prince speaks the English language with an accent, he is too thoroughly English in his feelings, not to be endued with the national weakness for lucre. How else can we account for his extraordinary course with regard to the farm? I would not voluntarily ascribe to the Prince an excess of wilful depravity. I cannot believe that he refused to pay his taxes, merely to enjoy the luxury of unparalleled baseness. Charity bids us to conclude, that he did not love honor less, but money more.

But, after all, when we remember the mean state of dependence in which Prince Albert is kept by the nation, as husband to their Queen, his reckless disregard of his reputation as a gentleman is, perhaps, more deserving of pity than scorn. Long-continued subjection, even to the thraldom of a petticoat, will in time destroy that proud feeling of independence, and chivalric sense of honor, so essential to manhood. Without duties or position—without honor or consideration, except what he borrows from his wife—indebted even for what he eats, and what he wears, to her bounty, it is not very extraordinary that His Royal Highness should be oppressed by a feeling of his own insignificance. A man should confer honor on his wife, as the sun lends light to the moon—not borrow it from her. He cannot change positions with her without being degraded. He loses all the dignity of his sex, when he sinks into the mere husband of his wife. The silken collar of matrimony must gall under such circumstances, and the necessity which compels any husband to wear it "cows within him the better part of man." He at once becomes as contemptible in his own eyes, as he appears despicable to other people. The sense of degradation often urges men into excesses they might not otherwise commit. The Prince may feel his humiliation more keenly than is generally supposed. He may be less anxious about the future opinions of the world, when he remembers what they must think of him now. He may be desperate, from the consciousness that his present position leaves him no honor to preserve. A debased spirit may safely burrow in the sordid recesses of avarice.

It is true that the huge pyramid of despotism which overshadowed Great Britain during the middle ages, has long since been demolished. But its ruins are still thickly strewn through her social condition. And in nothing can its former vastness be so distinctly traced, as in that relic of barbarism, ycleped the "Queen's Household." Although these household positions have no longer attached to them the magnificence which made them respectable, nor the duties which rendered them necessary, yet their names and their salaries are still preserved, at the same time, a mockery and a burthen to the people. But the sovereign and the nobility are solemnly leagued against their abolition. It is snobbish in the monarch to be tickled by the names—it is weak in the people to pay the salaries of these oppressive sinecures. The real object of their continuance appears to be, to put money in the purses of the already enormously rich aristocracy; and as, at the same time, the sovereign's ideas of his own importance are comfortably inflated by the presence of so many idle servants, the murmurs of the people will avail little against such a combination of interests. It is a condescension unworthy the theory of nobility, for its members to accept positions which even in name are servile —but how shall I describe the sordid instinct, which prompts them to pocket the pitiful price of their dishonor? These salaries, although they must appear contemptible to them, when compared with their own overgrown incomes, yet, taken together, form a serious oppression to the people.

The aristocracy contend that this formidable array of titled lackeys is necessary to sustain the dignity of the crown. But if they were sincerely solicitous about the pomp of royalty, the absurd superstitions of rank in England would enable them, at the same time, to amuse the monarch by the presence of these noble servitors, and to relieve the people from the expense of them. For the imaginary distinction arising from these hireling positions, the advantages of being fed and lodged free of expense in the palace, and of taking part in all the exclusive enjoyments of the court, would create among the highest nobility an eager contest for their enjoyment, although no pay were attached to them. But the grasping greediness of "the order" forbids so equable a compromise. Their Lordships cannot occupy even honorary sinecures without a remuneration. They pocket "what not enriches them," but makes the people "poor indeed." The Marquis of Exeter receives, as Lord Chamberlain, $10,000, and the Duke of Montrose $10,000 more as Lord Steward. The Earl of Jersey, as Master of the Horse, pockets $12,500, and the Duchess of Atholl, as the Mistress of the Robes, receives $2,500.

The venal eulogists of the British oligarchy must search in vain, through their bulky annals, for a single example of disinterested service to their country. I fear eighteen more centuries must elapse before a noble Englishman will be found to imitate the magnanimity of our Republican Washington, in declining the emoluments of his office. The refusal of money due him, even to win a name in history, seems a sacrifice an Englishman is altogether unequal to. Indeed, patriotism has become a profitable branch of trade in England, in which many dabble on a small scale, and a few are brilliantly successful. What bubble scheme, or railroad speculation ever proved so profitable to their originators, as the patriotism of Marlborough, Nelson, and Wellington. The profits of Law, or "Railroad King Hudson," were insignificant in comparison. Besides the distinguished patriots had divers and sundry monuments thrown in for good conduct. The royal family and the nobility have always been eager to sustain a lofty pre-eminence in the opinions of the people. It is alike their ambition and their interest to appear the elect of God's anointed. To stalk through life, as a superior race of superior beings, with superior instincts and propensities, is the difficult part they have assumed. Is it to be presumed, then, that, with such aspirations, they would willingly betray to the multitude the earthliest of earthly passions—a love of lucre? A mountebank would as soon expose his tricks, or an impostor confess his impositions. But their sordid inclinations have proved more powerful than their solitary ambition to appear superior to their fellows. Mammon has shown himself stronger than pride.

When we see the Queen violating the laws to protect her privy purse, and the Prince consort stooping to dishonor to save his taxes—when we find their Lordships scrambling for rich sinecures, and their honorable offspring monopolizing all the most profitable positions in the army and navy—when we know that the wealthiest nobles of the country, in assuming menial positions, become indued with a menial's weakness for wages, and take hire for idly loitering about the palace, it is but reasonable to conclude that the English aristocracy are not wholly insensible to the charms of money.

I believe that I have established the principle; for its action I refer my readers to the following extracts from English papers:

THE ARISTOCRACY AND CAB-DRIVERS.—At the Marlborough-street Court, on Tuesday, a cabman was fined 40*s.*, for behaving with violence at the house of Sir R. Peel. The defendant wanted 2*s.* 4*d.* as his fare for driving Sir Robert from the Brighton Railway to Pall-mall (which must be three miles), while Sir Robert would only give him 2*s.* The latter was said to be the legal fare.—At the same court, on Wednesday, Earl Fitzhardinge summoned T. Jones, driver and proprietor of a cab, for causing an obstruction in Davies-street, by loitering and wilful misbehavior. His lordship complained that the cab stood in the way of his carriage, and that, though the driver had no fare, he (his lordship) had to call out three times before the man would move. The driver told the magistrate that he was at Chiswick at the time. The groom, who confirmed Lord Fitzhardinge's statement throughout, when asked the number of the cab, said it was 2,326. The defendant's number being 2,336, the mistake was obvious. Earl Fitzhardinge said his impression was that the number of the cab was 2,336, but of course he would not contend that he was not liable to mistake. The summons was then dismissed.—*W. News.*

FRACAS.—At the Marylebone Police-court, yesterday, Major Cooke, one of her Majesty's Gentlemen-at-Arms, was charged, before Mr. Long, with illegally detaining an umbrella, the alleged property of Dr. Preston, M. D. Both are members of the Army and Navy Club. Mr. Long asked if the umbrella in question was produced, but was answered in the negative. A gentleman, who attended for complainant, entered into a statement of the facts, and, after proceeding for some time, Mr. Long said the simple question before him was, does Major Cooke detain the umbrella or does he not? Cannot a matter like this be settled between two gentlemen without going any farther? Dr. Preston said, on the 13th January last he missed his umbrella from the outer hall of the club-house, and saw no more of it until the 8th ult., when he saw it in the same place where he had left it, and took possession of it. On the same day, Major Cooke came into the room where he was seated, and claimed the umbrella as his, saying he had had it more than two years. Major Cooke seized it out of his hand and broke it in two. The value was 12*s.* After a deal of evidence, *pro* and *con.*, had been gone into respecting the identity of the umbrella, Mr. Long dismissed the summons, and said he regretted it had been brought there.—*Post.*

When the wealthiest commoner in England sues a cabman

for fourpence, and one gentleman accuses another of stealing his umbrella, and brings an action for the recovery of twelve shillings, its reputed value, no one can doubt that the sordid principle acts as smoothly as the *Amcrican reaping machine.*

It is a common habit with Englishmen to depreciate the intelligence, and ridicule the manners of the Americans, with whom chance brings them in contact, during their peregrinations in Europe, and the East. I rarely met with a number of Galignani's Messenger in which I did not find copied from English papers, some studied sneer at the ignorance and vulgarity of American travellers. They seemed unable to understand how people, of the comparatively limited fortunes of the Americans, could be actuated by a desire to see the world. They deemed it a much higher evidence of wisdom to remain quietly at home, and to spend their dollars in comfort and peace, than to go traipsing through strange cities, and foreign lands. They appear to regard travelling as one of the onerous necessities which pursue very rich men; men whose incomes surpass the entire possessions of our wealthiest citizens. Such principles were no doubt well suited to the sordid disposition and sedentary habits of Englishmen, but they but ill accorded with the enlightened energy of Americans. I shall make no observations on the character of travellers one meets from our own country; but I beg the indulgence of my readers, while I give some of my opinions and experience of the Englishmen I have met in my wanderings.

An Englishman travels for no better reason than that *everybody* does so. He visits the various capitals of Europe, lounges through their picture galleries, and dozes over their ruins, as he drags through the classics, and takes a degree at college: his position in society demands it. With him travelling is a stupid duty. and not the highest of intellectual pleasures; it is a necessary probation, which every Englishman of a certain degree of wealth is condemned to pass through. He submits to it as to any other inexorable necessity, but manifests his dissatisfaction by grumbling sneers at every thing, from Paris to Jerusalem. The French don't know how to roast "a joint," their conceptions of wash-basins are altogether too contracted in Germany, he is fleeced by rascally dragomen at Constantinople, and finds nothing but fleas and discomfort in the Holy Land. He solemnly protests that he has seen nothing that it was possible for him to eat, since he left England; and yet he retains his scarlet hues, and corpulent tendencies, in a manner wonderfully mysterious, if we believe he has lived on air. In his accustomed potations of malt liquors, he is more fortunate, as his bullying complaints and noisy censure have stocked every hotel in the East with stale ale and muddy porter.

He penetrates the parched depths of the desert to boast of having ridden a camel, and makes pilgrimages to the holiest spots, merely for the gratification of declaring his belief that they are not those which are designated in the Scriptures. It is *fashionable* in England to be skeptical about sacred localities! He discredits the wonderful events which attended the exodus of the Jews from Egypt. He coolly argues the impossibility of the Children of Israel passing through the bed of the Red Sea on dry land, and ridicules the idea of Moses' sweetening the waters of the bitter well of Marah, amidst the very scenes which witnessed the accomplishment of these miracles. He journeys to Mount Sinai to sneer, and enters the Holy Land with no holier motive than prompted young Sheridan to descend the coal-pit: merely to say he had been there. In a spot where I had thought that disbelief would be awed, and even blasphemy silent, in the sacred grotto of Bethlehem, I have heard an Englishman utter rude and indecent jests about the Virgin and her child. I was not surprised that he went to Jerusalem, a confirmed follower of that reverend apostate, Clarke, who has attempted to derange all the received opinions, as to the scenes connected with the crucifixion and burial of our Saviour. If he sincerely believed that the spots, which have for more than a thousand years excited the religious enthusiasm, and received the pious adoration of pilgrims of every sect, were in no way connected with the death of Jesus, then it was less impious for him to scoff whilst standing on Calvary, and to laugh within the site of the Holy Sepulchre.

What shall we say of the sacrilegious attempt of that worse than infidel to profane the Holy Places of our Faith? Though they might not have been what they are believed to be, it was an inhuman deed to destroy so pure a superstition—they should have been sacred as symbols of our religion, which the common consent of fifteen centuries has regarded as holy. Although Mr. Clarke had possessed positive proofs of their not being the scenes of our Saviour's death and burial, yet had he been as pious as he was desirous to appear learned, he would have spared them. Time and association have united in making them the most impressive emblems of the events they are designed to commemorate, and a sincere Christian could never have assailed their sanctity. Is the Lord's Supper to be considered as a less solemn rite of Christianity, because it is but the simple commemoration of His death? Are the wine and bread to be regarded as less holy, because they are not actually His blood and body? But the reverend Mr. Clarke was not satisfied with demolishing that beauteous structure, which the faith of fifteen hundred years had been building up. His ambition aspired to the distinction of a theory of his own. He made himself absurd by professing, after all the changes which time, and the different wars and dynasties, must have produced in the Holy City, to possess advantages for determining the sacred localities, very far superior to those enjoyed by St. Helena fifteen hundred years before. He did not simply deny the identity of the Holy Places, but had the audacity to select localities of his own. It would be difficult to discover so extraordinary a combination of folly, vanity, and sacrilege, as that presented by this pedantic divine. A monster so atrocious could only have been a Goth or an Englishman.

As our English acquaintance was an avowed disciple of Mr. Clarke, though he was a man of wealth and consideration at home—he was remotely and mysteriously connected with the Duke of Wellington—it was not surprising that he was not much impressed by a visit to the church of the Holy Sepulchre. But it is a little singular that the consciousness of being in Jerusalem, the unmistakable witness of so many extraordinary events, did not afford him some more appropriate topics of conversation than insipid anecdotes of the English nobility and wearisome complaints of the hotel—its servants and its fare. He went every where, and apparently saw every thing, but as an evidence of how slightly he could have been interested in the sacred objects around him, he had been eight days in Jerusalem, and his trunks were packed for his departure the next morning, but he was not *positive* as to the location of the Mount of Olives. He often wondered at his own folly in venturing into a country where there was so much discomfort—where there was positively nothing to see and not much to eat. He candidly acknowledged, that hearing so many of his acquaintances boast of visiting Jerusalem, had betrayed him into the weakness of wishing to say that he had been there too. But that if he could be forgiven for his rashness in coming once, that he hoped some terrible calamity might befall him if he was ever caught east of Paris again. He never ventured on his impressions of what he visited, but once, when after his return from a visit to the river Jordan and the Dead Sea, he thought he had passed *some* place famous for *some* battle, he did not precisely know which, but he *rather* thought it was near the brook from which David took the pebbles to slay Goliath. And yet every body who had ever visited Syria, or read the briefest account of the country, ought to have known that the identical brook was in exactly the opposite direction. At parting, he was peculiarly considerate in his admonitions, and most earnestly insisted on our visiting Mount Carmel. "Omit what you like besides, but you must go there." "For," said he—and I waited, with breathless anxiety, a burst of enthusiasm about the desolate grandeur and religious associations of the place—"For," repeated he, "the only tolerable dinner I have had since I have been in Syria, was at the convent of Mount Carmel." Shade of Elijah hear him! He had stood upon the sacred summit of Sinai—had ascended Mount Carmel—wandered along the banks of the stormy Jordan—visited Bethlehem—and was then in Jerusalem—and the only treasured recollection he was carrying away with him from the Holy Land, was that of having enjoyed a passable dinner at Mount Carmel. The celebrated John Hunter stated, as a curious fact, that the jawbone always predominated in proportion to the absence of brains. As this was a scientific observation of the learned gentleman, it ought not to be wondered at, that the only thing in Syria which our Englishman was able to appreciate, was the fare at the Convent of Carmel.

In mentioning the name of Greece, I feel a momentary forgetfulness of the sterile subject I have selected for my book. I no longer remember either Englishmen or their country. The name of Greece recalls to me countless joyous memories and delicious associations. The season in which I visited it makes nature in any form enchanting. It was in early Spring, when the year is too young to know aught else but gladness and sunshine: when the verdure is all freshness, the flowers are all beauty, and the birds all song. I had never known before the pain of feeling all a poet's longings, without the genius to embody them into words. The torrents from Helicon and Parnassus were full, and foamed furiously by. Every plain was dotted with flowers: every bush had its nightingale. A visit to Greece had been a pet dream since my boyhood. But its associations, its ruins and its battle-fields were what I thought would charm me. I was not prepared for the rare beauty of scenery which greeted me. Its storied mountains, where the Muses wandered and Apollo sung, with their beetling crags and crowning firs, possessed all the wildness and picturesque beauty that Switzerland boasts. Its classic vales and immortal battle-fields, of which I had read earliest, and dreamed most, were strewn with wild flowers,—so fair, so frail, so varied, that the Muses might have discarded their laurel to have garlanded their tresses with such loveliness. And then the music of the nightingale! But how shall I describe what is indescribable? All the glowing enthusiasm of Oriental romance; all that I had ever read of his poetic loves with the rose; all that I had ever dreamed of the music of "bright Apollo's lute, strung with his hair," which "makes heaven drowsy with the harmony," had given me no conception of the melody of the nightingale's song; and, when heard for the first time in Greece, by the side of a waterfall, with the beams of the full moon dancing in the spray, it afforded a ravishing delight I had never known before, and fear I shall never know again.

In Athens I met a couple of Englishmen, who proposed to join my party. As I was entirely alone, I, of course, consented, and we commenced a journey into the country together. I was somewhat shocked, in the beginning, by one of the gentlemen, who, in gazing for the last time upon the Acropolis, crowned with the shattered glories of the Parthenon, could give utterance to no less commonplace observation, than that Athens reminded him very much of "Edenboro'." But we jogged sociably on among classic ruins, glorious battle-fields, and sacred mountains, and paused at Helicon. I jumped from my horse, and eagerly traced Hippocrene's murmuring rill to its source. I could almost see the mark of Pegasus' fiery hoof, when, in stamping, he had called the bubbling fountain up. I could hear the minstrelsy of the tuneful nine in the warbling of every bird that twittered by. I could almost imagine that I saw Euterpe's laughing face peeping from behind a rock. The silence, the grandeur, and the associations of the spot seemed only suggestive to the Englishmen that "it would be a *capital* place to take lunch!" True votaries of Silenus, they could not forego their orgies here, but drank porter and discussed sandwiches as complacently in the favorite haunt of the Muses as if they had been seated in a London tavern.

I could forgive them for a want of enthusiasm, for I had seen too much of Englishmen to expect from them any great demonstration of sensibility. But, however much I might feel inclined to be lenient, I could not readily forget a degree of ignorance of the common history of Greece that would have subjected the dunce of a country school to a posterior application of birch. It seems almost incredible that men of any nation, who had arrived at the years of discretion, should have been so lamentably deficient in such ordinary knowledge. They thought that the battles of Marathon and Salamis had been fought on the same day. Hadn't the remotest idea who were engaged in the battle of Leuctra, but *had* a deep-rooted conviction that the Persians were in no way connected with Platæa. They went to Parnassus to *see sights*, and had a very vague impression as to what Delphi was celebrated for. But there was one subject on which they seemed profoundly learned: it was the highly interesting subject of "stinks." 'Tis their own generic term; and, if I write my annals true, I feel compelled to use their very words, although, I confess, I do so in violation of my own ideas of propriety. I beg the indulgence of those who feel like myself on this subject, for I am conscious that in illustrating the proneness of the English to vulgarity, I may myself appear guilty. Although these classical gentlemen entertained for the whole genus of bad odors the antipathy shared by humanity in general, yet they would nose them out, trace them to their origin, and classify them under their particular heads, with an avidity that was quite surprising. Their animosity for stinks, like that of terrier dogs for rats, prompted them to run down, and, if possible, catch every unfortunate of the species that happened to cross their path; and it really appeared to afford them the intensest satisfaction to determine whether their latest capture could be most properly placed in the positive, the comparative, or superlative degree of stinks. They were eternally going out of their way to stumble upon something "rotten," and were much given to having uncommonly "nasty" feelings even at meal times. The weather, according to their report, was frequently "funky;" the houses we were compelled to occupy were always "filthy;" and the fare was positively "beastly."

Englishmen pride themselves extremely on the off-hand frankness with which they always give things their *right names.* Those, whose associations with these people have forced them to hear such expressions as those quoted above, must feel thoroughly convinced of their strict adherence to the rule. Though I must confess that I think an occasional departure from it would be desirable, for the sake of delicacy, if not decency. The English ridicule Americans for their excessive particularity in avoiding offensive expressions. All must agree, however, that it is better to err on our side, than their own. We had better be over nice, than generally use, as the English do, such terms as I have felt compelled to disfigure my pages with, which ordinary refinement should banish from the conversation of every gentleman. I would advise the English to use expletives, even with the danger of being diffuse, rather than be so blunt, and so vulgar.

I am surprised that men, who had forgotten, or even never known the history of Greece, could have traversed its sacred soil, without becoming familiar with those brilliant events which have made her heroism a proverb. It is wonderful that men even of the most ordinary attainments could wander amidst "scenes that our earliest dreams have dwelt upon," so utterly ignorant of "man's divinest lore." But wonder becomes amazement, when I remember that these gentlemen, with whom I travelled, were a Fellow in Oxford University, and a Captain in Her Majesty's service. Although they might have forgotten, since there boyish days, much of Greece's history, yet it does seem strange that in visiting the country, they should have been too indolent to refresh their memories, more especially as they had one of John Murray's Red Books between them. It seems to me that Greece and her annals should possess a peculiar charm for the scholar, and the soldier. The precepts of her sages and beauties of her poets are as valuable to one, as the stories of her valiant sons should be interesting to the other. But how could an Englishman read even Murray, whilst he carried a bottle of porter in his saddle-bags, and sandwiches in his pockets?

National pride in Byron should have made them more familiar with his favorite Greece. I had myself traced the noble pilgrim through many wild and beautiful scenes. I had read his eloquent bursts of emotion, upon the classic spots which called them forth, and admired them more, because they had inspired such a mind. I could not forgive, *there*, his stockish countrymen, for their insensibility to both. But an ignorance of Byron is deemed becoming in the more exemplary members of society in England. It has become as fashionable to disparage his genius, as it was formerly to traduce his character. They have toppled him down from the niche which should have been sacred to him in the admiration of his countrymen, and are laboring to lift Mr. Alfred Tennyson into his place. Byron and Tennyson! What an unholy alliance of names! What sinful juxtaposition! He who could seriously compare the insipid effusions of Mr. Tennyson, with the mighty genius of Byron, might commit the sacrilege of likening the tricks of Professor Anderson to the miracles of our Saviour.

Most men have their peculiarities, and many their weaknesses. Our English scholar's particular passion was water-cresses. He was great on experimental consultation, and made it a rule never to put a question directly. He grew tired, and wished to turn back. He wondered interrogatively what there was to be seen at Parnassus; and when informed there was the view from the summit of the mountain, the grot of Apollo, and the ruins of the temple of the oracle at Delphi, he sorrowfully expressed his conviction that, after all the "bother," it wouldn't pay. But when the dragoman vaguely intimated that the finest water-cresses in the world grew in the immediate vicinity, he not only appeared consoled for the necessary fatigue, but even manifested an unwonted alacrity towards the end of the journey. Every breeze that breathed from the snow-clad peak of Parnassus, came laden to him with the refreshing odors of water-cresses. There seemed to be renovating influences in every whiff. As we advanced, his grim looks of dissatisfaction became more and more relaxed; and, on our arrival, he had not only succeeded in getting up a much better appetite than his ordinarily remarkably healthy one, but he found himself in a much happier frame of mind than common for the enjoyment of the lions of the place. A messenger was instantly dispatched for his favorite dish. He had cresses for dinner, cresses for supper, and cresses the next morning for breakfast; and, issuing forth under their mollifying influence, he seemed relieved from the harassing suspicion that, in coming to Parnassus, he had been the victim of "a regular sell." He rather thought that the temple "would do," and that the grotto "was not so bad;" but he had seen much finer views from Scawfell Pike, which he kindly informed me was the highest mountain in England, than from the top of Mount Parnassus. Oh, vanity and water-cresses! Absurdity and Englishmen! It seemed nothing to him to be where Apollo dwelt, and Byron had been. But in our ascent he alarmed me by expressing a distressing apprehension of being about to "funk." This mysterious intimation was more startling, as I was altogether ignorant of what terrible consequences might result from the unknown process of "*funking*." I was as much relieved as himself when he stopped at the grot, to be informed that "funking" was the briefly elegant acceptation of the word giving out. He did nothing during our entire stay on the mountain, but complain of great shortness of breath, and weariness of limbs. He blamed every body for inducing him to start, and could discover nothing to compensate him for such labor. He did not seem aware that even then nymphs, and fauns, and Pan with his satyrs might be frolicking along the banks of the brawling brook that dashed across our path. He never suspected that the Muses were timorously hiding in that leafy covert; and did not once hear the notes of Apollo's lyre mingling with the sighs of the moaning firs. But he was somewhat consoled on reaching the top, by disparaging Parnassus to praise Scawfell Pike. An Englishman seems never convinced that there is any thing out of England equal to what he boasts of in it. He will prefer an English mill-dam to Niagara, and compare one of our great Northern Lakes to some nobleman's fish-pond.

It is a favorite amusement of Englishmen to enlarge upon the peculiarities of our nasal twang, and to enumerate our "provincialisms." Because we have not imitated them, in the abuses of the language, into which vulgarity has betrayed them, we are pronounced guilty of "provincialisms." In alluding to the corrections we have made, of their own glaring improprieties of speech, they seem to forget that America is no longer a *province.*

In their attempts to be merry at our expense, they appear wholly oblivious of that *h*extraordinary 'abit of a vast majority of cockneys, of always making the *h* silent, and aspirating the vowels in the beginning of a word. On which of our remotest frontiers could they discover such an unpardonable violation of good grammar and good taste? Yet this habit of dropping, and adding the *h*, is universal among the lower and middle orders, from London to Wales, and is very prevalent among the highest and most polished. But whilst we are on the subject of "provincialisms," what shall we say of the heathenish dialects of several different shires in England, which neither Christians nor Englishmen, out of their particular counties, could pretend to understand? Where will they look for such in America? We may add to the significations of the words *clever* and *smart*, but it seems to me that the great national right, which permitted England to form her remarkable compound of Saxon and Norman-French, might confer on us the privilege of extending the acceptation of a few unimportant words. Even in our most figurative meaning of the word *smart*, we make a near approach to its original signification; how do the English force it into conveying an idea of showy, flashy dress?

But we often adhere to the strictly proper acceptation of a word, whilst they arbitrarily depart from it. *Plain* means, according to Johnson, simple, unadorned, and not *ugly* as the English would have it, in applying the term to women. *Stout*, if we can believe the same authority, signifies strong, brave, lusty, and not *fat*, as the English generally use it.

But of whatever indiscretions of speech we may be guilty, we are certainly saved the mortification of the insufferable vulgarity of applying the chaste term beautiful to greasy articles of food. This is a distinction reserved in undivided glory, for the most enlightened nation of the nineteenth century. "Beautiful mutton!" "Beautiful potatoes!" Ugh how shockingly disgusting! Who but a cannibal or an Englishman could discover any thing of the beautiful about what he had to eat? I can imagine an epicure of the Tongo islands remarking to a sympathizing friend, when some fair shipwrecked damsel had fallen into his hands, that she would make a "*beautiful* roast," but it requires the refined perceptions of an Englishman to appreciate the beauties of a cabbage-head. As my learned companion in Greece is an especial favorite of mine, I hope I shall be excused for again introducing him for the sake of illustration. The only wild bursts of enthusiasm into which he was ever betrayed, from "Sunium's marbled height" to the immortal pass of Thermopylæ, was whilst ogling a dish of "beautiful water-cresses." His soft, susceptible heart daily succumbed to an ecstasy of excitement, before a brilliantly green plate of his favorite salad. If there ever was an occasion when this excitement ceased to be utterly ridiculous, it was at Parnassus. For these were classic cresses. They had been culled on the poetical borders of the Castalian fountain. They had sprung from "holy, haunted ground." Protected by the shadow of Parnassus, and nurtured by the waters of the immortal brook, they might have borne about them, for aught I know, something of that poetical inspiration, anciently attributed to the fountain. They certainly possessed an interest for me from the charm of association; and I pressed in my pocket edition of Childe Harold a few leaves, as a memento of Apollo's favorite haunt. But they were cresses still! And how the Englishman could apply the term "beautiful" to them, as a wholesome and palatable vegetable, I cannot pretend to understand.

In America we conceive the highest evidences of beauty to be afforded by women and flowers; but Englishmen, more discriminating, chiefly delight in "beautiful roast-beef" and "beautiful porter." There is no accounting for tastes in this world, and an Englishman may really discover more personal charms, if I might use the expression, about a fat sirloin of beef, than in the loveliest woman. But in applying the term "beautiful" to beef and porter, he means not so much to intimate that they are pleasing to the eye, as that they are deliciously titillating to the palate. In this the extreme grossness of the impropriety consists.

Although I have acquitted the more refined and better educated people of Great Britain of being universally guilty of the vulgar liberties the middle classes take with the *h*, yet the disposition to indulge in them is very decided, in even the highest in London, and this habit, illiterate as it is, prevails very commonly in all the provincial towns. The most elegant and refined talk constantly of "*fried 'am*," although they are not often guilty of the atrocity of adding "the *h*eggs." They sentimentally insist that "there is no place like 'ome," and always salute a friend with "'ow d'ye do." They compliment a lady as being very "'andsome;" they invariably commence a question of time by "wen," and fearfully transform the simple relative pronoun into a "wich." These are but a few examples of the propensity of the most refined people of England to *h*adopt the general custom.

They seem very reluctant to *h*acknowledge this peculiarly *h*exceptionable 'abit, and *h*insist that *h*it *h*is confined to the low and *h*ignorant of the country. But it is universal among educated people, whose wealth far surpasses that of our richest citizens, and it is not at all uncommon among the highest and most polished circles. We don't *h*aspirate our vowels in America. Turn your *h*eyes *h*on this picture and *h*on that.

In a couplet of Ben Jonson, which I am sorry not to be able to recall, Thames is made to rhyme to James, showing that in those good old times the name of the river was pronounced as a Christian or a reasonable man would pronounce it now, instead of vulgarly mincing it into "Tems," as the present race of Englishmen do. They say Wool'ich and Green'ich, when they mean Woolwich and Greenwich. They metamorphose Alnwick into *An'ick* and Warwick into *War'ick.* The mighty "King-maker" is divested of a portion of his dignity, and "the Last of the Barons" loses some of his grandeur, when we hear him called the great Earl of War'ick. The abominable abbreviation smacks too strongly of cockneyism and smells of the ale-house. It is opposed in sound, as in association, to all our preconceived notions of the valiant Guy. The famous race of England is always spoken of as "the Darby." But the Earl of Derby, although in his ministerial relations he has been supposed to bear very close analogy to an old woman, has scarcely deserved of his countrymen to have his melodious title changed into such a sobriquet as *Darby*.

How can they force stone into "stun?" In this instance they are not satisfied with arbitrarily interfering with weights and measures, but do violence to all the ordinary rules of pronunciation, with "stun." They had much better pronounce it *ton* at once, more especially as this standard would be infinitely more convenient for determining the gross weight of Englishmen than either pounds or stone. But it seems the British nation are sensitive on the score of weight. In opposition, therefore, to every other nation in the world, they have adopted a stone instead of a pound, as the unit in ascertaining the gravity of British flesh and blood. To unsophisticated ears, 21 stone, 6 pounds, sounds infinitely less than three hundred pounds, which weight is a fair average of the avoirdupois density of the Sir Tunbelly Clumsies of the middle and upper classes. By the term "stun" they may possibly intend remotely to allude to the inevitable fate of any unfortunate person upon whom one of the *heavyocracy* might chance to fall. The crushed individual would most certainly be stunned, though the ponderous cause of the disaster could scarcely be called, in strict accordance with the English cant phrase, "a stunner." "A stunner" is generally supposed in England to be a gentleman, briskly astounding, rather than personally influential, from weighty considerations.

It is not surprising that an Englishman should assume the comfortable rotundity of a homemade loaf of bread, when it is remembered that few hops are requisite to make the latter "rise," and how much of the puffing ingredient the former consumes in the shape of malt liquors. In 1850 the crop of hops in England reached 48,537,669 lbs., which are capable of producing 24,268,834 barrels of beer. I will take the liberty of stating, as a matter of curiosity, the dimensions of a single brewery, that of Perkins & Co., the famous brewers of London. This vast establishment occupies some twelve acres of ground. There are employed between 450 and 500 men, whose burly forms and crimson and unctuous visages make each one a striking impersonation of John Barleycorn. There are 160 of those huge horses, whose ponderous proportions and great height seem the magic result of a mysterious cross between a giraffe and hippopotamus. There is a copper for steaming the malt capable of containing 400 barrels. There is a gigantic vat for final deposit of the liquor before it is drawn into barrels, whose wonderful capacity is 3500 barrels, and another of 1500. The quantity of malt annually consumed is 127,000 quarters, which will produce 317,500 barrels of beer. Quite a lively business, considering the amount of fermentation which must take place.

There is no one of our Americanisms at which Englishmen more frequently sneer, than the application of the name of "*cars*" to Railroad conveyances. They use the term "carriages." Grammar after all is but an arrangement of rules, which the general custom of the most intellectual authorities has declared to be proper. A Railroad was a new mode of transport, and naturally demanded some new name for its means of conveyance. *Car* was a word rarely if ever used in America, though it designates a species of wagon in England; and I think that both good taste and good sense would give the preference to its use, in connection with Railroads, rather than multiply to a mystifying extent the signification of the word carriage. Both cars and carriages have wheels, in common with the conveyances for passengers attached to locomotives—and as car was a word not in use with us, and carriage was already loaded with such general and various significations, I think that reason sustains us in the adoption of the former, though we possessed the right to assign, with perfect propriety, any name to the new mode of travelling, which general custom might have adopted. We can surely manufacture our own *names*, however many importations we are compelled to make from England. But Englishmen seem to insist upon denying us the privilege of travelling in "the cars" since they always go "by rail." Although "riding on a rail" is a mode of transport sometimes adopted on extraordinary occasions in America; yet its not being generally deemed the most reputable conveyance in the world is, I think, a sufficient reason for the adoption of some other term for Railroad travelling.

Among the standing heads for chapters, under which every English writer feels it incumbent on him to grow wordy and indignant, the dangers of our Steamboat navigation occupy a prominent position. All the flaming accounts of the accidents occurring on our Western waters, are eagerly collected by the touring English in America, and, after being properly colored to suit the taste of the market, they make up an important chapter for the forthcoming "book," which is the inevitable result of an Englishman's crossing the Atlantic. The best evidence of England's bitter hatred of America is her insatiable taste for slanderous productions on this country. The same complaints are repeated—the spitting—the same vulgarity—the same Lynch Law—and Steamboat catastrophes—are reproduced again and again, under new names and different colored binding, and yet the demand is always brisk for these villainous compilations.

Explosions of boilers—sinking from being snagged—burnings and collisions, are all joyously heralded, with terrible minuteness, by these English commentators on America. The frequency of such occurrences is adduced as convincing proof of the reckless disregard for life, and utter incapability of all grades of officials in America. It is true, that Steamboat accidents are extremely rare in England, for their boasted "Tems" would scarcely float a large-sized yawl, except when it is floated, as high as London, by the tide. Such limited aquatic facilities are certainly the safest protection against the frightful accidents, which have rendered the Mississippi so terrible to Englishmen. The great Father of Waters hurls his rushing current along a distance of 2800 miles, whilst the Missouri, with its junction to the Mississippi, measures 4100 miles, the longest river in the world. But the famous "Tems," with all its advantages of tide, locks, and dams, creeps but 233 miles to the sea.

But although there exists this almost impossibility against Steamboat accidents, yet never a week, and scarcely a day passes, without the announcement of one or more serious Railroad disasters. I will not crowd my pages with extracts from London papers in support of what I say, but I appeal to the habitual readers of the English journals, for the truth of my assertion. I have observed in the papers of the same morning notices of three different Railroad casualties. But Englishmen boast that the sufferers, on such occasions, are always amply remunerated for the injuries they may have sustained. It is true, that an accident rarely occurs, without the formality of a lawsuit, and that damages are almost universally recovered from the delinquent company. This may be all very well, after the mischief is done, but in most countries the remedy applied would be thought to come rather late. Who but an Englishman could be consoled for the loss of a near relation, by the receipt of a sum of money, which a jury had decided to be the equivalent of his intrinsic value whilst he lived? Who but an Englishman would be satisfied to compound for the loss of a limb, in shillings and pence? Money appears the panacea for every ill in England. It is applied with equal effect to bruised affections, and broken legs. So deliciously does this universal remedy act upon every patient, that the lucky individual is eagerly heralded in the newspapers, as a fit subject for congratulation, who can ascribe to some erratic locomotive a demolished parent, or pulverized limb. If a man should be unfortunate in his domestic relations, or receive a horsewhipping—they pay him: money being considered a salve, healing alike to wounded honor, and a smarting back.

If a young woman loses her reputation by slander, or a husband by "breach of promise," they hasten to pay her for the loss of both: money being deemed, in England, a desirable substitute for those two possessions, which are usually supposed to be absolutely essential to the happiness of the sex. But it is useless to multiply examples. It is a well-approved fact, that Englishmen have no sorrows that money cannot soothe.

Englishmen are stanch supporters of the principle that "vulgarity and rudeness" are the necessary consequences of "free and enlightened Republicanism." They may say what they like of the barbarous influence of mingling all classes in America, but a Republic is the only school for rearing gentlemen among the people. When there is a marked and inexorable distinction of classes, those beneath experience, in spite of themselves, a feeling of degradation, which produces a thousand little meannesses, inconsistent with the high-toned feelings of a gentleman. But where there is no social inequality, Democracy leaves room for the expansion of those principles, which, however rough a man's exterior may be, make him a gentleman in feeling and action. A proper pride is the first element of true gentility, and where there is no prescribed disability in the lowest to associate with the highest, this pride of independence produces a feeling of refinement, a regard for themselves, which very naturally produces a regard for other people. There is no danger of any brutal manifestation of disrespect towards those whose age, whose intellect, or whose wealth have placed them in superior positions. A man, who is perfectly assured of the equality of his rights with the highest, experiences no vulgar ambition to make an unbecoming display of them. The self-respect which arises from his position, teaches him that rudeness to those above him would be much more degrading to him, than it could possibly be to them. A man whose finer feelings are crushed by the consciousness of inferiority; who is compelled to submit to the insolence of purse-proud superiors, can have no self-respect; and in his debasement he is actuated by a mean desire to vent upon those beneath him the insulting injuries he has himself received. The more humbly he is forced to cringe to those whom the laws have made his masters, the more cruelly will he be avenged on those whom fortune has placed below him. The loss of independence, which makes him servile, makes him rude. Servility is as unbecoming as rudeness, in a gentleman. But so long as the present legal differences in the grades of society are maintained in England, her entire population must continue both obsequious and brutal. The 26,999,570 of the people must be basely submissive to the nobility, and the 430 titles must meanly cringe to the crown.

It has long been a subject of mysterious interest to me, to ascertain what peculiar qualifications conferred on a man in England the title of *gentleman*. Whether a certain amount of refinement, of fortune, of education, or noble blood were requisite, I never could satisfactorily determine. After much laborious research in books, and patient comparison of the various persons to whom this enigmatical title had been applied by Englishmen themselves, I have concluded that an English gentleman signifies any idle individual, who has inherited from his father or some other hard-working ancestor, fortune sufficient to live without active occupation. To be rich, and to do nothing, constitute an Englishman's somewhat contracted ideas of gentility.

This gentlemanly idleness of the so-called aristocracy, is an unnatural state of existence, which cannot subsist long without injury both to the individual himself, and the society in which he lives. Go back to the first gentleman, Adam in the garden. The experiment of idleness was satisfactorily tried there, and was found impracticable. Does any one imagine that the forbidden fruit would ever have been tasted, if Adam had been daily occupied in tilling the earth, and Eve, like a good housewife, in darning fig-leaf aprons for her husband and herself? Never. It was her utter idleness, which afforded the serpent an opportunity of using his guile, it was idleness which left room for his cunning suggestions to grow into uncontrollable curiosity. Had the lady mother of mankind been actively engaged in some domestic occupation, she would have had no time to listen to the serpent's wiles, much less to try afterwards the experiment he had suggested. This whole system of gentility is faulty. It is founded in error, and can never come to good. To make idleness, that fruitful source of every evil, the test of aristocracy, and yet contend that this unjust system is not ruinous to the nation in which it exists, is worse than folly. The condition of England is the happiest commentary upon this absurd despotism of fashion. "It is stated in the London Times, that, upon an average, one person out of twenty of this luxurious metropolis is every day destitute of food and employment, and every night without place for shelter or repose. It is a lamentable fact that in this town of London alone, the centre and core of British civilization, one hundred thousand persons are every day without food, save it be the precarious produce of a passing job, or crime."

The fortunate individual who is rich enough to live without labor in England, might be a blackguard, a fool, or a puppy, or all three at once, yet he would nevertheless be a gentleman, and could command, accordingly, the too ready deference of the money-ridden vassals of Great Britain. No refinement of manners, or cultivation of mind, are required to sustain his pretensions; no elegant accomplishments are expected of him: it is not even thought necessary that he should twirl his thumbs gracefully during his very many hours of unemployed leisure; but he must "box well," and "ride boldly," he must be able to "thrash the waterman," and to "take a five-barred gate" at top speed. Idleness is deemed his chiefest virtue, and ridiculous self-conceit, and brutal effrontery, are considered the most unimpeachable evidences of his gentility. An attorney or a surgeon are considered members of honorable professions: a banker or a merchant command high respect in society, but it would be deemed a shocking misapplication of terms, to speak of any of them as *gentlemen.*

How very different are our ideas in America of a gentleman. If I were called on here to give an American definition of a gentleman, I should say that he was a man easy, but unobtrusive in his manners, who never did any thing to offend the taste of the most refined, or wound the feelings of the most sensitive; and who possessed withal an income, sufficient to dress neatly, and indulge the simple habits of a man of cultivation. He should be modest without bashfulness, and firm, without an affectation of pugnacity. He ought never to attempt to attract attention by noise, or arrogance, nor should he allow any one to treat him in a manner which approached indignity. But let him be cool and civil under all circumstances. He should never be betrayed into any thing like a display of temper; there are much more effectual modes of manifesting spirit than in bullying. A woman might treat him in a manner to prevent his ever approaching her again, and a man might insult him so as to make it necessary to call him to an account, but he ought never to gratify either, by allowing them to think that they were capable of exciting a feeling of anger in his breast. He should be above such petty manifestations of weakness, as he should avoid such an acknowledgment to them, that they were of sufficient importance to disturb his equanimity.

Determination is stronger when cool, as the blade is keener from being polished. Above all, let him never condescend to bandy words with a woman. Her sex should be her protection even from attacks of his tongue. It is much more to his honor to maintain a dignified silence under the fiercest feminine assaults, than to elevate a shrewish woman into an equality with himself, by replying to her rudeness. He ought to be polite to her as long as he is in her presence, though he might avoid all repetition of the affront for the future. He ought to touch his hat to his opponent, with whom he was about to engage in mortal combat. He should be much more punctilious in his observance of etiquette with those whom he did not like, than with his friends. There is no surer way of keeping a man at a distance, than to treat him with studied civility. But I have allowed myself to say much more than I intended in alluding to this subject. The great animating principle of genuine gentility, is a delicate regard for the feelings of other people. Let a man remember this, and preserve his own self-respect, and he will be very certain never to do any thing unworthy of a gentleman. A refined perception of what would be disagreeable to his neighbors, will always prevent his being either coarse or rude in his manners; and he should not allow even a desire to appear witty, to betray him into a forgetfulness of the feelings of others, which would be much more unbecoming to him, than it could possibly be cutting to them.

Politeness is deemed lessening to the position of a gentleman in England; in America it is thought his proudest ornament. Englishmen say that we use "*sir*" too frequently in addressing our equals—to whom should we use it if not to them? The Englishman will reply to the civil question of a comparative stranger with rude abruptness, but should a nobleman chance to address him, "my Lord," or "your Grace," not only thickly garnishes all he replies, but smoothly rounds off the end of every sentence. Their excessive repetition becomes both absurd and disgusting. But it would be thought a want of self-respect in him to introduce "Sir" once, in answer to a man whose position did not look down upon his own. Yet the English declare that they so belabor the nobility with their titles, because it is *polite.* Their civility loses its rarest charm in ceasing to be voluntary; and their politeness becomes servility in making abject submission to a superior. Their truckling deference to nobles is a base acknowledgment of inferiority, and not that free, high-toned feeling, which produces a respect for the feelings of others; nor that generous affability of disposition which begets the desire to be agreeable. A man, actuated by the proper feelings of a gentleman, would be much more observant of his conduct towards equals, and inferiors, than towards those whose position commanded his respect; for although the former could not demand or even expect from him politeness, yet it is due to himself, if not to them, to treat them with consideration;—although he might entertain no very exalted respect for them, yet his own self-respect should induce him to extend to them such civilities as he could not omit with propriety. Politeness is justly expected from his position, though not demanded by theirs.

Many persons appear to think that a Lord must be a gentleman because he has nothing else to do. But an Englishman, even when possessing all the advantages of wealth in idleness, is so bundled up in his multifarious wrappings of selfishness and arrogance, that he possesses about the same faculties for being gentlemanly in his manners, that a suddenly resurrected mummy might be supposed to have for being sprightly in its movements. In England *gentleman* is a mere title, which is tacked to the tail end of a list of Dukes, Lords, Baronets, &c. It is not considered at all essential to a Duke to be a gentleman. But in France, where legal distinctions in rank are also acknowledged, the simple title of Gentleman, which a man must win for himself, is justly considered superior to all hereditary titles. They say Monsieur le President, Monsieur le Prince. The first title is descriptive of the man, the last of his father.

When an Englishman conceives it to be advisable to do a favor, instead of making it acceptable, he always succeeds in accompanying it with such an air of obliging condescension, as to render it extremely offensive. The supercilious smile on his lips seems to say, what an uncommonly good fellow I am, so extensively to patronize you. His anxiety always appears excessive to make you fully aware of the painful degree of self-debasement his pride has submitted to in doing you a trifling service. And as he is not often guilty of such indiscretions, he resolves to impress you with the importance of what he has done, and the overwhelming amount of gratitude due him in consequence. An Irishman can more gracefully refuse a kindness than an Englishman do one. The latter never appears so disgusting as when he attempts to be especially kind. As I said once before, in trying to seem affable, he succeeds in being condescending; in affecting to oblige, he becomes insulting.

I have met with some Englishmen who, after a long residence in India, or some other foreign country, presented but few of those national peculiarities which render them generally so forbidding. And I have known others in America whom you would never suspect of being Englishmen—they were such good fellows. But these had been early transplanted from England. If the sound oranges be immediately removed from a barrel in which decay has commenced, they may be saved; but if suffered to remain, they are all soon reduced to the same disgusting state.

The transient English travelling on our Western boats, make grievous complaints of the rude and vulgar manners of the passengers, when people of all classes—the educated and uneducated—the wealthy and the laboring—the elegant and the awkward—are mixed indiscriminately together. That many of them may have been rough in their appearance, and unpolished in their manners, I am most ready to admit; but that they made any display of indecent rudeness I do not believe. These hardy pioneers might not have been so meekly submissive as our stiff-necked Britishers were prepared to expect; but if they were at all rude in their manners, it must have been when these distinguished representatives of the old country were inclined to assert a superiority, which these independent Democrats were not disposed to acknowledge. No people know their own stations, or respect those of other persons more carefully, than Americans; but the respect which superior intellect or wealth generally receives, must be a voluntary offering, not a demanded right. The moment a man arrogates to himself superiority to his fellows, he is mortified by being made to feel that we are all born free and equal. It is this salutary humiliation of arrogance which makes Englishmen so bitterly hostile to the "brutal mingling of all classes in America."

English writers on America are eternally descanting upon the deteriorating effects of Democracy upon the morals and manners of a people, and yet they betray their insincerity by the comparisons they are constantly instituting between this country and their own. They denounce Democracy as destructive of all moral and intellectual excellence, and yet they appear dissatisfied that our worst do not equal their best. On some Western steamboat they are thrown into a sociable squad of cattle-drivers and horse-traders, whose manners are not elegantly polished, and whose persons may be redolent of other perfumes than Lubin's; and they express themselves disappointed because these rough but very good fellows do not possess all the easy presumption of their nobility. They rail at the Republic, and yet expect it to do wonders. They are fond of contrasting England and America, but they always place our roughest citizens beside their richest nobles. Indeed, to hear an Englishman talk, one would very naturally conclude that the nobility embraced the whole nation, and London the entire country of Great Britain. In discussing the manners and customs of the English people, he invariably cites what my Lord what's-his-name says, or His Grace of what-d'ye-call-it, does. And people in the largest cities of the provinces and remotest parts of the kingdom, in alluding to London, speak of "going to town," just as a man living in the outskirts of one of our villages speaks of going "down in town," when he proposes a walk to the principal business street. If their 430 individuals of title really do monopolize not only the virtues and accomplishments, which might be reasonably expected to be distributed among the twenty-seven millions of people of Great Britain, but those of the 830 millions of the universe, it would be extremely unjust to compare our most refined classes with a circle so peculiarly favored. According to the British standard of excellence—money—our wealthiest citizens are very far inferior to their rich middle classes, and could not consequently be contrasted even with them, without injustice. But the English are much too cunning to be just; they will not exhibit their commercial and agricultural classes in opposition to ours, though even then they would have immensely the advantage in wealth. These are the only classes of society in the two countries between which there exists a parallel. According to their own theory all classes in America should be infinitely inferior to their nobility. We have no hereditary aristocracy, with their vast advantages of wealth, of idleness, and legal superiority; but our merchants, our planters, our farmers, and members of the learned professions are our best; but these are always compared with their nobles, instead of their corresponding classes in England. The "cits" of England have always been regarded with scorn, and treated with contempt. They were the fools and cuckolds of every farce from Wycherly to Garrick, and still continue the bulls for the sharp authors and titled blockheads who aspire to be witty. But our more refined classes of citizens are thought to present too favorable a contrast with their nobility, and our roughest Western pioneers are therefore selected as a suitable foil to aristocratic excellence. But what can produce so extraordinary a difference between the commercial and agricultural classes of the two countries, if it be not the Republic? I have made the suggestion, and leave the rest to the reflections of my readers.

It is surprising how difficult it is to discover the basis, on which rest pretensions so ample as those of the British aristocracy. It is true that custom numbers all the nobility among "the mighty men of Israel." Each noble Lord boasts himself vastly superior to the untitled of the universe, though the evidences of his superiority still continue a mystery. Less simple than Samson, he has never betrayed to the world in what his strength really consists. He studiously conceals its sources. Probably apprehending the treachery of some new Delilah, he considers it safer to talk about, than to display his immeasurable superiority. All are ready to admit that his estates are much more extensive, and his income much ampler, than those of ordinary individuals, but surely he cannot found his pretensions on his fortune, for he professes heartily to despise money, and never omits an opportunity to sneer at those who are toiling to possess it.

When we consider the fact that they possess all the advantages that wealth, uninterrupted leisure, and the superstitious awe of rank can give, it is strange how few scions of noble families have in the last two hundred years occupied distinguished positions. And if we except Lord Byron, not a single hereditary possessor of a title has made, during that period, a name that will live. The government wisely leave the nobility to sport the broad ribbons of the different noble orders, and to sustain the arrogance of the country, whilst her honor is protected, and her battles fought by the great minds that spring from the commons. The only instance in which an attempt has been made to force distinguished rank into supplying the place of distinguished abilities, the Duke of York committed such blunders, as Commander-in-Chief in the Low Countries, as to be court-martialed for misconduct. When a Prince of the blood royal is subjected to such a mark of the nation's disapprobation, his incapacity must be gross indeed.

The world had a beginning, as every thing in it must have. The basis of aristocracy is money. It is useless to attempt to conceal it. Money founded, and money sustains the noble families of Great Britan. James I. enjoys the honor of establishing a basis so worthy of the order. The vilest of monarchs, for the vilest of purposes, erected the stepping-stone, by which low-born opulence is wont to climb into nobility.

When all those oft-tried extortions of tonnage and poundage, compulsory loans, and miscalled benevolences had been exhausted, when every possible expedient to raise money had been resorted to, except its legal appropriation by parliament, James I. created the order of Baronets, and retailed the titles at £1000 apiece. Yet this despicable tyrant, without a single redeeming quality, this King without dignity, and pedant without sense, this unnatural son and cruel father, this treacherous friend and pusillanimous foe, in order to overturn the constitution of the country, and trample upon the rights of his subjects, became the hucksterer of these new means, by which rich parvenues might assume the coveted ermine of the aristocracy. To evade the constitutional presence of parliament, and bid defiance to the laws, James established this traffic. And for filthy lucre, paid to such a monarch, in such a cause, a large majority of the founders of the present proud nobility of England gained their baronetcy, which was then, as it is now, the antechamber of aristocracy, from which upstart wealth may peep, on tiptoe, into the half-curtained windows of fashionable revels. Those who will observe the enormous increase of the peerage since the reign of Elizabeth, may form some idea of the number of persons who compounded with James. It is not surprising that the nobility should be so fond of tracing back their genealogies. An origin so worthy of their tastes, so in accordance with their habits, is naturally regarded with fond affection. They are right, piously to hoard the pelf to which they owe so much. With James I. as an example for conduct, and money as their chief object in life, they will probably continue to be worthy of their illustrious origin.

It is true that the refinements of society of the present day would be outraged by the audacity of James's shameless bargain and sale. Modern etiquette has changed the form of proceeding, but the principle which characterized the transaction then, stamps it now. *Cash* is still the password, which admits any enterprising individual into those mysteriously exclusive circles, which are professedly guarded with Masonic watchfulness.

But greater changes, than in the refinement of the people, have taken place in England. It is "the order," not the King, whose coffers now require replenishing. Since the secure establishment of the English constitution, servile parliaments have always been too zealous in filling the exchequer of the sovereign, to make it necessary for him to resort to those extraordinary expedients, alike degrading to the monarch, and injurious to the subject, which commenced under Henry VIII. and ended with Charles I. Both his public and private wants being thus happily provided for, it is not on his own account, but to pour new and vigorous blood into the exhausted veins of "the order," that the sovereign now graciously admits the bloated vulgarity of rich snobs within the magic circle of aristocracy. Money is a perishable sort of thing, and will not stick eternally to noblemen's fingers, however convulsively they may clutch it. But money is the life-blood of the aristocracy, and money must be had at every sacrifice, to bolster up its greatness. Whenever therefore a despised citizen becomes rich enough to make his wealth desirable, or his opposition feared, the Queen, who dotes on the order, as every sovereign ought, ingeniously discovers some long-hidden virtue, which suddenly makes him worthy of Knighthood. From that happy day the Cit belongs soul, body, and more than both, purse—to the nobility. He already dreams of a coronet, and looks forward with fond expectation to the intoxicating period, when he can speak of the privileges of the nobility as his own.

But it frequently happens, that the rare virtues and distinguished merits of well-fed aldermen are so securely buried under the ample folds of fat acquired in green-turtle indulgences and civic potations, as to escape even the inquiring penetration of the Queen. Not even modesty could forbid, under such circumstances, that the deserving individual should give some gentle intimation of his having money enough to insure him the possession of every earthly virtue. A huge donation to some royal charity—to the crystal palace, or some other chimera from the Prince Consort's brains, at once makes the Queen sensible of his hitherto unappreciated excellence, and he becomes a Baronet. The progress from Baronet to Earl is easy and natural, when gold paves the way. And although the fortunate aspirant may not himself do so, yet his son or his grandson are certain to enjoy the ineffable felicity of breathing the balmy atmosphere of those elevated regions, where both *money and trade are so heartily despised.*

Mr. Carlyle has particularly designated us as "eighteen millions of the greatest bores ever seen in this world." I greatly fear that his retired habits have not permitted the distinguished gentleman a very extended acquaintance with his well-fed countrymen. Had he been more general in his intimacies at home, I feel assured that candor would have compelled him, in defiance of his known courtesy to America, to award to his own countrymen a pre-eminence so well earned, and universally acknowledged.

There exists a ponderous sympathy between the minds and persons of Englishmen, which renders them unrivalled as "bores." Unwieldy and inert, neither is much addicted to unnecessary exertion. They infinitely prefer eating to talking. Indeed I may say that they are opposed to conversation on principle. They regard even a limited indulgence in words as an unjustifiable interference with their dinner, and condemn it as a serious interruption to digestion, after dinner is over. Conversation is something therefore to be eschewed by all sensible people. A Briton is emphatically a silent animal. But we commend his silence since, like that of the ass, it relieves us from the terrors of his bray. He can, however, talk upon occasion, but woe unto him whom he deems worthy of being talked to. For however disinterested, or even complimentary, the intentions of the innocent persecutor may be, the sufferings of his victim are not the less acute. Surely the English must imbibe stupidity with their food. Veal and lamb must certainly possess some chemical affinity for their oleaginous brains, which, when thoroughly established, forms a sluggish solution that must prove an opiate for any mind that comes under its influence. Their liveliest conversation is a drowsy compound of beef and porter, enlivened by oft-told tales of England's glory, and stale slanders of America. Their highest appreciation of fun is to make Ireland's sufferings the subject of some senseless jest. The peculiarities of the bullock, and the sheep have, through the magnetic influence of continued absorption, made themselves much more prominent in the dispositions of the people, than those distinguishing Anglo-Saxon peculiarities, of which we hear so much, and know so little. They have not become woolly, nor do they universally wear horns, but the nobility are eternally bellowing forth the astounding deeds of their ancestors, whilst the muttonish middle classes bleat a timorous approval. Such subjects constitute their fund of amusing small talk, their agreeable conversational recreation, their lively hits at the passing unimportant.

But interest or vanity sometimes makes him hold forth in more serious strains. He often talks as "Jack" was wont to "sing"—"for his supper." It is an established rule of his life never to omit an opportunity of feeding at another's expense, and the remote prospect of an invitation to dinner will make him bore his intended host, with the intention of making himself agreeable, by a rigmarole of vapid nonsense, that would deafen a miller. His vanity, too, will prompt him to great efforts to impress distinguished strangers with his sparkling entertaining powers. His topics for conversation for such extraordinary occasions are hidden and deeply buried, but if once you reach them, like the Artesian wells, they are inexhaustible. If he conceives you to be a man of consideration, he will dilate on steamers and railroads, in voluminous discourses, possessing all the fatigue and *ennui*, without the expedition of those conveyances. He will assail you with prodigious accumulations of information on coals, and overwhelm you with statistical tables concerning them, as dark and fathomless as their own native pits. He will spin you tedious yarns about Manchester manufacturing, as endless as the thread of fate. He will kindly favor you with an elaborate price-current of hops for the past twenty years, which shall be warranted destitute of all the sprightly qualities of that article. And, after having put you comfortably into a doze by his learned disquisitions on trifles, he will arouse you by retailing the kitchen gossip of every noble family in the kingdom, which is rather enlivening, as a pretty considerable dash of scandal gives something like piquancy even to his dulness. The English are undoubtedly strong believers in the substantial. Their minds, their persons, and their conversation are all of a solidity which nearly approaches the *heavy*. But they are not "bores," for Mr. Carlyle, a man of decided discrimination, has never discovered them to be so; although ill-natured people might insinuate that his opinion was formed upon the principle which induced the owl to believe her nest-full of owlets the prettiest lot of young birds in the world.

Mr. Carlyle, in common with the rest of his nation, complacently boasts of the acquirements of a few of his countrymen, and raves about the wonders they have achieved. It would be strange indeed, if from such vast pools of stagnant stupidity, some bright spirit did not occasionally arise, as the Jack-o'-lantern springs from fetid bogs. It should be remembered that these huge puddles have, for eighteen centuries, been in a state of progressive preparation for such phenomena, and yet the world has been dazzled by no illumination of Will-o'-the-wisps. A leading spirit, every hundred years, is no great things, even for lumbering Britain. The intervals between Chaucer, Spenser, Shakspeare, Milton, and Byron, are rather long for England to sneer at

America, because she has not yet produced their equals. But Great Britain possesses the happiest faculty of making much out of little. The nation is never at a loss for the bluster of a genuine bully. John Bull's course towards us has always been that of an overgrown, lubberly lout, towards a very young boy. He dares not measure his strength with those of his own age, but, prompted by aspiring cowardice, he delights to assume airs of superiority in derision of our youth, and to boast of his own exploits in comparison with our inexperience. But when people recollect what we have accomplished in our short national existence of three-fourths of a century, the world will not laugh with, but at the British bumpkin, in his giggling self-complacency.

Mr. Carlyle suddenly turns upon America, and tauntingly demands, "what great, noble thing, that one can worship or loyally admire, has yet been produced there?" I am free to acknowledge, that the activity and widespread intelligence of our people are too great, to produce the brilliant phenomena alluded to above. And it is not at all surprising that their natural sprightliness should cause them to be considered "bores" by a man of Mr. Carlyle's sedentary habits and phlegmatic disposition. It is true that we support no magnificent Archbishops at $75,000 a year to "worship;" nor do we annually invest $1,925,000, in order to have a Queen whom we may "loyally admire." But we can boast that our country presents to the assembled world 23,000,000 of the freest, happiest, and most enlightened people the sun ever shone upon.

But Mr. Carlyle asserts that "America with her roast goose and apple sauce for the poorest working man," is still "not much." We have at least shown ourselves a match for Great Britain in every contest, and, according to the evidence of the distinguished essayist himself, we have every reason to feel satisfied with our position. He pompously announces that "America's battle is yet to fight," that we have done nothing. Is stilling the rushing currents of rivers, and making them obedient to our arks of steam nothing? Is it nothing to tame the withering lightning, and lead it harmless by the habitations of men? Is it nothing to annihilate space, and whisper with our antipodes? "If these be nothing," then Fulton, Franklin, and Morse are nothing, and "the world and all that's in't are nothing." Let Mr. Carlyle array all his Heroes of History, and show the world another Washington. Where will he find more fervid bursts of eloquence than our Adams, our Henry, and Randolph have startled a nation with? Where will he find the aims of history writing better accomplished than by Prescott and Bancroft? General Jackson taught the British at New Orleans what our armies could accomplish. And although the English nation, on every festive occasion, may shout with maudlin glee, that "Britannia rules the waves," yet all the waters of all the oceans will not wash out the records that Decatur, Perry, and Stewart have made in the naval history of the world.

The English are eternally alluding to our national vanity, and disposition to exaggerated boasting. These are qualities which England appears to consider exclusively her own. That she is immeasurably superior to all the nations upon earth, she holds to be a corollary which no one would dare to dispute. And she has always been so magnificently grandiloquent in self-glorification, that she deems it presumption in any nation to attempt the same strains. If England really be what she boasts, we ought to be excused for feeling some little national pride; for we have overcome her in every contest—whether by sea or land, whether contending with muskets or cannon, yachts, clippers, or steamers, patent-lock pickers, or reaping machines, we have always been victorious. But her supremacy on the ocean has been her chief source of pride. I shall not be invidious in enumerating the exploits of Paul Jones, nor shall I be unkind in dwelling upon our brilliant naval victories during the war of 1812; I shall base our claims upon the peaceful victories of competition. It is scarcely necessary to allude to the victory gained by the yacht America; but I will remind my readers that we have the fastest time ever made by sailing vessels. The Witch of the Wave, an American clipper of 1400 tons, made the voyage from China to England in 90 days, the fastest on record. Her greatest run in one day was 389 miles, whilst the greatest run in one day ever reported by an English ship was less than 370 miles. The Racer, of 1700 tons, made her first voyage from New-York to Liverpool in the unprecedented time of 14 days; but the Washington accomplished the same voyage in 13½ days. It is scarcely necessary to allude to the glorious victory achieved by the Collins steamers over the Cunard line. John Bull is not much given to acknowledge himself surpassed in any thing; he must be completely whipped before he will confess it himself. As an evidence of how badly he feels himself beaten I give the following extracts.

English Yachts and American Clippers.—Yesterday evening Mr. Scott Russell delivered a lecture before the Royal Institution on English Yachts and American Clippers:—

"England, he observed, wrapped up in her prejudices, had been excelled in the art of ship-building by the Americans, who followed in this matter common sense and the laws of nature for their guides. He, however, believed it was only necessary for us to be assured of our present inferiority, to produce a stimulus that should result in placing us first in the competition. A premium under the old British law of tonnage had been held out to the construction of bad ships, and our yacht clubs adopting this law had increased the evil. There was a time when speed need not be considered a necessary quality in merchant ships, which were held to be good in proportion to the amount of cargo they would stow away—with no reference to speed—and but little to safety. Now, however, since the discovery of gold at the antipodes, speed was more than ever an object, and therefore under the stimulus thus begotten, the lecturer predicted the building of ships within the next ten years very far exceeding in size and speed any we had already seen. Twenty miles an hour, he believed, would be not an extraordinary speed for the new race of vessels, and their length might amount to 500 feet. In point of fact, the longer a ship, the safer, the swifter, the better was she, provided only her materials were strong enough to withstand the increased strain. By adopting iron instead of wood as a shipbuilding material, this necessary degree of strength might be secured."—*Observer.*

And the following from the Times:

The truth must be told—the British steamships have been beaten, and the most rapid passages ever achieved between the Old and New World have been accomplished by the American steamships. None but an American steamship has ever yet run from Liverpool to New-York and vice versa in less than ten days. The average passage of the Asia and Africa may, perhaps, nearly equal those of the Pacific, Baltic, and Arctic of the Collins line; but the Americans have achieved the positive victory in speed, their steamers—the Pacific, Baltic and Arctic—having made the fleetest voyages. On the part of the Americans the contest has been carried on at vast cost, and additional grants from Congress, ostensibly for the mail service, but in reality from the national spirit of rivalry, have only recently been obtained to prevent the project from perishing by reason of an enormous inequality between receipts and expenditures. On the part of the British, while heavy amounts have been paid by the exchequer, and a large profit has been made by the contractors, the Messrs. Cunard, the defeat had been accepted only to renew the attempt in the hope and expectation of mature and eventual success.

A great change has recently occurred in the tone of the daily press of England towards America. She is evidently waking up to the consciousness of who we really are. I hope my readers will bear with me in offering some extracts from daily papers in illustration of this somewhat mysterious change in the style of addressing America. The following are from the Times, with their dates and subjects attached, about the period principally of the Boundary question, and the McLeod difficulty.

We have boundary questions, which, it is too manifest, that the North American republic will struggle hard to convert into means of our injury and humiliation.—*Times Leader on the Ministry,* February 24, 1840.

The enlightened and upright portion of the North American people do not form the *ruling power* therein; the supreme power is in the numerical majority. The numerical majority of the United States are, we apprehend, and the impression is a mournful one, among the least enlightened and the least conscientious of communities calling themselves "civilized."—*Leader on Reduction of the Navy,* March 7, 1840.

We are bound to resist this overbearing demand of the United States, and, if the demand be maintained on their part *vi et armis,* England, *vi et armis,* must repel it.—*Leader,* April 18, 1840.

Save only when that government had placed itself in an attitude of indirect, though obvious, offence towards England, by totally failing to check, and *scarcely* failing to encourage, the criminal outrages of large bands of armed villains upon the provinces of the Queen of England, into which they carried fire, blood, and desolation.—*Leader,* April 23, 1840.

The conduct of the people of Maine has proved that their purpose is to establish a system of encroachment in *all* directions; to push us to the wall wherever they meet with British subjects, or can find them; to wring from us first one specific concession, and so habituate us to the practice of yielding, that whenever they begin to *bully,* we shall prepare to yield, and, at last, not have one acre of ground to stand upon.—*Leader,* April 27, 1840.

Circumstances have been stated, which justify a presumption that the report of Colonel Mudge and his colleague is to be relied upon by Lord Palmerston, as one of the main vouchers, in the nature of an apology, for concessions of British right, more abject and injurious than this country has yet been sufficiently humbled to suffer.—June 27 1840.

Any person who paid attention (and who has not?) to the clamors of the republican newspapers, must have been persuaded, had he not known better, that the citizens of the State of Maine were a set of the most oppressed and ill-used of God's creatures,—lambs worried by the prowling wolves of England,—turtle doves fluttered in their nest, —stricken and sighing sufferers under wanton injury. —*Leader on Boundary Report,* July 31, 1840.

For a specimen of solemn gravity, bordering on the ludicrous, a parallel to this has seldom presented itself:—"How men pretending, as it is to be presumed these do, to any share of public character, could come before the world with such an exhibition, is past all comprehension except their own."—*Leader on Correspondence between Webster and Biddle,* September 16, 1840.

The Oregon Question has once or twice already been alluded to by Mr. Van Buren in his official messages, though in language *sleek and sly,* so that in fact it becomes a matter of serious inquiry whether the safer policy might not be to fight like men for all our rights at once, than, after a dozen pettifogging disputes, to sacrifice them all in succession.—February 19, 1841.

He was as good as any other British subject for a *peg* on which to hang a provocative to war, and plenty of conscientious Yankees, it would appear, were at hand to swear his personal presence on board the Caroline.—*Our relations with France and America,—Mr. McLeod,* —February 19, 1841.

What will be the course of the British Government? Need we ask the question? Yes, we must; although it be one which the country, if not the ministers, will promptly answer. The consequences of Mr. McLeod's judicial murder must be *War.*

The attempt, therefore, to shuffle off the obligation of redress for a wrong perpetrated upon Great Britain, in the person of her subject, from the United States Government, which originally claimed jurisdiction over the whole question, upon the shoulders of the State of New-York alone, is adding levity and ridicule to insult and oppression.—*Leader,—McLeod,*—March 5, 1841.

A document, which we do not scruple to describe as the most virulent, unprincipled, and revolting, that has ever disgraced the records of any people, hower immersed in the rudest or most corrupt vice.—*On Report of Committee on Foreign Affairs to the House of Representatives*, March 9, 1841.

As far as the American people have had time to degenerate from their British origin into a distinctive national character, we are afraid that that character consists, for the most part, in empty pretension and *puff*. Having began their republican career with a deep tincture of vanity, occasioned by their successful struggle for independence, and having afterwards enjoyed considerable mercantile prosperity, as the principal cotton growers for the European markets, they seem to have strutted into a precocious and unnatural self-importance, as if their political and commercial resources had attained a maturity, which, under the guidance of democratic infallibility, rendered every chance of miscarriage an inconceivable thing.—*Banks*, April 16, 1841.

But that as long as the American Government find that we may be trifled with, with impunity, they are willing to gratify the passions of the populace, by anticipations of the judicial murder of one of the Queen of England's officers: If by any fatal mischance that monstrous act should ever be consummated, the horror and disgust of the whole civilized world will fall as heavily on the statesman by whom it was tolerated, as on the savages by whom it was committed.—*McLeod*, August 5, 1841.

It requires we fear a stronger arm than that of the existing Federal Government of America, to control the arrogant, unjust, and turbulent spirit which the "pattern democracy" is apt to carry into its controversies and negotiations with foreign states. The Boundary Question has awakened a spirit of direct hostility to England on the Northern frontier, the emancipation of the black population of the British colonies, in the West Indies, has been witnessed with feelings of rancor and dread by the slave States of the South. In private life the nefarious abuse of British capital, too confidingly intrusted to a people of speculators, has led the Americans to get up a cry against the nation they have plundered.—*On Relations between England and America*, August 18, 1841.

But in spite of all this fume and sputter, we would give the Amerians any favorable odds they please in betting on the security of McLeod's life. We know the infirmities of transatlantic citizenship tolerably well. It is astonishing what big talk and what undaunted temerity they will make use of in a case like this.

With such a Minister, equally temperate and uncompromising, we cannot doubt that if actual hostilities be providentially averted, the Americans will at least be taught a lesson which in future will lead them to a truer estimate of their self *conceit* and *arrogance* than they yet appear to have formed. Pompous bombast in this quarter of the world has not gone out of fashion.—*McLeod,* Oct. 12, 1841.

If the Americans cannot repress their insolent aggressions upon British territory, the Queen of England will assuredly do it for them. If a systematic series of outrages must needs be inflicted on the British Crown, Her Majesty's forces, instead of abstaining from doing the duties of the Alburgh magistracy, will in all probability find ways and means of asserting her great national rights under the *walls* of New-York itself. And if it must come to that, God send us a good deliverance.—*Leader, on General Affairs,* Oct. 18, 1841.

Poor Judge Gridley,—one can scarcely read his elaborate summing up, without a compassionate smile; conceiving that he had to deal with the most important cause that had ever agitated the world, the anxious functionary seems to have been literally bowed down to the dust under the weight of his fancied responsility. The quiet and humble apartment he set in, became, in his excited imagination, "the solemn temple of Justice," the presence of a few straggling Canadians, whom curiosity had attracted to the spot, was felt to be so flattering to the solemnity, that the judge publicly complimented them as "distinguished actors in the scenes of blood and suffering," connected with the suppression of the McKenzie rebellion: ——— and after indulging in a long and wasteful expenditure of profound judicial *saws*, the complacent luminary was constrained, at last, to let the jury retire.—*McLeod's Acquittal,* Nov. 1, 1841.

We have our laws, and it is mere arrogant impudence, mere presuming on English gullibility, to demand of us to govern by any other.—*Detention of the Brig Creole,* March 21, 1842.

A generous concession to a generous claimant is one thing; to invite Brother Jonathan to help himself from our pockets is another: we are ready to be liberal, but we must not be bullied into giving half-a-crown to a known swindler.—*Leader,* Feb. 6, 1842.

Frenchmen are sometimes impertinent, Irishmen impudent, Welchmen voluble, Englishmen blustering, Scotchmen cool; but the conjoint coolness, blustering, volubility, impudence. and impertinence of a true Yankee, has a height, and depth, and breadth about it, which "flogs" each of these nations, in their most characteristic accomplishment.

The Pennsylvanian farmer or merchant, knows that his creditors, grumble as they may, cannot pocket the Canadas, or ship off the railroads. He puts his hands in his pockets, and his feet on the chimney-piece, hugs himself in comfort over his growing income, and takes care to look for a repudiating representative, in the State Legislature.

This is, was, and will be the American cry, "give! give! give!" but the English counter cry will be "pay! pay! pay!" Before you expect us to entertain a single argument you use—"pay your debts;" till then you have no right to a place among honest nations. Unless you come with your money in your hand, and pay down upon delivery, buy not at all, barter not at all,—and if you must needs be negotiating, negotiate with the convicts of Botany Bay.—*Leader*, Nov. 14, 1843.

That such views as these should be current among the people, is, perhaps, what the holders of Pennsylvanian bonds might expect, discreditable but natural: but that they should be deliberately promulgated by the highest authority in the United States, in his most solemn official manifesto, is an additional and unnecessary dishonor, arising, as we have said, from the practice of requiring from that personage an annual palaver *in extenso* for the satisfaction of an unprincipled though "*free* and *enlightened*" public.—*On President's Message*, Dec. 29, 1843.

The change in the tone of the Times from that period, is almost startling in its abruptness. They can now talk of "consideration for the feelings of a people so nearly connected with ourselves." They seemed formerly ignorant that we had any feelings at all—and I must confess, that considering the intimacy of the connection, they have been somewhat tardy in making the discovery. It appears that the danger of the fishery question plead much more powerfully in our behalf than these tenderly chronicled ties of consanguinity. The rest of the press following in the distance the bolder strides of their leader, now honor us with the appellation of "our rivals in commerce and arms," and courteously discourse upon the sort of consideration with which "so powerful a nation" should be treated. The Times can now pathetically enlarge upon the probable inconvenience to American fishermen, which must arise from the hasty proceedings of the Derby administration, and in a tone of chiding remonstrance to the government, they observe:

It is more than probable that American fishermen have been trespassing, but their trespass has been so far unheeded, that notice of altered resolutions on our part might have been fairly expected, while the true interests of both countries are so plainly dependent on good understanding and reciprocal concessions, that the very last resort should have been to any proceeding which might resemble a menace. Least of all should a crisis have been selected for the experiment, when the preparations of the fishermen were too far advanced to be stopped, and when the ordinary good sense of the community was so suspended by constitutional incidents as to leave it at the control of even an Irish mob.

It appears that even the Times can be extremely mild and conciliatory in its tone towards America, though discussing a question calculated to develope all its proneness to vituperation. What could be gentler than the following extract, in which they remonstrate more in sorrow than anger with the Americans for their somewhat intemperate proceedings. "The sweet south" would scarcely breathe more softly "o'er a bank of violets," than comes the bewailing censure of the following:

Long usage, previous concessions, and even arguments of a broader and more general kind, suggest that the question should be treated in a liberal and conciliatory spirit; but the law of the case, to which the Americans have so intemperately appealed, is decidedly against them; and while we regret that measures calculated to irritate a sensitive nation should have been so hastily adopted, we are constrained to observe that their own proceedings have been equally precipitate, and that such views as were expressed in the Senate are ill adapted to promote a settlement of the dispute. It is no credit to either State that its first step on an occasion like this should have been to equip war-steamers for action, and we trust that the awakening sense of both countries may speedily dispatch the affair by a more reasonable appeal.

To speak of England and America as equals, is certainly a novel idea—and actually to appeal to our "sense," as if we were reasonable people, is a condescension in Mr. Times, of which we bowie-knife barbarians should feel properly sensible. It certainly didn't use to be so.

What a change in their notions of our importance is developed in the following from the same paper :

The Disastrous War at the Cape.—While all eyes are intent on the threatening aspect of the storm which seems about to break upon us from the north-west, our attention is for the moment diverted by one of the periodical accounts of the tempest which has been so long raging in the south-east. From the icy shores and stormy seas of Newfoundland and Nova Scotia we are abruptly recalled to the desert plains and burning rocks of South Africa. Sandilli takes the place of Mr. Webster, and the capture and recapture of sheep and cattle replace the contest which is going on for the possession of unconscious cod and mackerel.

They seem suddenly made aware, that America *can* raise a storm. No "tempest in a teapot," but a veritable squall along the "icy banks and stormy seas of Newfoundland and Nova Scotia," fierce enough to make "Britannia" slightly apprehensive, though she does "rule the waves." They seem to consider us of too much importance to be wholly despised—and have actually elevated us to the rare distinction of being mentioned in the same category with the rebellious Hottentots and savage Caffres, who have been summarily thrashing all the commanders-in-chief the government has successively sent out for the last twelve months.

It appears from the following extract, that even the Times has concluded that our just ire cannot be excited with impunity—and has recently become convinced that "it cannot be the part of sound statesmanship" to "arouse the temper" of our people.

If we have rights, which, after long negligence, we now choose to enforce—well and good; but it at least behooves us to afford the adverse party fair notice of, and full reason for, our altered proceedings. Especially this behooves us when dealing with the United States, whose government is influenced, whether it will or not, by every prevalent temper of their people. To arouse the temper of that people by any unexpected proceeding, wearing a hostile aspect, cannot be the part of sound statesmanship. Unfortunately our "Conservative" statesmen, in dealing with the Americans, are apt to miss the just and dignified medium, between truckling and bullying. Where Lord Aberdeen betrayed alacrity to capitulate, Lord Malmesbury indicates velleities to menace. Mr. Webster communicates to the *Boston Courier* the copy of a dispatch from Mr. Everett, United States Minister in London in 1845, transmitting a note of Lord Aberdeen, to the effect that the British government had come to the determination *to concede to American fishermen the right of pursuing their occupation within the Bay of Fundy.* If this document is cited accurately, a pretty picture is presented of that school of statesmen who, seven years back, made our American friends a gratuitous present of those very rights which they now, all of a sudden, send vessels of war to vindicate.—*Globe.*

How anxious they now are to claim us as relations, whom they formerly most delighted to villify, appears from the "Globe" comments :—

Whatever abruptness there has appeared in the manner of proceeding on our part, no substantial ground of offence has been given by that proceeding to our republican kinsfolk. It can be no substantial ground of offence to enforce admitted rights—rights infringed admittedly. But it is *convenient* to infringe them! It is. In such cases, rights must either be appropriated by robbery, or obtained by purchase.

The "Republican kinsfolk" are growing in importance.

and consequently in the intimacy of the family ties, that they have been something less than a century in recollecting. They can *now* acknowledge superior enterprise to Americans in something at least.

We are induced on good information to believe, that the superior success of the Americans is mainly attributable to the superior method they adopt in capturing the fish. Whilst the operations of our fishermen are limited to the boat-shore fishing, they are engaged in the bank and deep-sea fishing. In the net and seine fishing they are likewise in advance of our fishermen. The superior system adopted in the cod and mackerel fishery by the Americans, would of itself account for the disparity between their prosperous voyages and the scanty catch of the Colonial fishermen of those descriptions of fish. In Sir Charles Lyell's "Second Visit to the United States," we find the following passage [vol. II., p. 356], which affords additional illustration of the like sources of success as those above indicated in Brother Jonathan's fishing and other enterprises. Brother Jonathan "looks alive," and keeps awake.

It seems indubitable that there is "*danger*" in disturbing the amicable relations according to "the Chronicle."

But in addition to the injury which his selfish and unconstitutional course is inflicting on the commercial interests of the community, we have, in the pending dispute on the subject of the American fisheries, a still more striking proof of the mischief and danger of prolonging the present political uncertainty. In the first place, with regard to the fiscal part of the question, Sir John Pakington has taken a step which gravely compromises the relations between this country and our American colonies, and which is in direct contravention to the spirit of that Free-trade policy which it is certain that the new Parliament will decidedly maintain. If the legislature had been sitting, would it have permitted the Colonial Secretary to sanction the Colonial proposition for bounties? And if it would not, is it not plain that the country has been jockeyed, against its deliberate will, into this little trick of Transatlantic protection? But this is the least important aspect of the affair. As regards the more serious question of our amicable relations with the United States, the imminent danger of intrusting so delicate a negotiation to a "moribund" Government is but too apparent.

But this question of the "*danger*" of trifling with America, is put beyond all cavil by the "Times."

We are informed upon the authority of Ministerial organs, that the whole question has now been virtually settled by liberal negotiation; and so easy and desirable was such a result, that we can scarcely discredit the report; but the intelligence of Monday announces that American cruisers are actually on their way to the fishing grounds, and no limit can be put to the danger of a policy which brings the ships of two such nations as Great Britain and the States into menacing, if not hostile presence.

The two following are from the "Chronicle."

The grave misunderstanding between this country and the United States, to which the question of the American fisheries has given rise—and which appears to be daily growing more serious—will go a long way to dispel any amiable prejudices which enthusiastic persons may entertain in favor of improvising Secretaries of State. Sir John Pakington and Lord Malmesbury have contrived, by their ignorance and folly, to blunder into a position in which it is impossible for them either to advance with justice, or to retreat with honor.

Even if we judge the conduct of ministers from their own view of what is expedient, they might at least have known that the Americans are about the last people in the world from whom any thing is to be obtained by bluster and bullying. There are no two countries in which national jealousies take fire so quickly, or rage so fiercely, on questions of foreign politics, as in England and the United States. In dealing with a free people like the Americans, it is above all things necessary that, before a claim is preferred—and, much more, before any attempt is made to enforce it—its exigency and validity should be clearly ascertained and established. It appears, however, that Lord Malmesbury has proceeded to the extreme measure of seizing American vessels, on grounds which are totally inadequate to justify such a step. It is impossible to contemplate without painful uneasiness the consequences of so rash and foolish an exploit.

These extracts from the Chronicle intimate a rather more flattering estimate of our national importance than

English journals were wont formerly to contain. But it would be the height of injustice not to allow the Times to "sum up" on this subject. Hear him and wonder.

Late Dispute with America.—*The Colonies and Protection.*—By this time we hope our dispute with the United States of America is over, and we trust that all parties will return without delay to those amicable feelings and friendly relations which our Government has so needlessly disturbed. It is not, however, of the obvious and glaring errors of the Government of England, or the wild and precipitate proceedings of the American Legislature, that we wish now to speak. Our desire is to make the danger we have just escaped the subject of a few practical reflections, which we submit to the good sense of the English nation. We have been on the verge of a war with a nation which, from its identity in race and language with ourselves, would have proved a truly formidable enemy—a maritime and commercial people who would have met us with our own arms, on our own element, and visited our commerce with mischiefs similar to those which we should have inflicted upon theirs. So closely are the two countries united, that every injury which we might inflict on our enemy would have been almost as injurious to our merchants as bombarding our own towns, or sinking our own ships. And yet it is no exaggeration to say that with this people we were on the very verge of war, for, had we persevered in carrying out with a high hand, by seizure and confiscation, our own interpretation of the treaty, a collision with the American Commodore was unavoidable; and such a collision must almost necessarily have been followed by a formal declaration of hostilities. Now, what is the question which has so nearly led to such serious results? It is simply whether a certain quantity of the salt fish consumed in these islands shall be caught by citizens of the United States or natives of our own colonies. The question whether American fishermen shall be allowed to spread their nets in the Bay of Fundy is one in which the people of this country have no imaginable interest; they will neither be richer nor poorer, stronger nor weaker, more admired or more feared, should they secure the monopoly of fishing in these northern waters to the inhabitants of the sea-coast of our North American colonies.

I find a very appropriate termination for my extracts in the Examiner.

The Retreat.—We said last week that the English ministry would have to beat a hasty and disgraceful retreat in the American brawl. Already it has done so. The act of cowardice has followed hard on that of bluster and defiance, and the Americans remain not only masters of what they had, but gainers of considerably more. It is announced by the organs of the ministry that the matter in dispute has been amicably arranged between Lord Malmesbury and Mr. Abbott Lawrence, the former agreeing to throw open to the United States all the British fisheries at greater distances than three miles from our coasts, and the latter making the same concession to England of the American fisheries. Thus every point in question is given up on the English side, while at the same time, by what the *Standard* calls "an arrangement of perfect reciprocity," the Americans give up nothing at all, and get a great deal. If there had been any other fisheries worth naming in these American waters except those off our own coasts, the brawl could never have arisen.

I shall make no comments on the miraculous change of tone towards America, in the press, or rather in the Times, which is a synopsis of the press, from 1840 to 1852. The extracts I have made at the two periods speak for themselves. I will simply ask my readers whether they believe this very perceptible change to result from the fact of England's having more interests to protect now than then, or from her having, by some mysterious process, become aware that we are rather more powerful than she imagined when she talked blood and powder about the Boundary question and the McLeod difficulty? Was it the sense of danger, or gentle "consideration" for our "feelings," which has produced so marvellous a contrast in the style of addressing us? Was it prudence or affection which dictated the change? Have we grown so much better, or so much more powerful in the opinion of the English press, that we are now treated with something like the respect usually extended towards other nations? Has "the Times" became more tolerant of a nation of swindlers, or has policy suggested a little flattering deceit? Again I say the extracts speak for themselves.

CHAPTER VI.

ENGLISH MANNERS.

IT is not surprising that an Englishman should be awkward, and reserved in his manners. In his apprehension of addressing some one above or below him, he lives like a man on a sharp fence between a mad bull and biting dog. If he rashly ventures down on one side, some haughty superior may contemptuously toss him; and if he cautiously slides off on the other, he incurs the danger of being pulled down and worried by an inferior. Either catastrophe would be equally terrible in its results to him; and his only alternative is to remain mum, and bolt upright. How could an individual under such circumstances be otherwise than constrained, unnatural, and ill at ease.

Such is his life, his only consolation being in venting his ill-humor on dependents. He delights in creating a sensation in public places by blustering among the waiters. He is fond of displaying his breeding by ordering unusual or impossible things. Nothing seems to afford him such exquisite enjoyment as setting a whole establishment in commotion. It is ludicrously terrific to witness the emphatic fierceness with which he will thump the table, and noisily declare his determination not to leave it, till his demands, however absurd or unreasonable they may be, have been complied with. Such conduct cannot fail, in his opinion, to inspire all beholders with respect, and to impress them with high notions of his aristocratic rearing. He grumbles on principle, and finds fault in order to be well served. He makes it a rule never to express himself satisfied with any thing that is done for him. He is afraid to appear pleased. He laboriously avoids manifesting any thing like enthusiasm in public places of amusement, and never acknowledges the slightest pleasure at any entertainment however sumptuous. If he did, people might suppose that he had never been accustomed to any thing better; whilst it is his darling wish to produce the impression that he was "born so high," that nothing gotten up by inferior mortals for his amusement could merit his approbation. His tastes are too refined, his habits too luxurious to be gratified among the herd. Content is plebeian, and applause decidedly vulgar. A peasant can feel one, "the groundlings" do the other. An English gentleman should consequently know neither. How could he be guilty of such injustice to his caste, as to appear amused by what other people took interest in? And besides, if he should so far forget himself, as to appear contented with what he ordered of a menial, the English would immediately conclude that he was not much accustomed to being waited on. So after all, if an Englishman was not morose by nature, the trammels of the society in which he lives would inevitably make him so. Circumstances compel him to be noisy, blustering, and bullying, with those whose services his money temporarily commands; whilst it is equally incumbent on him to be silent and forbidding among those whose position in life he is not perfectly well assured of. It would be as shocking to his sense of his own importance in encouraging the advances of others, to be contaminated by familiar intercourse with an individual of inferior pretensions, as to be snubbed in too boldly addressing somebody, whose rank conferred on him the privilege of being rude. He can never approach a stranger without braving this double danger;

consequently the delicate nerves of snobbishness make him keep his distance and hold his peace.

During my wanderings in the East, I became acquainted at Jerusalem with a wealthy English banker, whose chief delight was to boast of his noble connections, and aristocratic associations. He had travelled much, though with no decided advantage to a naturally contracted and violently prejudiced mind. He was far from being either intellectual or well informed; and yet he was an extremely entertaining companion, from the unsuspecting display of such a catalogue of absurdities, as is rarely possessed even by an Englishman. Among very many extraordinary and highly amusing disclosures he was daily in the habit of making to us, with regard to himself and his country, he on one occasion alluded to the inexorable nature of the laws governing fashionable circles in England. He informed us that it was destruction to a man's position in society to wander, even inadvertently, beyond the confines of his particular class; and in illustration of his remark, related a little adventure which had once occurred to himself. He was one night during the fall of the year going from Dover to Ostend. It was bitterly cold, and sleeting in that driving-piercing sort of way, only observable in England and off her coasts. Scarcely had they emerged from the dock when they discovered it was extremely rough. Our banker found it impossible to remain in the cabin below, which was soon rendered noisome by the number of seasick passengers, who had taken refuge there from the weather. His only alternative therefore was to continue on deck, exposed to the pitiless storm that was then raging. During the somewhat melancholy reflections produced by his situation, for, singularly enough, he happened to be without an overcoat, a strange gentleman of remarkably prepossessing appearance approached him, and discovering his forlorn condition, politely begged his acceptance of a heavy coat which he had with him, in addition to the one he himself wore. The proffered coat was joyfully accepted by our shivering acquaintance, who sought in vain for words sufficiently to thank the unknown passenger for so unexpected a kindness. So agreeable an incident very naturally led them into conversation. The banker was charmed with the other. He discovered that in addition to his unusually graceful manners, he was a man of decided intelligence and rare information. So much was he delighted with his new friend, that they spent the night together on deck, conversing on a multitude of different subjects, of all which the stranger possessed the same familiar knowledge. The banker was as much impressed by his appearance and address, as he was charmed by the very extraordinary powers of conversation he continued to display during the whole voyage. In parting with him on the pier at Ostend, he warmly acknowledged his indebtedness to his kindness, and expressed a hope to have the pleasure of his farther acquaintance. But previous to his making some effort to show his appreciation of the obligation under which the stranger had placed him, his caution suggested the propriety of making some inquiries as to who he was, as he might possibly compromise himself by some unworthy association. "What," continued he in his relation of the anecdote to us, "was my consternation in discovering that he was a rich *linen-draper*, who was about to make a short tour on the continent. The presence of such a man I could never acknowledge even by a bow, without seriously endangering my own standing. So I determined if possible to shun him, not wishing to be the occasion of any unnecessary mortification to a man who had been polite to me. But the fates had ordained it otherwise. What was my horror when, that very morning, I met him face to face in the street. What was I to do? I remembered I had a position in society to maintain, so *I cut him*, and returned his polite bow with a surprised stare, that was meant to inquire what insolent fellow presumed to bow to me without an introduction? I was sorry to do it, for I must acknowledge that I have rarely met a man with whose manners and conversation I felt so much pleased; but his *occupation* precluded the possibility of my so far demeaning myself, as to acknowledge that such a person had had it in his power to oblige me. Besides, if I had even coldly returned his salutation, he might on some future occasion have had the impertinence to bow to me at the opera, or in Regent-street, which would have ruined me with all my West-end acquaintances. The only course left me, was the one I pursued—to cut him in the beginning. It very probably saved both of us much future annoyance." This wholesale shaver—this man of flint, who preys upon the necessities, and lives by the misfortunes of his fellow men, felt contaminated by receiving a kindness from a haberdasher, because, forsooth, *he* was dignified by the elephantine title of *Banker*. What opinion must we entertain of the mind and heart of a man, who could unfeelingly insult another, whose bearing had so favorably impressed him, simply because he pursued an occupation less fashionable, 'tis true, but equally as respectable and far more honest than his own? What estimate can we place upon the refinement of the society which compels its victims to descend to low-bred vulgarity and brutal rudeness in order to retain in it their positions? A position so precarious, as to be endangered by the simple acknowledgment of a favor to the humblest man who was honest, seems to me to be scarcely worth having. Had there been any thing peculiarly repulsive in the man's appearance, or obtrusive in his manners,—had the banker discovered upon inquiry, that he had been engaged in some disreputable pursuit, or that suspicions however vague had ever been whispered against the integrity of his past conduct, he might have been excusable for formally expressing his thanks, and afterwards treating him with sufficient coldness of manner plainly to intimate that he desired no greater intimacy. But when he himself had declared the stranger to be a most delightful companion, and had candidly acknowledged the decided suffering from which his polite offer of his coat had relieved him, his conduct was a barbarity which an Englishman only could perpetrate. How insecure must be the basis of that rank, which could be toppled over by a nod of recognition to a man whose only offence was in being a retail merchant. What contempt must we feel for a nation who professes to despise trade, when trade made England what she is. How completely must all magnanimity be enveloped in the fog of absurd superstitions about rank, when honest industry can be regarded as a disgrace.

It would be folly to express a doubt of England's widespread influence. It would be worse than prejudice to deny the honor, with which her representatives are received at all foreign courts. Her flag is known and respected in every sea. Her power is acknowledged, and her resentment feared by every nation of the older continents. The rights of her humblest citizens are respected in the remotest countries—for her subjects bear with them into the most distant climes assurances of her protection. She has always redressed the injuries done to individuals, as outrages to herself. The affair of Don Pacifico and the Greek government is too recent to require more than a passing allusion. I was in Athens during the embargo by the English fleet. I saw a king harassed—a friendly power threatened—and the whole nation distressed, because the Athenian mob had been pleased incontinently to batter Don Pacifico's pet warming-pan. Yes, that immortal Bay, which had witnessed the destruction of Xerxes' thousand ships, I saw desecrated by the presence of a hostile fleet, because the ingenious Don considered it safest to throw himself upon the protection of the English government, on the authority of an antiquated passport, dated some twenty or thirty years back, at Gibraltar. So far as regarded the proof of Pacifico's citizenship, the passport might just as well been dated in the moon, or some other distant planet. But England showed to the world that a man, even professing to be an English subject, could claim, and receive her protection. Even in the last few months, a prime minister has been hooted by all classes of his own countrymen, and two friendly powers have been kept in hot water, because young Mr. Mather had been maltreated by an Austrian officer, in Florence. And although redress was sought, and obtained, yet the almost entire press of the country united in reviling the imbecility of Lord Derby's government, in not insisting upon some retribution, more in accordance with the offence.

The civilized world has reason to be grateful to England for the promptness with which she has always punished any nation, that dared to assail a citizen of hers. This influence is felt in the remotest countries of the East, into which travellers ever penetrate. I have, myself, enjoyed the advantages of it, and here make my acknowledgments. In Turkey, Syria, and Egypt, all Franks and Howadjis are confounded with Englishmen. And Germans, Frenchmen, and Americans, profit by the mistake. The summary manner in which British representatives have more than once proceeded, has taught these bigots that their nation, at least, must be sacred from persecution and insult. These semi-barbarians seem apprehensive, that the English fleets will come stalking across their sandy plains, like the wooden horse up to the walls of Troy. And so exaggerated an opinion do they entertain of England's power, that the curse of their Prophet is scarcely more dreaded than the terrors of her ire.

Previous to the conquest of Syria by Ibrahim Pasha, the heroic son of Mehemet Ali, no Christian was permitted to enter the gates of Damascus on horseback. All Franks were compelled to assume the most abject humility in the presence of a native, and they were altogether excluded from certain quarters entirely occupied by the residences of Turks. When Ibrahim asserted the conqueror's right to the direction of affairs, he very greatly alleviated the condition of the few Christian inhabitants of the city, and decidedly diminished the annoyances of travellers, All these absurd restrictions were abolished, and never resumed, although the citizens of Damascus still continued the most bigoted of the Turkish dominions. On a certain occasion, some years ago, an English traveller was curiously peering into the outer court of the principal mosque in Damascus. He did not enter, as he was well aware of the insane fury of the Mahometans against any Frank, who should dare to desecrate their fanes by his presence. But the bigoted people in the neighborhood determined to regard his inoffensive conduct as a pollution of the sacred character of the place, and immediately commenced an assault with mud and stones, which, becoming fiercer every minute, must have proved fatal, had not the poor tourist fled for refuge to the house of the English Consul, which fortunately happened to be not far distant. The Consul at once demanded satisfaction for so flagrant an outrage. The Pasha was apparently most active in his inquiries, but professed to be altogether unable to discover the perpetrators of the insult. The Consul promptly demanded the arrest of every male inhabitant of that quarter of the city, and insisted upon subjecting them all to the punishment that some of them had so richly merited. The Pasha demurred, but finally he attempted a compromise, by proposing that the punishment should be inflicted in private. But the Consul would listen to no such proposition; and England being a name of fear, the Pasha was compelled to submit, and some two or three hundred of these bigots were bastinadoed by a detachment of soldiers in the Public Square. The example of several hundred delinquents undergoing this fearful punishment at the same time, was not soon to be forgotten by the Damascenes; and England, and Europeans, have been respected highly ever since. The proceeding must seem harsh and unjust to us, but it was altogether in accordance with Oriental notions of justice, which makes whole sections of the country responsible for the crimes committed in their boundaries. The apprehension of a general punishment makes of all the inhabitants a vigilant police, for the detection of thieves and murderers. Some such act of severity too, was essentially necessary to impress these zealots with becoming ideas of the inviolability of the persons of the Franks.

Nineteen hundred years ago Cæsar found Britain the puny possession of savages—and the Romans left them more civilized, 'tis true, but still, unable to defend themselves from the attacks of their more powerful neighbors on the other side of the Tweed. From an origin so humble, she has risen to be the most powerful nation on the globe. Once an inconsiderable island, with an area about equal to our State of Missouri, her colors now float from the citadels of 44 colonies, scattered over the known world, besides her vast possessions in India. Her rule is acknowledged by nearly 200,000,000 of people. She sustains a standing army of 100,000 men, and a navy of 198 ships in commission, with 33,759 seamen and marines. Her merchant service is estimated at 4,144,115 tons, and she sustains a vast national debt, whose interest alone annually amounts to $141,269,160. For a nation, who from such a beginning has produced such results, I can but feel an exalted admiration. But my contempt surpasses my admiration, when I remember that they are ashamed of what has made them great. Instead of erecting statues to commerce in every public square—instead of placing tablets at the corners of all the principal thoroughfares, expressive of the nation's gratitude to trade, they pitifully profess to despise those engaged in commercial pursuits. What were they till commerce lent her helping hand? Alternately the defenceless prey of Romans, Picts and Scots, Saxons, Danes, and Normans, England was only known among nations, as the convenient conquest of any marauding horde of barbarians, whose own possessions were too narrow, or too poor to content them. Commerce first taught them the art of self-defence, and gave them strength to maintain it. Commerce brought them wealth. Commerce made them powerful, and ministered to their glory. Yet in their degradation, they have branded commerce as unworthy to associate with the descendants of their Norman enslavers. The poverty of their language never appears so lamentable as when we seek for expletives worthy of such meanness. What shall we call such conduct? 'Tis littleness in Titan mould!

A genuine Englishman delights in rendering himself conspicuous by the multitude of his wants. If on board a steamer, where the number of servants is necessarily limited, he will send one waiter for roast beef, another for a bottle of porter—will order a third, as he approaches the gentleman sitting next him, who has had nothing to eat, to hand him the radishes, and then complains to the head steward that he can get nobody to wait on him. In the meanwhile, he helps himself successively to every thing he can reach, by sticking his elbows into other people's faces, and pronounces all he tastes unbearable. His beef arrives, which he eyes scornfully, and with upturned nose pushes off from him. He once more bawls for the head steward, and sarcastically asks to be informed what he calls that on his plate. "Roast beef, I think, sir." "Roast beef, is it? Well, I should say that, whatever it may be, it is not fit to be put into a gentleman's mouth." He then continues confidentially to announce to the whole table—whilst professedly addressing the steward—that the cook does not understand his business, that the carvers do not know how to carve, and that he has found nothing since he has been on board that he could eat; although he has been daily in the habit of employing two-thirds of all the servants within call, and devouring every thing he could lay his hands on. The eager haste, amounting almost to a scramble, with which an Englishman seeks to have himself helped before everybody else, appears to me strangely unbecoming in a gentleman,—especially in situations where the wants of all are certain to be attended to, with the exercise of a slight degree of patience. But he seems to imagine there is distinction in being first served, even when he is compelled to resort to unseemly haste to secure the doubtful honor. He considers selfishness knowing, and a total disregard of the comfort of other people as eminently indicative of an aristocratic turn of mind. He is nervously apprehensive of showing the slightest attention even to a lady at table, such, for instance, as passing her the salt or filling her wine-glass. He is haunted by the spectral fear that somebody might construe such an encroachment upon the duties of the waiter into evidence of his having emerged from some obscure position. Such scrupulous attention to the preservation of his rank would naturally imply the consciousness of being in a new position, of which he was not altogether secure. What man among us, really entitled to the consideration of a gentleman, would be agitated by such absurd apprehensions. A man, really certain of his position in society, would scarcely fear a sacrifice of it by so simple an act of politeness. An Englishman is always excessively anxious to have his seat near the head even of a public table, as in England the rank of the guests is determined by the arrangement of their seats. But it seems to me that true nobility would confer honor on the place—not borrow honor from it. Whatever its position at table might be, there, it appears to me, would the seat of distinction always be. And when a vulgarian does succeed in rudely elbowing his way to the head of the table, the mere fact of his being there could scarcely impose him even on Englishmen as a gentleman.

In ordering his wine, he always pronounces the name of the brand in an unnecessarily loud voice, that the whole table may be made aware of "what an extravagant dog it is;" but he at the same time takes good care to add in an undertone to the waiter, "*a half-bottle*, mind ye." He is peculiarly knowing in all the varieties of wines, especially after having examined the brand on the cork. He first sternly regards the waiter who has just filled his order, and then proceeds minutely to inspect the bottle, with a sapient wag of the head, which plainly indicates that he suspects some trickery, though it is altogether useless to "try it on so old a stager" as himself. He never appears to think of *tasting* the wine to ascertain its quality, and seems altogether oblivious that new wine is sometimes put into old bottles. When satisfied as to the identity of the brand and bottle, he smacks his lips with affected gusto, and never fails to remark for the edification of the company generally, that he is just then engaged in drinking the very best wine ever exported. What a lucky chap it is, not only to know, but to be able to order the very best wine that is exported. He is never so happy as when descanting upon the rival merits of high-priced wines. He professes to be intensely interested in the dates of the different vintages, and uncommonly well posted up on the yield of the various *chateaux*. He will order some French dish among the *entrées*, and pronounce it in such a manner that nobody can understand him. He will have all the servants on board, and both stewards, in confusion, running to him with the different side dishes, till he has succeeded in collecting them all in stately array before him, when he finds himself in the mortifying predicament of not knowing what he wants himself. He, however, flies into a passion, abuses the servants, "talks sharp" to the steward, and seems proud of the staring attention he attracts. He is marvellously discriminating in cheeses, and particularly nice about tea. It is his ordinary custom to kick up a daily rumpus at the table because the waiters will persist in confounding Wiltshire with Stilton, the latter of which he always prefers, and usually ends the uproar by having all the cheeses on board, English, Dutch and American, passed in grand review before him. He travels with his own private tea-caddy of Russian tea, which he orders forth every morning at breakfast with an imposing loftiness of manner one might ascribe to his tea-drinking Highness, the Emperor of China. Whilst pouring on the hot water, which he always does himself, to avoid the possibility of tricks with his precious Russia, he sympathizingly wonders how human beings can endure the dishwater stuff with which they drench the rest of the passengers. As an act of Oriental condescension, he will occasionally invite some peculiarly favored individual to come sit beside him, and imbibe honor and inspiration from his squat black teapot. He will inquire *en passant*, if it is a regulation of this particular ship *never* to change the napkins on the dinner-table. He is eternally fussing about the number of towels furnished in his room, and invariably appropriates, in addition to his own, those intended for his room-mate. He appears impressed with the notion that it is his bounden duty to busy himself about the general management of the vessel. He is constantly reporting delinquent servants to the head steward, and is apparently the only person among a hundred and fifty passengers who never can have any thing done for him. Of course, a gentleman who requires so much waiting on, and makes such a noise, must necessarily be an individual of distinction and importance, and he impresses the English flunkies and the English waiters accordingly,—though the disgust he inspires is almost universal among the American passengers. He will volunteer a stupid song, and sing it badly, and tells long stories, at which nobody laughs but himself. After dinner, he cracks nuts and disgusting jokes, for the amusement of those who have been sea-sick and still feel a "leetle uncomfortable," and regards it as quite a triumph to drive some unfortunate from the table. Notwithstanding his disgust for every thing put on the table, he never omits a meal, but breakfasts, lunches, dines, takes tea and sups, with a regularity, and to an extent, truly surprising. Actuated by the generous impulses of a public-spirited individual, he seems resolved that the captain shall have no delicacy on his table which he himself cannot share. He will order some rare dish, and, when told that it is not on the bill of fare, he will declare his conviction that he saw it on the captain's table at lunch, and rudely express a determination to have it if it be on board. He manifests his admirable sense of decency and neatness by eyeing with frowning distrust his plate, which he proceeds furiously to rub, and then diligently scours his knife and fork, in nervous apprehension of lurking dirt. He throws his head back with a knowing jerk in the accomplishment of this interesting proceeding, and looks around for applause among the passengers, as much as to say, "follow my example, gentlemen; I am an old traveller, and am resolved not to be unnecessarily hastened in taking 'my peck of dirt' by being confined to these filthy steamers." He will permit no waiter to help a passenger from a favorite dish which happens to be near him, but he helps plates himself, and the unconquerable greediness of the man protrudes itself in the very ample manner in which he piles up his own plate, and the rather dainty provision he makes for other people. I cannot resist the temptation to allude to the somewhat extraordinary conduct of an *official* personage from England, whom we happened to have on board the Baltic, in crossing the Atlantic last spring. He never omitted at a single dinner during the entire voyage to display his extravagant profusion, by ordering the most expensive description of champagne, but, with the usual prudence of an Englishman, he was always particular in taking it in a *half-bottle*, which he swallowed in solitary grandeur. He had several friends, but no one of them was ever invited to take wine with him. Indeed, having early discovered that the allowance of wine which his parsimony permitted him to enjoy was insufficient to be shared even with his wife, he earnestly insisted that this meek-minded person should drink *porter*, as it was so much more "wholesome" than champagne. The poor little woman was an American, whom he had just married, and evidently did not like porter; but she submitted without a murmur, though she could not resist making a wry face at the *cheap* beverage her husband had so considerately prescribed for her *health*. This continued till the last day of the voyage, when wine is furnished by the captain gratuitously to the passengers. Immediately after taking his seat on that occasion, our official gentleman drew one of the bottles to his side, from which he refused to permit the waiters to help other persons. He found no difficulty in disposing of the wine which he had so unceremoniously appropriated, and soon ordered another bottle to be brought. The peculiar wholesomeness of porter was forgotten, and his submissive little wife was allowed to take as much champagne as she pleased. He suddenly remembered that he had friends on board, with all of whom he successively took wine, in the generous exhilaration of his feelings. And, finally, reaching over for the *third* bottle, he ordered the waiter to carry it with his compliments to the surgeon of the ship, as he desired to take wine with him. I wonder if he remembered, whilst he was nodding with condescending familiarity, that it was the *captain's* wine he was being so liberal with. But the doubt implies a suspicion of his prudence, which I acknowledge to be unjust. Of course, he recollected the fact, for he would never have been guilty of the folly of sharing with others what was his own. I was delighted with the whole proceeding. I felt happy to make the discovery that even an Englishman was profuse in his generosity when he could be so at the expense of other people.

When on deck it is the unceasing struggle of the genuine English tourist to ape the ways of an "old salt," and he seems to think that having a stomach like a cassowary that nothing can turn is something to boast of. He is always by very far the busiest man on board. He interrupts the officers in discharge of their duties by his impertinent suggestions; he goes "*aft*" to inspect the compass, "*forerd*" to superintend the steerage passengers, and *below* to torment the engineer. In rough weather he always wears a "sou'-wester" and an oil-cloth coat. He eyes the sails askance, sagely discourses of "royals" "top-gallant" and "*main sels*," and speculates profoundly upon a probable change of wind. He is intensely ambitious of appearing learned about trifles. He can always tell you the tonnage of the ship, her length, her cost, and quickest voyage. He keeps himself posted up as to the *log*, invariably knows the number of revolutions the wheels are making to the minute, and is certain to be earliest informed of "the last twenty-four hours' run." He is foremost in all marine auctions and lotteries, and intensely delights in instructing new-beginners in the occult science of "shuffleboard." He is charmed to play the oracle; and talks most glibly for the edification of a crowd. He is never so contented as when recounting to a squad of greenhorns the adventures of former voyages, the whales he has seen, and the icebergs he has encountered. If any thing a little out of the ordinary routine of the ship happens to occur, he immediately pronounces it nothing to what happened to him, during a certain voyage, on a certain ship, with a certain captain, and forthwith proceeds to spin interminable yarns without point, of his past personal experience. If not otherwise employed he will hang about the quarter-deck, in order to enjoy the satisfaction of impudently replying to questions asked by passengers of the captain with regard to his ship, and her management. He seems as destitute of delicacy as of modesty, and does not hesitate to answer for anybody, though the gentleman addressed was present, and might very naturally be supposed to prefer talking for himself. He will intrude himself into any conversation where an opportunity occurs of showing what he thinks he knows, and seems altogether to forget that he may occasionally display his ignorance, as well as his rudeness, by such gratuitous favors. If remonstrated with upon such conduct, he will reply, " Oh, *everybody* knows me; why, my dear friend, this is my twentieth voyage!" Being an Englishman, and *such* a traveller, gives him of course the privilege in his own opinion of sticking his nose into every company without incurring the danger of having it pulled, as it often deserves to be. He indulges himself in the liberty of treating everybody as an acquaintance, since he considers himself not at all bound to acknowledge on shore the acquaintances made on board of the ship. In throwing aside his checked travelling coat and cap, he conveniently disremembers all the passengers, whom he has treated with such patronizing familiarity, unless there happens to be among them somebody of distinction whose casual acquaintance he is certain afterwards to take advantage of if he can. It is amusing during the first few days after leaving port, before he has succeeded in discovering the residence and occupation of every one on board, to watch the effect produced on him when the captain happens to take wine with a passenger. He immediately puts down the fortunate individual as worthy of being inquired after, and should he prove to be of the preconceived degree of importance, the Englishman unhesitatingly commences a system of toadyism despicable to behold. But insolence and servility are usually united. One is rarely discovered in a superlative state of perfection without the other. He is never slow in arriving at his conclusions, for, notwithstanding his violent condemnation of "Yankee curiosity," he possesses a peculiar facility for picking up personal details, altogether surpassing any thing presented among other nations. He contrives in this style of his own invention to be correctly informed as to name, birth-place and occupation of every man, woman and child on the steamer, without once resorting to the exploded fashion of direct interrogation. He delights in being appealed to for the decision of bets and disputes; and generously gives the advantage of his opinion to any one who is willing to receive it. He seems to consider nothing troublesome that affords him an apology for hearing himself talk. Indeed an Englishman appears to have two characters when on ship-board and on shore. Silent as he always is in the latter situation, in the former he is decidedly garrulous, though not the less stupid. When he can find nothing else to meddle in, he interferes with the prescriptions of the ship's surgeon, by recommending some infallible nostrum of his own which he has known in over a hundred cases to relieve sea-sickness; and insists on cramming the stomachs of nauseated passengers as full of his quack doses as his own pockets. He never misses a chance of throwing all the passengers into an unnecessary commotion by intently gazing for half an hour through the spy-glass on vacancy. Of course such a proceeding on the part of an old salt, is sufficient to make every man advance in turn seriously to ogle the clouds through the glass; for, though the "old salt" assures each one with chuckling satisfaction, that he has seen nothing, absolutely nothing, yet every one remains firmly convinced that there *must* be "something ahead." He finds too an inexhaustible fund of amusement in pointing his prophetic finger to imaginary "sails," which passengers cannot see because they have neither acquired their "ocean eyes," nor their "sea legs."

CHAPTER VII.

ENGLISH DEVOTION TO DINNER.

CEREMONY and dining constitute the melancholy recreations of an Englishman's life. Eating is the only thing which he is permitted to do heartily, and as if he enjoyed it. He cannot talk, he cannot think, he cannot dress as he pleases, there is an inviolable rule for them all. He is never free till armed with a knife and fork, indeed he is never completely himself without them. Even the order in which he must place himself at the table, and the manner of occupying his seat, are both prescribed by law. He only escapes restraint when he feels the familiar touch of those domestic weapons of offence, which may be as properly considered integral portions of an Englishman as claws are of a cat.

I once said that an Englishman's dinner "was not only the event of the day, but the primary object of his life." With the English eating is not simply the highest enjoyment of their existence, but it has become the great national mode of commemorating social incidents and public events. From birth to death a prolonged set-to at the table marks the principal occurrences of an Englishman's life. He is joyously ushered into the world, and solemnly escorted out of it, by a feast. A child is born, a christening follows, and a huge lunch Frenchified into "*déjeuner*" is the consequence. A man gets married, and his father-in-law feels a hungry sort of necessity to feed all the friends of the family on the day of the wedding. A man dies, and his relations and friends assemble to read his will, and devour a solemn dinner at his expense. They write cards of condolence to his family and send their empty carriages to attend his funeral, but take good care to be at his "wake" in person. Englishmen do almost every thing by proxy but eat—that is a duty which they religiously perform themselves. The professions of distress they deem it proper to make upon these funeral occasions, are as heartless as the notes of consolation they write to the family. The outward forms of sorrow they consider it decent to observe, are as empty as the mourning coaches.

If a great Lord makes a great speech, all the corporations immediately honor him with a great dinner. If a distinguished diplomatist negotiates an important treaty, they *fête* him by feeding him. If a mighty General gains a mighty victory, he must at once pass through the ordeal of a mighty repast, where more fatigue must be endured than in his whole campaign, and more wine must be drunk, and indigestible turtle swallowed, than the blood he has shed and the lead he has wasted in the battle. If an Englishman wishes to be respectful, he gives a dinner; if he desires to be polite, he invites you to dine; and should he wish to be sociable, he insists upon your joining the family circle at the important meal of the day. If a stranger brings a letter of introduction, a dinner is the result, unless the man who gave the letter has the meanness to write privately to your host that you are unworthy of such an honor. From such premises we can readily determine the value at which the friendship and attentions of these people are to be estimated, when it is a precept especially enjoined upon them, that, if they give a letter of introduction to an improper person, 'tis their duty to write at once by mail, warning the person to whom it is directed of the fact. We know not whether to feel the greatest contempt for the man's conduct when he shows himself so destitute of all manliness of character as to be unable to refuse an introductory letter, to an improper person, or when he descends to this clandestine mode of confessing his own meanness.

Englishmen not only regard eating as the most inestimable blessing in life, when they enjoy it themselves, but they are always intensely delighted to see it going on. The government charge an extra shilling at the Zoological Gardens on the days that the animals are fed in public, but, as much as an Englishman dislikes spending money, the extraordinary attraction never fails to draw an immensely increased crowd, even with the advanced prices. I mean not to intimate that there is any thing objectionable about social conviviality. There is something comfortable and agreeable in the simple act of taking a glass of wine, which, like the coffee-drinking and pipe-smoking among the Turks, produces at once a genial feeling of good fellowship; and I know that if two boon-companions get drunk together, they are sworn friends for life. It is not my desire to interrupt that "feast of reason and flow of soul," which these enthusiastic lovers of "belly-cheer" will not agree can occur elsewhere than at the dinner-table. I can myself conceive of few things more charming than a small, well-assorted party, gathered sociably about a round table. But I am opposed to the idolatrous tenets of those who can worship at no shrine save that of the hungry spirits of their vasty stomachs. The man whose soul is confined to the limits of a paunch, however capacious, could find little use for a heart, when a gizzard would answer all his purposes so much more admirably.

The frigid ceremony, the weighty forms and solemn deportment at an English dinner-table, must exclude every thing like mirth or social chit-chat. They assemble to eat, and all conversation of a light or amusing character is regarded as an unpardonable interruption to the business of the meeting. As I said before, an Englishman is never wholly himself until armed with the carving-knife. He takes to the weapon as naturally as Indians to bows or Spaniards to stilettoes. The formal rules of English society do not pretend to extend to the dinner-table. There even Englishmen are free. Each bold Briton can gorge himself to his own private satisfaction, provided he does not interrupt his neighbors by irrelevant remarks, but leaves them to the enjoyment of the same much esteemed privilege. Silence and stuffing are the distinguishing characteristics of a grand dinner party. And so apprehensive are they that the very few civilities which Englishmen feel it incumbent on them to offer to ladies, might too seriously interfere with the swilling and cramming proceedings of the day, that the ladies all retire at a given signal, leaving the men to force nuts and guzzle wine till their stomachs or their legs rebel against the unnatural imposition, when they once more repair to the parlor to pick their teeth, and stare in maudlin silence at "the women."

It is fashionable to extol the English as the countrymen of Shakspeare and Milton, as if, with their language, they must necessarily have inherited the elevation of mind which distinguished those worthies. But each sleek modern head will be found to be much fuller of pudding than poetry. Upon examination, all must confess that the English public are decidedly more familiar with the living on the rival lines of steamers than the beauties of the old English poets. And the comparative excellence of Parisian restaurants and London chop-houses, constitutes a study much more congenial to their taste, than musty incidents in the lives of dead celebrities. What do the English nation possess in common with Shakspeare and Milton but their birthplace and their language? The first was the heritage of chance, the last they have debased by confining it to the mean uses of gormandizing triflers and chaffering hucksterers. The Mahometans for many centuries were in posssesion of the holiest places of the East, and as an evidence of how worthy they were of the succession, they changed churches into stables, and shrines into pedlers' stalls. The fact of the English nation's speaking the same language as Shakspeare and Milton, only makes the absence of every other noble quality the more startling.

If the greatness of men be estimated by their circumference, and their reputations rated according to their appetites, then England has a just right to be proud of her progress. The wan figures of Shakspeare and Milton might well hide themselves deeper in their shrouds, appalled by the prodigious masticatory performances of the modern race of Britons. For their exploits as trenchermen would astound their Saxon ancestors themselves, whose tables habitually groaned under the weight of whole roast porkers and integral sheep. But he who assigns a higher destiny to man than, after huge dinners, to crack nuts and swill wine, must acknowledge that the nation have tumbled from the summit to the foot of Parnassus. He must confess that they are not only destitute of the genius to produce, but the taste to appreciate, such works as have rendered the Bard of Avon and his blind successor immortal. Nonsensical shows in crystal palaces, and the silly plots of Italian operas, have usurped the places, in the taste of the people, of the historical plays and divine poetry of the great masters of English verse.

When it is remembered that the richer portions of the English people consider themselves happy in proportion to the dainty gratification of their appetites, it seems strange indeed that in the gastronomic science, at least, the nation have not excelled. They are not original even in their gluttony.

Possessing the utmost capabilities to devour, they are destitute of the ingenuity to invent the gross dishes with which they cram themselves. They owe to a foreign nation the mean privilege of bestial indulgence. No one can doubt the eminent qualifications of Englishmen to show the rest of the world how to *eat;* but France has taught them how to cook. But still, if digestion and not genius be the chiefest blessing to intellectual man, as the universal practice among Englishmen would seem to indicate, then the modern triumphs of mind have not been inferior to those of steam, in Great Britain.

Frenchmen live to dance; Englishmen to eat. About what is a Briton so anxious as his kitchen? of what is he so proud as his cook? with regard to what is he so solicitous as his dinner? Here all his hopes are concentrated, here 'tis his highest ambition to excel. His cook is the stage-manager, his kitchen the green-room, and dinner-table the stage of the theatre on which the drama of his existence is played. The gorgeous decorations of his theatre, the assembling fashionable audiences, and the successful performance of the stupid pantomimes usually porduced there, constitute the exciting employment of a lifetime. Lively comedies are banished, as unbecoming the awful dignity of the place, and even the stately periods of the heaviest tragedies are eschewed, as interruptions to "the stage business," which is cheifly conducted by means of knives and forks. The proprietor of the establishment displays an enthusiasm altogether unknown among the most enthusiastic of his brethren, the professional players. If he toils to be rich, it is to acquire means of purchasing plate, liveries, wines and delicacies for his play-house. If he cringes, begs and bribes, in his efforts for a title, it is all done to secure noble personages to grace his front boxes.

Almost every man, of every nation, cherishes in his

dreaming moments of reverie some pet scheme of ambition or enjoyment, and no exertion seems too great, no privation too terrible for its realization. Mahomet, to coax into paths of virtue his vicious followers, presented to their warm imaginations the black-eyed houris, the brimming wine-cups and shady fountains of paradise. But an Englishman needs no keener incentive to exertion than a glimmering glance of the happy period when he will be rich enough to do nothing but eat. Ambition, pleasure and excitement are all stowed away, like apples in a dumpling, in this superlative gratification. The voluptuous paradise of Mahomet appears incomplete to English eyes; there is no dinner-table and no provision made for regular meals. Without dinner heaven itself seems scarcely worth possessing. An Englishman's imagination can revel in no sweeter Elysium than having plenty to eat and an appetite to enjoy it. His antipathy to chameleons may be attributed to the fact of their living on air. His neglect of Shakspeare may be accounted for by his never having dedicated an ode to the charms of roast beef.

Englishmen may well feel proud, with the rest of the world, that human nature has produced such specimens of her handicraft as Shakspeare and Milton. But each bold Briton should blush to claim them as countrymen. He should shrink from the mortifying example, that he himself presents, of the degeneracy of the nation since the days when Shakspeare wrote, and Milton sung. *Their* genius was only bounded by the limits of creation; *his* mind revolves in the orbit of his plate; his fancy never soars, but on the fumes of some favorite dish. He knows no intenser joy than a plum-pudding, and rarely suffers a keener infliction than an overdone beef-steak. He is erudite in sauces, and deeply versed in pies. His vast amount of kitchen statistics is really imposing. Though he is hopelessly ignorant of the general lierature of France, his noddle is tightly packed with French cookery receipts. His thoughts are much more absorbed in the mysteries of roast beef and boiled mutton than the beauties of the rival measures of verse. His ingenuity is much more deeply immersed in the composition of a new gravy than the comparative charms of Hexameters and Alexandrines. In short, he is just the sort of fellow, who, in reading Paradise Lost, would be intensely curious to know whether Lucifer was addicted to night suppers, who would give the first joint of his little finger to find out what Adam and Eve had for lunch; a man to wonder that Macbeth should have supped on "horrors," when his royal exchequer might have afforded him the means of procuring so much more digestible stuff. "The Housekeeper's own Cook," is his text-book, whilst poor Shakspeare remains the gilded ornament of neglected shelves.

Nature only seems beautiful to an Englishman when she ministers to the cravings of his belly; he never courts her society but to alleviate the pains of table indulgences. Waving woods and lowing herds are only suggestive to his mind of blazing fires and roast beef. Babbling brooks and placid lakes do but remind him of the inestimable blessing derived from the application of steam to the culinary art. Great ocean himself has no grandeur in his eyes, except as the boundless means of importation of foreign edibles. He climbs towering cliffs and wanders beside sparkling waterfalls in search of an appetite. He makes romantic tours to escape from the gout, and frequents picturesque and inaccessible places as the best cure for the dyspepsy. He makes runs into Scotland for the sake of oat-meal cakes, and sojourns amidst the wild beauties of Switzerland, in order to be convenient to goat's milk. He goes to France to replenish an exhausted purse, and to Italy to repair a broken constitution.

If guts could perform the functions of brains, Greece's seven wise men would cease to be proverbial, for England would present to the world twenty-seven millions of sages. If the English people did every thing as they eat, we should no longer have to turn to Rome for examples of eloquence and heroism. 'Tis true they have produced no eminent feeders whose gluttony has become a proverb; they can boast no Vitellius and Heliogabalus; but it would be difficult indeed for a single individual to eat himself into celebrity in a country where every ordinary citizen surpasses, without effort, the immortal table exploits of the imperial voluptuaries. The English nation seem much more deeply impressed, than were the Romans themselves, by the force and eloquence of Menenius Agrippa's fable of the belly and the members, by which he succeeded in coaxing the rebellious plebeians from the Mons Sacer back to deserted Rome. In their admiration of the truth and beauty of this famous fable they appear to have forgotten the figurative meaning intended to be conveyed, and to have taken it in its literal sense as their motto, sacrificing the members and every thing else to the all-devouring belly. Intellect, honor, ambition, pleasure, are all swallowed up in this vast receptacle of plum-pudding and roast beef. In their enthusiastic devotion to their voracious idol, they appear to have grown unmindful that there are higher duties for man to perform than to eat, that there are nobler aims for him to live for than the gratification of his appetite. To eat, to drink, to look greasy, and to grow fat, appears to constitute, in their opinions, the career of a worthy British subject. I mean not to insinuate that "to be fat" is "to be hated." There is something comfortable about a portly corporation, and genuine mirth it seems to me delights to lurk in the folds of a double chin. Flesh acquired in the merry circle of friends, the joyous result of laughter and good cheer, is always the best evidence of a kind heart and liberal disposition. But corpulence without jollity whispers of *self*, it is eloquent of the meanness of secret stuffings and solitary potations. To be gross without being good-humored is to be swinish, and consequently to be shunned. But an Englishman is never so silent as when eating. Like other carnivorous animals he is always surly over his meals. Morose at all times, he becomes unbearably so at that interesting period of the day, when his soul appears to cower among plates and dishes, as if with the suspicious dread of being called upon to divide that which it clings to, even more fondly than to money, his dinner.

An Englishman is like all well constructed guns, he never goes off into any displays of animation until completely loaded with the good things of the table and primed with good wine. And when upon such auspicious occasions he does go off into something like gayety, there is such fearful quivering of vast jelly-moulds of flesh, something so supernaturally tremendous in his efforts, that like the recoil of an overloaded musket he never fails to astound those who happen to be near him. Eminently sensual, he is not even enthusiastic in his sensualities. He gloats rather than exults over those exquisite delights of the table, which, in his opinion, are so soul-stiring. Though he gorges his food with the silent deliberation of the Anaconda, yet in descanting upon the delicacies of the last "capital dinner" at which he was present, he makes an approach to animation altogether unusual with him on other occasions. He loves to dwell with lingering affection upon the roast beef and plum-pudding he ate and the porter he swallowed. And in discoursing with tender minuteness upon the charms of these delicious viands, he displays a touching earnestness which might almost be considered eloquence.

He deems no friend worth having who does not give fine

dinners; and no individual unworthy of being cultivated who is known to have a good cook. Every Englishman is a systematic "diner-out;" and as assiduously intrigues for invitations to dinner, as ambitious politicians for sinecure preferments of state. He delights in entertainments prodigiously expensive, but, like Vitellius, he makes it a rule to enjoy them at his own expense as little as possible. Thus every private citizen in Great Britain enjoys the honor of uniting in his own person the two qualities which have rendered this Roman Emperor immortal: parsimonious as Vitellius, he is much more of a glutton. With two such genial traits as a basis, 'tis not strange that such a pyramid of social peculiarities has been reared as to crush all kindly feelings towards the English in every foreign country. When it is remembered that of all the vices, avarice is most apt to corrupt the heart, and gluttony has the greatest tendency to brutalize the mind, it no longer continues surprising that an Englishman has become a proverb of meanness from Paris to Jerusalem. The hatred and contempt of all classes of society as necessarily attend him, in his wanderings, as his own shadow. All those whose positions make them subservient to his ill-humor as cordially hate, as other citizens and travellers despise him. His passions for gold and eating have so entirely swallowed up every other feeling, that he appears really ignorant of the existence of many of those pleasing little refinements which even savages instinctively practise. His unnecessary harshness to inferiors, and his arrogant assumption among his equals have cut him off from all sympathy with his kind. Equally repulsive to every grade, he stands isolated and alone, a solitary monument of the degradation of which human nature is capable. Destitute of all consideration for those beneath him, he appears to believe that they were created, like other domestic animals, for his pleasure and convenience. But in his treatment of them his cruel nature is restrained by no salutary apprehensions of punishment by those numerous humane societies which are established in England to prevent cruelty to animals. The charities of the nation expend themselves in tender solicitude for horses and asses, without experiencing one sympathizing throb of kindness for those of their fellow-creatures who have had the misfortune to be born poor. But as I have before remarked, poverty is the only crime in England which admits of no palliation. The delicate nerves and nice sensibilities of English charity, would be shocked to penetrate into those sinks of hungry wretchedness, where starving thousands are driven by necessity, rather than destitution of moral principles, into open warfare with that society, from whose selfish system of regulation they have suffered so much, and from whose sympathy they can hope so little. The extremely proper regard for cleanliness and acute sense of smell in Englishmen would entirely prevent their descending into those loathsome dens, in which despairing misery is wont to hide itself. Contact with rags and filth is vulgar. They reserve their kindly offices for the well-washed and newly-combed inmates of model prisons, and new-fangled houses of correction. These dapper philanthropists shrink with loathing from misfortune, when arrayed in the frightful paraphernalia of woe. But let a man pick a pocket, or rob an orphan box; let him by the frequent repetition of crime prove himself utterly destitute of every moral principle, and he immediately becomes an object of especial interest to the benevolent of both sexes in England. Men of genius are employed to construct commodious and healthy places of confinement for these hardened rascals. Rival philanthropists vie with each other in suggesting plans of prison discipline which shall most conduce to their social improvement. The scoundrel-sympathy which distinguishes the ostentatious charity of Englishmen, provides humane keepers to minister to their personal comforts, skilful physicians to watcn over their health, and pious chaplains to superintend their religious culture; every attention is paid to the cleanliness and airy situation of their rooms; every precaution is taken to secure for them a healthy diet; good Samaritans of the gentler sex are constantly visiting the prison wards to distribute tracts and consolation to these irreclaimable villains. All this is done for these corrupt scoundrels, whilst gaunt starvation is permitted to stalk unheeded among those of the wretched, who have as yet secured no claim upon the charity of these benevolent benefactors of thieves, by the commission of crime. Does it not seem strange, that some gold and so much solicitude should be employed for the benefit of these daring renegades from law and religion, whilst the really deserving objects of charity are left to die uncared for and alone? Does it not appear remarkable that all the benevolent impulses of the British nation should exhaust themselves in exertions for these hopelessly vicious outcasts of society, who have so unmistakably shown themselves "the stony ground" in which the seeds of righteousness could never take root? But they shrink in disgust from really suffering innocence, which, if properly cared for, would be found to be "the good ground that did yield fruit that sprang up, and increased, and brought forth some thirty, and some sixty, and some an hundred." The ambitious Pharisees of England have not even the mean apology for their conduct, of a fellow-feeling for these malefactors. They do their alms before men in order "to be seen of them." The benefactors of public criminals get their names into the papers; their bounty is eulogized by "the *Times*." The liberal founders of model prisons, and the charitable advocates of reformed houses of correction, "have glory of men," whilst the modest doer of good relieving in secret the wants of the obscure pauper must await his recompense in Heaven, where "thy

Father that seeth in secret himself shall reward thee openly."

An Englishman entertains a high scorn for every man who does not eat hugely, and drink well. He respects individuals according to their abdominal, rather than their mental, capacities. He observes with admiration their corporeal, not their phrenological, developments. People who have weak digestive organs he regards with that pitying sort of contempt with which a youthful literary pretender might be supposed to look down upon some half-witted unfortunate. And those who are unable to gobble food to the same extent as an ostrich, he feels sorry for, as being deprived of man's divinest faculty. An enormous stomach, and a plentiful supply of gastric juice, he regards as just subjects for congratulation. Being convinced that to eat is man's highest destiny on earth, he assiduously cultivates the powers which most conduce to its ample accomplishment. The dilating power of the anaconda, and the gizzard of a cassowary, are the pet objects of his ambition. He leaves inexperienced sages to preach the importance of a mind well stored with useful information, and a powerful mind to digest and apply it, whilst his only care is a stomach well-stuffed with dainties; his only anxiety a generous flow of the digestive fluid. True wisdom, in his opinion, indulges in mastication, rather than meditation. In his judgment, the seat of all heavenly joys is the belly, not the mind. He wonders how men can ever be unhappy whilst they can eat and drink. There is no disappointment so bitter, no calamity so great, that it cannot be comfortably smothered with roast beef and porter. He knows no excitement so intense, or joy so thrilling, as a smoking plate of ox-tail soup, backed by the usual beef and potato accompaniments of an English dinner. And when his eyes close, and his skin becomes distended, under the sweetly soothing influence of these savory viands, his soul is filled with a "content so absolute" that he has nothing more to live for till dinner-time next day. 'Tis true that he breakfasts, that he lunches, takes tea, and sups, for there is music to him in the clatter of knives and forks that cannot be heard too often to be amusing; but the "tocsin of his soul is the dinner-bell;" it is his national anthem which arouses within him all the ferocious heroism of his nature; its stirring notes make him eager for the assault. Its inspiring harmony awakes him from the lethargy, and, armed with a knife and fork, "Richard is himself again." The daggers of the patriot conspirators were not more fiercely wielded against Julius Cæsar, than are these natural weapons of an Englishman, in his eagerness to get the "first cut" from "the hot joint." The position as well as the appetite of people is reckoned according to the order of "cuts" in which they come, and he who obtains the "first" enjoys the honor that Englishmen most dearly prize. The secondary meals an Englishman takes to while away the dozing hours that must elapse before the period of the great event of the day arrives; and, besides, a certain degree of repletion is absolutely essential to his comfort. But dinner is his grand climacteric; for dinner he reserves himself, at dinner he makes his great display; to him dinner is the concentration of life's rarest joys; for dinner he elaborately prepares himself; for dinner he purges, bathes, rubs, and dresses; to dinner he looks forward with the intense longing of the weary sentinel awaiting the corporal's guard that is to relieve him; of dinner he makes his existence a dream; he talks, he cares about nothing but his dinner; his only regret seems to be that he is so constituted that he cannot pass his life at the dinner-table. The only annoyance which ever seriously disturbs his digestion is, that the process of stuffing is not as harmless to him as to a Bologna sausage. But alas for the happiness of British nature! not even the innocent amusement of eating is to be indulged to excess without retributive pains. Misery and mineral water are as certainly the results of gluttony, as of the more active vices. The devotion of the English to eating is an excrescence upon their national character, which, like the carbuncles on Bardolph's nose, makes it hideous and glaring. Its presence disfigures their more serious literature, and it unpleasantly protrudes itself from their romance. Their modern poets condescend to describe sumptuous repasts with the technical minuteness of a pastry-cook; and their best novelists are vain of their knowledge in the culinary art. Their fairy tales are always crowded with ogres, who eat hugely and drink well. And the romance of chivalry is outraged by having greasy thoughts of dinner lugged in on King Arthur's round table.

Nothing is too heroic or too refined to be associated in their minds with eating. An English lover is never so sentimental as when discussing in solitude the "first cut" of a "hot joint." He plies his lady-love with doughnuts instead of flowers, and believes there is no bridal present like something good to eat; he brings her a cornucopia of chocolate drops as much more provocative of sentiment than a copy of Lalla Rookh; he has no anxiety to discover her taste in poetry, but is intensely curious as to what she prefers to eat; congeniality of soul is never sought for in their fondness for the same music, but is developed by their devotion to the same dish. He never asks if she admires Donizetti's compositions, but tenderly inquires if she loves beef-steak pies.

This sordid vice of greediness is rapidly brutalizing natures not originally spiritual. Every other passion is sinking, oppressed by flabby folds of fat, into helplessness. All the mental energies are crushed beneath the oily mass. Sensibility is smothered in the feculent steams of roast beef, and delicacy stained by the waste drippings of porter. The brain is slowly softening into blubber, and the liver is gradually encroaching upon the heart. All the nobler impulses of man are yielding to those animal propensities, which must soon render Englishmen beasts in all save form alone.

CHAPTER VIII.

ENGLISH GENTILITY.

IT has been declared in England, that as a nation, our manners are unformed: indeed that we have none. I certainly consider it much more desirable to be without any, than to have such as every man who pretends to be a gentleman should hasten to get rid of.

Both civilized and barbarous nations have united in considering certain pleasing little forms essentially necessary to the preservation of society. We have all felt, and are familiar with the charm of politeness, and yet few of us could describe in what it really consists. I have yielded to the influence of this nameless fascination in my intercourse with French, Germans, and Italians; I have observed its action among Greeks, Turks, and the wild Bedouins of the desert, but I have sought in vain to discover its existence among the English. They seem to glory in disregarding the rules which the politer portions of the world have agreed upon adopting. But not satisfied with banishing all graces of manner, they unceasingly labor to suppress those natural instincts which teach the swarthy sons of the desert to be courteous, and the North American Indians to be polite. They are terrified by the flunky apprehension, that being polite might render them liable to the suspicion of imitating the French, whereas they are eager to appear peculiarly *English*. In their ignoble ambition to stand alone, they have succeeded in making the name of Englishman synonymous with almost every term of reproach in the language, among the mildest of which may be numbered those of glutton and blackguard. They have become odious in their anxiety to be unique; and I doubt whether a single individual could be found, from Paris to Constantinople, who would not indignantly deny the imputation of possessing a single social quality in common with an Englishman. The nation seem deluded into the belief that their violations of decorum are evidences of independence, and really appear to hope that brutality can be mistaken for bravery. They are not ashamed to acknowledge, that money or fear can induce them to do little things, contributing to the enjoyment of others, which, though costing them nothing, they would never dream of performing from a polite desire to oblige. An Englishman can be forced or paid to do any thing; he may be coaxed to do nothing. Rank or money applied to his impenetrable shell of sullen reserve produces the same effect as a coal of fire placed on the back of an obstinate terrapin; the application invariably occasions in both instances a display of awkward animation very unusual in the animals.

It would be difficult in circumnavigating the globe, to discover a nation presenting so much that is peculiar, and so little that is attractive, as the English. *Outré* in dress, repulsive in manners, and selfish in nature, they have withdrawn themselves into an unsympathizing seclusion from the rest of the world. Yet each self-conceited Englishman is proud of his isolation, and exults in his surliness. He has peopled the social solitude which his selfishness has made, with cheering illusions of his own superiority. He knows no ties of sympathy, and has no friends; but each lonely egotist gloats over the belief, that the universe contains no associates worthy of his excellence. He sees that all the world shuns him, and he fondly imagines that he has *cut* the world.

The English people render themselves ridiculous by assuming airs that but ill accord with a stockish nature. In affecting the noble they succeed in being simply arrogant, and are morose when they would be considered exclusive; in attempting to appear complaisant, they are always supercilious, and never fail to be rude when trying to seem free and easy. Yet they imagine the universe to be deeply impressed by the graceful sublimity of their deportment. They affect an eccentricity of costume, as most becoming the solitary elevation of their position. Whether in the unusually scant habiliments in which they array themselves, they are desirous of imitating as nearly as possible, the costumes of their ancestors about the time of Cæsar's invasion, or whether they have simply made the most of their cloth, I know not, but certain it is that their prominent peculiarities of dress and disposition are in admirable accord. Hat and head tendencies may be pronounced decidedly sharp. Collar and general bearing, stiff, awkward, and unbending. Cravat and pretensions, very ample. Vest and regions about the heart, exceedingly contracted. Coat ample, but short; indicative of their lavish expenditure upon their own persons, but the extremely limited distance their liberality ever extends beyond. Pants very full about the seat and waist, to match their great natural advantages for prolonged sittings, and vast accommodations for extra supplies of food; but the pants about the legs very tight, in accordance with the extreme closeness of his disposition, and natural aversion to waste, whether in cloth or shillings. His shoes and movements, to sum the matter up, are always thick, heavy, and clumsy.

An Englishman cannot escape the hallucinations peculiar to folly in seclusion. People shrink from him in disgust, and his vanity ascribes their conduct to a becoming awe for his pre-eminence; he imagines the silence which arises from contempt to be a deferential respect for his opinion; he mistakes sneers for smiles of approval, and believes instinctive repugnance to his person to be a reluctance to intrude upon his reserve. Indeed he entertains too exalted an opinion of himself, to doubt another's appreciation of his surpassing excellence. He can comfortably ascribe any course of conduct to some feeling flattering to himself.

We could forgive the absence of all politeness in an Englishman, if there was one single generous quality to redeem his incivility. We could not anticipate much gentleness from the most affectionate toyings of the hippopotamus, nor could we reasonably expect any great display of elegance in the manners of an Englishman, however affable he might endeavor to make them. We often smilingly submit to the most serious annoyances, when we feel convinced that they proceed from no evil intention on the part of those who inflict them. Roughness of manner no more indicates an unkind disposition, than servility evinces a polished mind. And if an Englishman was the same thing to all people, charity might attribute his brutal effrontery to hardy ignorance; or partiality might ascribe his total disregard of every precept practised by a gentleman, to bluff independence. But he is as sensitive to the influence of a title, as a high-strung instrument to the touch of its performer. A close observer may always determine the position of a man with whom he is conversing, by the tone in which he addresses him. In taking him through the gamut of behavior it will be discovered that he sounds A natural with the same facility as G sharp. Insolent and overbearing to his inferiors, rude and laconic in his intercourse with those he considers equals, but softly cringing to persons above him, tortured catgut itself, scraped by a skilful hand, cannot give utterance to tones more various. The harsh twang of the wired chord, the growling discord of the middle string, and the soft whining of the treble, are all uttered by him as if each one was his own especial note. No man professes to entertain a more punctilious regard for etiquette, in all its minutest ramifications, than an Englishman. His clothes are constructed on angles. His manners are apparently regulated by the square rule. For the most elaborate laws upon the refinements of society, a stranger may safely consult English books; for their grossest violations, he may be referred to the English themselves. They attempt to preserve the letter, whilst they sacrifice the spirit of their written code of gentility. An Englishman's ethics consist in seeming not being. His career in society is a laborious attempt to deceive, a noisy parade of what he does not possess. His feelings are professedly influenced by the dictates of a refinement he cannot appreciate. His manners are formed on principles he does not understand. His existence is made up of ponderous formalities, full of pretension, and signifying nothing.

Among the numerous passengers of the steamer returning home, was an interesting young sprig of nobility—an Honorable Mr. Somebody, the eldest son of Lord Something, as an Englishman patronizingly informed me one day, immediately after he had enjoyed the honor of proffering a light for the honorable young gentleman's cigar. He looked, and was dressed precisely like ninety-nine out of every hundred Englishmen one meets in travelling. He was pursy in person, and very red in the face; he had short bushy whiskers, and parted his hair behind, brushing it forward with the utmost particularity. He wore the universal gray check, and sported a very small cap, and very large shoes. His near approach to a title made it incumbent on him, I presume, to maintain a mysterious reserve to the passengers; but he favored the captain, for hours together, with what seemed most eloquent discourse. That delighted functionary would then devote the balance of the day to retailing to

11*

every one who would listen to him, the various profound observations this remarkable young man had been pleased to make. Although he indulged in the easy dishabille, ordinarily affected by cockney tourists, he never omitted to make a grand toilette for dinner. He lounged about all day in his check suit, but he always appeared just before eight bells, in the afternoon, rigged out in black dress-coat, white cravat, and white kid gloves, as if he had been invited to a dinner-party. He was invariably the earliest at the table, and the latest to leave it. And when he did leave it, it was a remarkable fact that he always demanded of his friend the captain, "if there was not *more sea on:*" the ship appeared to roll so confoundedly, he found it difficult to keep his legs without the support of the captain's arm. A man who ate and drank, as he habitually did, could hardly expect to reserve much room for breath, and he was consequently nervously anxious about the proper ventilation of the ship, as the supply of air he was able to keep on hand was necessarily limited. We were off the Banks of Newfoundland, and it was—as it always is even in summer—bitterly cold, and very uncomfortable. The passengers all looked blue and were shivering at the table in their overcoats; but the Honorable young man looked as red, and perspired as freely, as if he had been roasting eggs in the crater of Vesuvius. He insisted upon having his window opened to its utmost extent, regardless of the chilled condition of his neighbors. Opposite him sat a lady evidently in extremely bad health, who coughed almost incessantly; and so injurious to her was the piercing wind blowing in at the window, that her husband ordered a waiter to close it. The man of the roseate visage instantly opened it again, and looked around with a frowning stare, meant to inquire who had had the audacity to give orders in *his* presence. The husband of the sick lady then sent the waiter to him, with a polite request that he would allow the window to be closed, as he apprehended his wife might suffer seriously from the effects of it. Without ceasing to cram his mouth, he informed the waiter, it would perhaps be advisable for him not to "bother" about that window any more. The gentleman then rose himself, walked across the saloon to the rubicund son of a Lord, and, with the greatest suavity of manner, explained to him the critical situation of his wife, and begged of him, for her sake, to permit the window to be shut. Then the *Honorable* did look up from his plate, but briefly replied, with his mouth full, that he could not consent to be suffocated though his wife was sick. The lady retired—but this worthy representation of English nobility continued to stuff and swill till his shirt collar, which seemed a sort of thermometer of the degree of spirituous heat to which he subjected himself, ominously drooped, warning him of the maudlin state to which strong potations had reduced him. The English people, who have declared the deference shown to females in America to be very vulgar, would probably consider such conduct spirited, and worthy of applause. But I do not doubt that every American will agree with me that it was more than contemptible, and richly deserved a kicking.

His scrupulous regard for his toilette only rendered his rudeness more conspicuous. We were prepared to expect better things from a man who sported such evidences of a cultivated taste. The proof he presented in his dress, of his having at least a vague idea of what is becoming in a gentleman, deprived him of the single apology for his conduct that innocent ignorance might have afforded him. He deemed it due the position of a son of an English nobleman to appear daily at the dinner-table in a dress-coat, white cravat and white kid gloves, but he considered it no stain on the title of his father for him to refuse so simple a request to an invalid lady. His code of manners prescribed, with rigid particularity, the style of dress, but said nothing, apparently, of what is due the other sex. According to its sage refinements, it would be considered an outrage for a man, not in full dress, to appear at dinner-table, but he is permitted to insult with impunity a sick woman—and his conduct is applauded as a proof of manly spirit. A beautiful code! A worthy people! to profess to be the most refined nation of this enlightened half of the nineteenth century. They are a huge sham; an elaborately ruffled "dickey;" a bladder of ostentatious emptiness.

That people, like the English, should regard gloves and a dress-coat essential to gentility, does not appear remarkable, but it does seem very extraordinary that they should believe them its sole elements. They constitute without doubt the garb in which it ordinarily clothes itself—but surely politeness is the spirit which quickens gentility into the charms of life. When the vital spark is wanting, the gay habiliments it wears whilst living, only render the ghastly corpse the more disgusting. It is like arraying a festering inmate of the dead-house for a ball. Fashionable articles of dress prepare us for a courtesy whose absence is more keenly felt; as the sight of an empty fireplace, on a cold day, makes us shiver by reminding us of a fire.

But his indulgent countrymen might offer many very plausible excuses for the ill-mannerly stubbornness of this very *honorable* gentleman. In the first place—among men by whom white kid gloves and a dress-coat are esteemed such irresistible evidences of superior breeding, their fortunate wearer might have been justly indignant that any one should presume to address him without having previously enjoyed the honor of an introduction. It might have been considered proper for the husband of the sick lady to have first gone to the captain, and begged to be presented to the distinguished young man, before he ventured to ask so important a favor as the closing of a window when the thermometer was little above the freezing point.

Besides, immense importance is attached in England to the amplitude and stiffness of a neckcloth—incalculable influence lurks in its tie. And an Honorable might have considered it degrading to the dignity of a white cravat to sacrifice his rights as a passenger to the whims of a sick woman. He had certainly paid his money, and thereby purchased as maintainable a pre-emption on the windows as any single individual on board. Then, too, he was a son of a Lord.

No people have, in the organization of their government and society, submitted to greater impositions than the English. Immeasurable awe of their oppressors makes them silent under public oppressions. But selfishness has made them such inflexible asserters of the most trivial personal privileges, that they are justly regarded as nuisances on every steamboat and railroad on which they happen to be passengers. After the surrender of all the rights that humanity holds dearest—and the loss of every privilege that manhood should defend, they render themselves ridiculous by their watchfulness over those that only old women should deem worthy of preservation. With them, the location of an umbrella, or the arrangement of a hat-box, are matters of tremendous import. These are the proud prerogatives for which they battle—these are the glorious rights they defend. In the protection of these precious advantages, every social compromise and genial feeling are forgotten. The ferocious determination with which they maintain them, puts to flight the spirit of accommodation—and they would not, for all the women in Christendom, abate of them one tittle, unless some more powerful incentive could be offered, than the mere fact of their being of the gentler sex.

Our aristocratic young cockney might have apprehended

like a veritable flunky, soiling his immaculate kids by doing a favor for an unknown individual who did not sport the same indispensable badges of gentility. For there can be no doubt that the true reason of his rudeness was, that he dreaded the possibility of compromising his own position, and that of his noble family at home, by obliging an ordinary sort of person. What means had he of ascertaining her rank in society? 'Tis true, her manners and appearance were those of a lady—but appearances are deceitful—and she might have been some mechanic's wife, which would have caused his friends in England to quiz him a little about having been "sold." Besides, what possible claim could she have on him? He did not know her, and could therefore derive no benefit from inconveniencing himself on her account. Had she been reputed rich, or noble, no one who has ever been in England, could doubt his alacrity to oblige her. The remote prospect of future possible advantage would have justified, in his eyes, any ordinary sacrifice. But could he have claimed the honor of a bow from a lady, who was known to be rich, or noble, he would have smilingly endured prolonged suffocation, rather than have seen her lapdog shiver. Hot, but eager, he would have vowed in an agony of short gasps, what infinite honor he considered it, to be able to manifest his deep respect for her ladyship's slightest wish. And after the infliction had passed, he would have embraced the earliest opportunity afforded by the recovery of his wind, to express to her ladyship the hope, that her ladyship's charming little pet had suffered no inconvenience during the gusty weather of the previous afternoon. To us, among whom a lady always receives the deference due the sex, whether she happens to be a stranger, or an acquaintance—rich or poor—such reflections must seem somewhat extraordinary—but they are, nevertheless, eminently English.

Prudent as he is by nature—economical and penurious

in all his habits, as education has made him, there is no outlay an Englishman makes more reluctantly, than that of politeness. He often invests it, 'tis true, but always cautiously and with hopes of usurious interest. Gratuitous displays, like his other charities, are but rarely indulged in. He may perhaps be somewhat excusable upon the principle that where little has been given, not much ought to be required. He has certainly not been endued with so large a supply of the article as to be at all lavish in its expenditure. Being conscious, I suppose, of his deficiency, he reserves his politeness, as he does his best wines, which are only to be served when he is honored by the presence of his betters. He deems it a reprehensible degree of wastefulness to display either, except on extraordinary occasions. His civility is, consequently, like the Sunday-clothes of a man, who only indulges once a week in the luxury of a clean shirt—and sits ill upon him. His smile of welcome fades into servility, and his attempts at good-humored cordiality dwindle into obsequiousness.

In venturing among the various tribes of semi-barbarians, that they appear to think inhabit the different States of America, Englishmen find it convenient to leave behind them the unwieldy mass of formalities, by which they have been all their lives oppressed—and generally come among us in the undisguised nakedness of their vulgarity. Wholly freed from the restraints imposed upon them at home by the different grades in society, they indolently luxuriate in the inherent brutality of their nature. They constantly violate not only all rules of decorum, but the laws of decency itself, with the apparent belief that we know no better than to submit to it. They abuse our hospitality—insult our peculiar institutions—set at defiance all the refinements of life, and return home lamenting the social anarchy of America, and retailing their own indecent conduct as the ordinary customs of the country. They will invite themselves into private houses—go to an elegant ball in soiled overcoats—take liberties with perfect strangers by a minute catechism, that they would not dare to venture on in England—and then abuse us as aspiring savages, utterly ignorant of the most ordinary usages of society. But the cool assurance with which they attempt to patronize us as inferiors—and the intrepidity with which they do the most outrageous things, ceases to appear so remarkable, when it is remembered how many there are among us who believe, with these upstart cockneys, that a titled Englishman could do nothing, and an ordinary cit very little, that might be justly objected to as low-bred, or indecent. According to such people, if an Englishman is insulting in his familiarity, he only means to show us republicans that he is not proud of his superiority—if he is rude to a lady, he only means to be playful—if he is impertinent to a man, 'tis only a way they have in England. These anglicized Americans will insist that a Briton can do no wrong. He may revile our country, and yet be guilty of nothing more than a little innocent badinage. He may perpetrate the most startling offences against refinement—and yet he does it all in his laudable anxiety to be sufficiently supercilious and condescending to the obliging toadies who surround him. His clumsy attacks upon his entertainers pass for wit—his scurrilous abuse of Americans is declared to be sarcasm—and an insufferable blackguard is ingeniously metamorphosed into an elegant gentleman by these degenerate Americans, who only require the livery to render them such admirable lackeys, that even their English friends might approve their servility. An Englishman, who arrives in America, is generally beset by just such despicable specimens of freemen, who consider *any* Englishman greatly preferable as a companion to the most accomplished American gentlemen. And so long as such unworthy sons of our

Republic are permitted to infest unpunished our larger cities, so long will our whole nation be confounded with these straggling renegades. When these Britons are surrounded by such fellows, eager to submit to every indignity, and receive any insult to enjoy the advantage of their society, they would surprise one if they did not presume upon the supposed obsequiousness of the nation. These American flunkies are thus instrumental in involving their entire country in their own degradation. They ought to be mounted upon the pillar of infamy, like the bankrupt merchants of Venice in old times,

> ——"for the hand of scorn
> To point his slow unmoving finger at."

It should be the duty of every good citizen to revile them. They ought to be denounced in every newspaper, and hooted by every crowd, till they were convinced that the simple dignity of an American citizen was somewhat preferable to playing the snubbed serving-man to any Lord in England.

During my first voyage across the Atlantic we had on board the old Caledonia two rich London merchants and West India sugar-planters, who had been out to the West Indies to endeavor if possible to relieve their estates from the ruinous effects of the general emancipation of slaves. The elder gentleman kept a journal filled with absurd complaints of America, but containing much valuable statistical information respecting omnibus fares up and down Broadway—the comparative expense of boot-blacking in the different cities in the Union; and the price of every ride and every meal the gentlemen had taken during their sojourn in America. After having advanced every possible objection to the country and the people, he went on to state that "Niagara was no great things after all; that he had seen infinitely finer waterfalls in Scotland or Wales—that the Americans made 'a great blow' about Niagara, but that he had discovered more water in a little book that he had paid sixpence for, than he had been able to find at their boasted 'falls.'" We might place a just estimate upon this grumbling tourist's opinions of America and Americans, from this objection of his to the greatest wonder of the Western Hemisphere. Had he found fault with the grandeur of the Falls—the picturesqueness of the scenery; had their height or shape not suited him, there would have been some plausibility in his objection; but to complain of the quantity of water tumbling into the river below, exposed at once the absurdity of the man, coming to our country resolved to disapprove of all he saw. So successful however had this gentleman been in the management of his diary, and so eager was he to read it in detail to every passenger on board, that he was, soon after our sailing from port, dubbed *Mr. Pips.* His friend, who affectionately followed him about, listened to him as an oracle, and kindly offered himself as a butt for his witty sayings, was familiarly known as "My Child." One day, when they were in a greater gale of merriment than ordinary at the dinner-table, "Mr. Pips" challenged "the Child" to mortal combat, in a chicken fight. The challenge was instantly accepted, the fight to come off immediately after dinner. I was exceedingly curious to find out the manner of proceeding in this "chicken fight;" and great was my astonishment when I discovered that each gentleman sat himself down on the deck, and clasped his hands over his knees, that were drawn up as much under his chin as possible. His wrists were in this position securely tied together, and a strong stick run through the elbows, and under the knees, completing a process known among boys at school as "bucking." When this somewhat extraordinary arrangement was completed of each gentleman, he was left entirely without the power of motion except a slight spasmodic movement about the head and toes. The sport was, when the two were placed face to face, for each one to endeavor to insert his toes under the soles of the other, and thereby tumble him over on his back, when he rolled helplessly till his "bottle-holder" had sufficiently recovered from his laughter to pick him up.

The fearful hum of preparation is heard in the distance. Excited men and anxious women crowd the cleared deck. Every thing betokens that some deed of dreadful note is to be done. All eyes are turned towards that end of the ship from which the rival combatants are to issue forth. No word is spoken, and the nervous fidgeting of the passengers alone denotes the intensity of their suspense. At last the little knots of particular friends appeared, and in their midst were the two combatants arrayed for battle. Slowly and majestically the impatient rivals are bumped noiselessly along the deck by their attendant backers. Their eyes gleam dazzlingly upon each other, as they approach. Each one bears his head proudly erect, and his dilated nostrils seem to indicate that the souls of a thousand heroes are being stirred violently within him. When finally prepared for their work, each ambitious aspirant to Olympic honors sat silent, solid and immovable as the grim statue of Memnon. Indeed, however sprightly he might have been in his intentions, a very slight distortion about the head and toes was the utmost extent of locomotion, of which he was capable. They are now face to face. During one awful moment they pause, for a last mighty inhalation of breath and valor, when, with the agility of the lightning's flash, they join hostile toes, as angry bulls lock horns, and at once the promiscuous skrimmage begins. Never was such animation among toes witnessed before; the Highland fling was a minuet compared to it. Such scrambling and scrouging — such squirming and screwing it was really exhilarating to behold.

The unusual exertions of the untrained champions seem strangely overcoming to both, as they swell and grow red like turkey-cocks. Their fight soon demonstrated the fact, that *bottom* does not always indicate *wind;* for however amply endowed each gentleman might be with the former, in the latter he was not long in showing himself lamentably deficient. Brief but violent was the conflict. Each corpulent champion wheezed like an overcharged locomotive. "Science however must prevail." The right foot of "the Child," possessing a cunning that the too confident "Pips" knew not of, by a dexterous flourish suddenly toppled his puffing opponent from his centre of gravity. Exhausted, the ponderous Pips tumbled upon the resounding deck. Overthrown, not vanquished, he wildly glared upon his triumphant foe, who essayed to flap his pinioned arms, as he loudly crowed in exulting mockery. The peculiar manner of doing up was naturally calculated to produce a considerable stretch both of hide and breeches. And when by the casualties of battle a champion was, like a cracked dinner-pot, turned bottom upwards, with both skin and cloth drawn tight as à drum-head, the exposition was immense. No one, but those who witnessed it, can conceive of the very ludicrous appearance of a plump middle-aged gentleman, tightly trussed up as a Christmas goose, and convulsively wallowing on his back. He afforded an "aspect" as unusual and much more startling than that presented by the famous frizzled chicken, of fabled memory.

Rolling in helpless agony—deaf to the jeers of the bystanders at the absurdity of his exposed position—the fallen combatant is only eager for a renewal of the fray. At last his convulsed bottle-holder so far recovered the command of his muscles as to lift him first into a sitting position, and then bump him along as before, till within reach of his rejoicing foe, when they again joined toes, as if life depended on the result. Once more commences the shuffling and scuffling, the rearing and pitching—each gentleman creating as much noise, and kicking up as great a dust, as if he had been miraculously metamorphosed into a centipede, with his hundred feet, instead of a single pair. Fierce continues the doubtful contest. Black and turgid, the big veins start from their glowing fronts. Their knotted muscles writhe and twist in the desperation of the fearful struggle. Their sinews crack, and nerves quiver in that tremendous strain. Renewed wriggling and twisting—sliding and slipping, announce the intensity of their final efforts—when the swollen cheeks and protruding eyes, accompanied by the shortening gasps of *the Child* seemed ominous of his approaching fall. By a sudden sleight, the toes of *Pips* are surreptitiously inserted under the weary soles of *the Child*, whose heels unexpectedly salute the setting sun. Heavily he rolls from side to side, like a high-pooped Dutch brig in a storm; affording during his prostration, to the curious among the spectators, an admirable opportunity for studying prominences, which are certainly not laid down on *phrenological* charts.

The laughter again subsiding, the Child is put into a fighting position, and at it they go, as if this was but the beginning of their conflict. The assault renewed, encouraging acclamations incite the flagging foes. The noisy bustle once more shakes the trembling deck, as whirling, twirling, rumbling, tumbling, they writhe in the agony of their struggles. Hot and furious raged the combat. The laughing cheers of the excited spectators, ringing merrily forth, threw the laboring combatants into spasms of exertions, still more terrible. Their suppressed breathing and clenched teeth told of the earnestness of their endeavors. As regardless of "all around, above, beneath," as two infuriated ants locked in deadly conflict—they heave, they slide, they roll. in the fight, frightening women, and overturning campstools, in the violence of the onset. By heaven it was a noble sight to see! The heroic strife of these valiant Englishmen, contending for the smiles of approving beauty, was worthy of the chivalric days of Britain. I feel abashed whilst making this feeble record of their exploits. They deserve some modern Homer to sing their prowess, and embalm in Epic verse their fame. The story of their deeds should become a part of history; their names should be the battle cry of the *Erring* knights of every cockpit in Christendom; and the details of this dread combat, between doughty *Pips* and his illustrious *Child*, should be as familiar to "heeler" and "pitters" as the cant phrases of the mug. Frantic were still the efforts of both. But the invidious God of battles semed still to favor the boastful Pips. The Child seemed stricken by some sudden fear, a panic crept through every limb, his muscles became relaxed; his nerves shook, his eyes rolled fearfully, and he would have fled had flight been possible. Escape was hopeless. He struggled yet awhile feebly on, when again he rolled at the feet of the redoubtable Pips. A hundred straining throats hail the victorious hero, whose visage, resplendent with smiles and exertion, beamed forth his thanks.

Both gentlemen had arrived at that respectable period of life, when certain corporeal developments become rather prominent. And now "the Child," with his bluntest extremity turned towards blushing heaven and the ladies, exhibited a portion of his person, which, however *honorable* it may be deemed, is usually considered most presentable, when veiled by the mysterious folds of a coat-tail. But it may be altogether proper, or even fashionable, for aught I know, for gentlemen in England to make these somewhat remarkable exhibitions to the public. All this may have been English gentility, indulging in a little ground and lofty tumbling, merely to show us innocent republicans, that the thing had joints, and could sometimes use them—but to a plain man, like myself, it seemed much more like what I should now designate as the quintessence of cockney vulgarity. Suppose that during the tour of Mr. Dickens or some other scribbling Englishman, a couple of our western pioneers had been suddenly seized with the immodest desire of exhibiting, in this extraordinary way, their fair proportions, in the ladies' cabin of one of our Southern steamboats. We should never have heard the last of it. It would have been heralded from one end of Europe to the other, as irresistible evidence of the vulgarity of the American character, and obscenity of American taste. Even the heinous crimes of spitting and bolting would have paled into petty vices, beside this fearful outrage of decency. We should have had lengthy dissertations, in every language in Europe, upon the indecent license of American manners. Our men would have been denounced as devoid of all modesty, and our women of all shame. English journals would have piously regretted the fearful influences of vice and corruption, which have always existed in republics; and English philanthropists would have seriously debated the propriety of sending out missionaries to improve our morals. We should have been held up to the world as a warning example of the avenging curse of heaven, for those twin abominations, slavery and democracy. All pious, moral and discreet people would have been considerately put upon their guard, against us lawless republicans. They would have been earnestly warned against all connection, public or private, with a people, whose total disregard even of the decencies of life make them such dangerous companions for the true friends of law and order. Our influence would be deprecated, our society shunned, and our principles condemned as inimical to all that good men love, because forsooth, a couple of western hunters had taken it into their heads to make an exhibition, which it seems an Englishman can make daily without exciting either surprise or comment.

The English aristocracy have issued their edict, which all flunky Americans obey, that the wearers of linsey-woolsey and broadcloth can have nothing in common. Their language and actions, though they may happen to be identically the same, are placed in widely different categories. The pranks, which in a backwoods American would be stigmatized as shocking obscenity, become, when perpetrated by a rich Englishman, charming evidences of sportive humor. The English and their echoes still persist in reversing the scriptural precept, and always judge most harshly of those, who have enjoyed fewest advantages. A backwoodsman might do something offensive to refined taste, for which his ignorance should be a sufficient apology. But these illiberal judges would vituperate him, but blandly smile upon the improprieties of a man, whose wealth and associations in society ought to have taught him better. In a western American "the chicken fight" would have been an abomination; but when enacted by a rich West India merchant, and planter, it was but a playful acknowledgment to the ladies and gentlemen on board the steamer, that the proportions of his person had not materially changed, but only become more fully developed since his days of tight breeches and round jackets. From the American, similarly situated, every woman should fly in blushing confusion; but any lady, who should have the delicacy to feel shocked by the graceful exposures of an *English Gentleman*, would be ridiculed as affecting a false modesty, that nobody but Americans are guilty of. I am not very familiar with the science of anatomy, and there may exist a sufficient difference between the conformation of a lean pioneer, and a corpulent Englishman, to justify the distinction they seem inclined to make in favor of the latter. And the English may very probably be right, in supposing that there is something much more alarming to ladies in the angular projections of a lank western hunter, than in the plump proportions of one of their own beef-fed countrymen.

CHAPTER IX.

ORIGIN OF THE CHURCH OF ENGLAND.

THE high-churchmen, always great sticklers for birth and pedigree, are somewhat squeamish as to the origin of the Established Church of England. They are loath to attribute their greatest blessing to their greatest tyrant, and would fain discover in the various excesses of the old religion, the causes of the Reformation, which were snugly stowed away in that bloated budget of atrocities, fat Henry himself.

If there be any of that importance about mere origin, which English churchmen are eager to attach to it, they may be somewhat excusable, perhaps, for their solitary belief in their own infallibility. The Church of England certainly owes its existence to the most exalted source, and has never disgraced its lineage. If Henry could return to earth, he would have no reason to blush for the degeneracy of his offspring. It has always borne about it unmistakable marks of its descent, and still continues to practise some of the peculiar virtues of its founder. The easy indifference, with which the earlier primates could turn from the terrible scenes of their persecutions to the touching offices of religion, bears a startling family resemblance to the indelicate haste of the tyrant in marrying Jane Seymour, the day after the execution of Anne Bullen, when the latter had so recently been the object of his tenderest solicitude. Does not the malignity, with which they pursued both Puritans and Catholics, seem but the reflection of Smithfield's blazing fires, which Henry kindled alike for the followers of Luther, and the adherents of the Pope? And do not the ostentatious regard for forms and the hollow ceremonies of the modern Church, the fondness of its ministers for display, and their eagerness for riches, still recall some of the prominent attributes of the corpulent Henry?

When it is remembered how much this modern Blue Beard was given to matrimony and extravagance, it no longer continues surprising that he quarrelled with the Pope in order to take unto himself a new wife, and that he destroyed the monasteries to satisfy his avarice. To gratify his old passions, and acquire the means of indulging new, was too much in accordance with Henry's disposition to need any ghostly advisers in hurrying on the Reformation. Once commenced, the work went bravely on. The dispute with the Pope, begun to gratify the king's love of Anne Bullen, was carried to extremities to gratify His Majesty's love of gold. Rich monasteries were pillaged. Their confiscated lands were divided among worthless court favorites—their treasures squandered in idle court shows. The lazy monks were expelled—their well-stocked larders destroyed—their saintly images broken—and altars overthrown. Their old tenants were loaded with heavier tithes to support a new clergy, who hankering more after lawn and lucre than venison, substituted in their worship the king for the Virgin Mary, and filled up the calendar of abolished saints with a long list of their titled patrons.

It was a gloomy omen for the future purity and toleration of the Established Church, that it had sprung from the lusts, and been founded in the rapacity of a tyrant. From such a beginning, it appears but natural, that bigotry should color its doctrines, and persecution mark its course. It seemed necessary to infect it with every species of worldliness, in order to render it worthy of its royal progenitor, who had the sacrilegious audacity to clothe his vices in the holy garb of religion, and to make his *conscience* the vile pretext for a viler action. The divorce from Catherine, Henry assures us, was the result of pious alarm; his having so long violated a canon of the Church, founded on the Levitical law, was certainly well calculated to produce it. But during the eighteen years of his marriage with Queen Catherine of Arragon, the king's scruples had comfortably remained in the profoundest slumber, and they were only awakened with love for Anne Bullen. It is surprising, after so long a nap, how amazingly sprightly His Majesty's conscience became. Its delicacy and refinement may be justly estimated, by the somewhat prolonged period of its torpidity.

Had Henry, apart from all religious considerations, been actuated by a single noble impulse,—had he simply rebelled against the encroaching tyrannies of Rome, or only attempted to curb the excesses of her arrogant priesthood, the origin of the High Church of England might have still possessed something of that nobility, which its zealous adherents would fain ascribe to it. But up to the period of his outbreak against Rome, no prince in Christendom had appeared more steadfast in his devotion to the Pope, than his corpulent Majesty. In the mildness of his enthusiasm, he had descended from his kingly dignity, laid aside his royal robes, and entered the public ring of theological wrangling to contend, in behalf of the Pope, with that cunning wrestler, Martin Luther himself. The rude reformer did not receive him with that tender consideration that a royal personage might reasonably have expected; but though he richly deserved the rough treatment his temerity exposed him to, his zeal merited all the "mouth honor" conferred on him at the time. And after having been publicly complimented by the special commendation and affection of the Pope, he could sport the sonorous title of "Defender of the Faith," with the blushing consciousness of having won it.

After the eighteen years of uninterrupted connubial quiet with Catherine of Arragon, the king's religious scruples became suddenly alarmed at having so long lived in the holy estate of matrimony with a brother's widow. Being at last awakened to the enormity of his crime, it was but natural that a tender conscience like his should have been assailed with all sorts of sulphurous visions of purgatory, and that his fragile frame should have been fearfully shaken by superstitious horrors of every shape. What mortal could calmly endure the intense anguish of such remorse? He flew to Rome for relief. And it was only when Pius VII. hesitated by granting him a divorce to set aside the dispensation of a venerable predecessor for the solemnization of the marriage, that Henry's devotion was turned to bitterness. In the excess of his virtuous indignation he resolved to defy the authority of that church, whose canons he had such holy horror of breaking, even with the connivance of its head. He felt there was a higher power whose simple fiat should outweigh the indulgences of all St. Peter's successors together. The Levitical law was more sacred to him than the accumulated bulls of a thousand Popes. Alone he stood forward the champion of morality and religion, the avenger of outraged decency and the advocate of civil rights. Such distinguished sincerity, such refined delicacy, it seems to me, should entitle their possessor to the highest admiration of posterity. The churchmen whose fortunes he founded should be eternally grateful for the illustrious example of piety he gave, in shrinking from so sinful a connection; they should unceasingly thank him for the admirable evidence of intrepidity he afforded, when he resisted that power, which would have forced him to continue it. Since they cannot canonize him, but are allowed to indulge a passion for heraldry, they might, at least, quarter his arms over the door of every established church in the kingdom. The factions might, however, declare that it was a little remarkable that Henry was never disturbed by those praiseworthy apprehensions of sin till he had grown weary of the person of his wife, who was some years older than himself. But surely such a coincidence should not stain the purity of his conduct. Because he had passed eighteen years of his life in evil-doing is no reason why he should not have experienced the greatest eagerness to atone for past faults. He never pined for a divorce till he had wholly yielded himself up to his unruly passion for Anne Bullen. That should not have lessened his anxiety to free himself from a connection, revolting alike to his pious feelings as a Christian and his moral sentiments as a man. He never questioned the divine right of the Pope till he refused to minister to his vices. But ought this fact to tarnish the glory he won in freeing England from the rule of the spiritual tyrant? Such a monarch, actuated by motives so pious, so holy, so exalted, the Church of England may well feel proud of, as its founder.

But there are churchmen so little orthodox in their estimate of Henry's religious character, that they would willingly prove the church a foundling, the mysterious results of a happy combination of circumstances, instead of allowing her all the advantages of her distinguished parentage. The atrocity of the attempt is only equalled by its folly. History fortunately furnishes facts which establish the illustrious pedigree of the church as indisputably as if it had been recorded in the Herald's College. These skeptics may declare that the public mind had been gradually prepared for the great religious revolution, and that Henry, for the only time in his life, consulted the wishes of the people in breaking his allegiance with the Pope.

There can be no doubt but that the overgrown power of Rome had become extremely irksome in England. Many of the nobles were anxious to see the country freed from the inordinate riches and encroaching disposition of the clergy. Although the rival forms of the two churches were, to them, matters of supreme indifference, as the accommodating elasticity of their consciences during the rapid religious changes under Mary, Edward and Elizabeth abundantly proved, yet they both feared and hated the arrogant priesthood, whose superior opulence overshadowed the magnificence of their own order. The immense riches accumulated by the six hundred and forty-five monasteries, the ninety colleges, the two thousand three hundred and seventy-four chantries and free chapels, and one hundred and ten hospitals which Henry was pleased to plunder, are almost incredible. One of their own partisans concluded that they possessed little less than one-fifth of the entire landed property of England, besides their enormous revenues arising from other sources. When it is remembered that in addition to wealth so unusual, all tonsured persons enjoyed an immunity from civil punishment for crimes, it is no longer surprising that they should have been regarded with fear and suspicion, even by their own party. Possessing, as they did, such extraordinary means of every vicious indulgence, without the restraint imposed on other members of society by the civil law, it is not improbable that their excesses merited the exaggerated reports made by Henry's commissions of visitation. But so far was this natural desire for an improvement in the morals of her priesthood from inciting any alienation from the old church, that when Henry first attacked her, by his daring spoliation of the smaller convents, a rebellion convulsed the north of England, and disturbances occurred in various portions of the kingdom. What better evidence of strong attachment to the Catholic Church could be adduced than that the tyrant, with all the terror of his name, was unable to quell the indignation of the people at his officious tampering with their faith? The dissatisfaction was much increased upon the destruction of the larger convents in 1540. Even Henry, whose fierce nature seemed to delight in warring against God and man, became alarmed, and he attempted to enlist the most powerful of the nobles on his side, by bribing them with the confiscated estates of the monasteries. Does such universal disaffection, from so despotic a government, evince any eagerness, on the part of a nation, for religious changes? No, no! It was Henry, not the people, who had quarrelled with the Pope. His vices and not their devotional feelings were to be gratified by the Reformation. If Catherine of Arragon had been younger, or Anne Bullen less beautiful, England might have become Protestant, in the lapse of ages, but she would have escaped the crushing weight of the hierarchy.

When Henry, after his rupture with the Pope, gracefully resigned the magnificent title of "Defender of the Faith," and assumed the one no less imposing, of "Protector and Supreme Head of the Church," he conducted himself as step-fathers, on such occasions, are wont to do. He at once commenced a rigid inquiry into the morals of his adopted charge. The monks were reported to be somewhat loose and erratic in their habits. Their tender guardian declared them incapable of managing their own affairs, and wishing, I presume, to present to the world a startling example of his superior justice and piety, coolly robbed them of all their possessions, and would himself have pocketed the money, if he had dared. Every friend of law and order felt outraged, by the king's glaring violation of the sacred rights of property. Admitting that the monasteries harbored individuals who were guilty of excesses, and even crimes, before what legal tribunal had they been arraigned? By what jury had they been condemned? By what right had the king become censor of the morals of his subjects? What stretch of the royal prerogative had given him this sweeping power of confiscation, to regulate the private lives of the people?

The monks, too, with all their jolly vices, had many and warm friends in the kingdom. The great mass of the population, who would have hailed with joy a decent reformation of their morals, were alarmed into resistance by this terrible blow, struck, through the monasteries, at the Church itself. Besides, there were many who continued to entertain an affectionate weakness for the religious houses, in spite of all their failings. Those who had dead friends to be prayed for, those whose sinful courses made them look forward with trembling eagerness to the masses that were to be said for their souls, after they had been called to their final reckoning,—the benighted travellers who missed the cheering hospitality of the scattered monks, and the beggars who daily received alms at the gates of the monasteries,—all assisted to swell the wail of timorous indignation at the sacrilege of Henry.

The pious haste with which he devoted the incontinent abbots and their followers to destruction, was no doubt increased by the gratifying prospect of their confiscated treasures, which were by no means unacceptable to a spendthrift of his expensive tastes and improvident disposition. But, with the impious audacity to strike the blow, he lacked the moral courage to enjoy the fruits of his wickedness. Bewildered by the storm of opposition which assailed him, he was compelled to dole out the pilfered estates of the church to the nobility, hoping, by making his crime their interest, to enlist these ready allies of evil on his side.

Thus cowardice defeated the only possible benefit that might have arisen to the state, from so flagrant an outrage in its head. Had Henry retained these immense treasures, his subjects might have been relieved, at least, from the burden of "supporting the dignity of the crown," and "providing for the public defence"—two favorite pretexts, in despotic governments, for squandering the money of the people. But, what he did not lavish in idle parade, having become the victim of his own fears, he distributed to covetous courtiers, to swell their large fortunes, whilst he remained as needy and craving as before. His successors, backed by these powerful nobles as their friends, and supported by the numerous party of reformers who had sprung up in the kingdom, possessing all the facilities he had afforded them for completing the work he had himself commenced, were still unable peaceably to establish the High Church of England. Rebellion and insurrection followed the attempt, and Burnet admits that Edward was forced to send over for foreign soldiers, to intimidate the obstinate bigotry of the people.

When Henry, with all his terrible machinery for awing discontent into silence, had been unable, without outbreaks, to interfere with the religious opinions of the nation, it is scarcely to be supposed that Edward, or even the more resolute Elizabeth, could ever have established the new church, had he not prepared the way for them, by wholly changing the estate of the upper house of Parliament, when he destroyed the monasteries. The abbots and priors, to whom writs of summons had been previously issued, added to the twenty-one Bishops, had always given the Spiritual Lords the majority in the House of Peers. These, whether actuated by attachment to their belief, or by worldly considerations, would always have firmly resisted every attempt at alterations in their form of worship.

Who can doubt that it was Henry's will, and not the general desire of the people, which commenced the Reformation in England? Who can pretend that the destruction of the monasteries was not the immediate cause of its accomplishment? Had the expelled churchmen been allowed to retain their places in the House of Lords, the Protestant successors of Henry could never have obtained that powerful influence over the nation which was derived from a decree of Parliament. And, though the people murmuringly submitted to despotic power, when sustained by the instinctive obedience to law with which they had been reared, they would never have yielded rights so dear as their religious belief to tyranny alone. So tremendous a revolution could never have been effected in England, but for Henry's destruction of the monasteries.

The tyrant's unholy love for Anne Bullen first induced him to set up a church of his own; his spoliation of the monasteries enabled his successors to sustain it. Henry's lust produced the Church of England; his rapacity established it.

CHAPTER X.

PERSECUTION UNDER THE ESTABLISHED CHURCH.

BLOODY Mary has never lacked a chronicler of her wicked deeds. Her cruelty and bigotry are themes, upon which historians of successive ages have dilated with increasing eloquence. All persons of rank, who suffered during her reign, are thrust into prominent places in history, and even obscure mediocrity is lighted into immortality by the flashing fires of Smithfield. Every state trial is noted with eagerness, every fine recorded, and the list of the martyrs burnt at the stake is preserved with commendable accuracy. Leaders of rival parties have vied with each other in heaping obloquy on her memory. But no politician ever sought popularity, or author renown, by dwelling on the persecutions which followed under her Protestant successor.

Yet the implacable fury of Elizabeth was not directed against a single sect. The omission of the surplice and the use of the crucifix were crimes, in her eyes, equally deserving of punishment; and Puritans and Catholics both became the objects of her remorseless bigotry. It seems the anxious wish of Englishmen, of every grade, that the lurid glare of persecution under Elizabeth should pale before the vaunted glories of her reign. In remembering the eloquence of Shakspeare, and the learning and wisdom of Bacon, and boasting of the intimidation of their Scottish neighbors, and the continued subjugation of the Irish, in exulting in the deeds of Drake and Hawkins, and the destruction of the Spanish armada, men are too prone to forget the religious intolerance of their favorite sovereign.

No record has been kept of the obnoxious sects who perished in prison from privation, nor can we tell how many were reduced to beggary, by the infliction of enormous fines or the entire confiscation of their estates. But we do know, from undoubted authority, that under this wise, chaste and most Christian princess, two hundred and four Catholics alone lost their lives for opinion's sake, and that the fearful clank of the rack was rarely silent during the latter years of her reign.

In obsequious Parliaments, that knew no law but the Queen's pleasure, statute succeeded statute, robbing them of every right an Englishman holds dear. The strict prohibition of all public enjoyment of their religion was not deemed sufficient. The most clandestine performance of their rites was strictly forbidden; priests were banished from the kingdom on pain of death, and those were punished who were aware of their presence, without giving immediate information. Ingenious tests were contrived, by which the persecuted Catholics were excluded from all offices of trust and honor. The sacred precincts of their homes were invaded by spies and informers, armed with a revolting oath, the refusal of which hurried the inoffensive victims to prison, or subjected them to ruinous fines and confiscations. The terrible tribunals of the Star Chamber and High Commission Court deprived them of those only guarantees of personal freedom—the habeas corpus act and trial by jury. But even when allowed, by an ostentatious parade of clemency, the benefit of the ordinary course of law, what hope had they of receiving justice in a community in which men regarded a Papist as a dangerous criminal? Elizabeth, however, when she occasionally made these specious exhibitions of pretended justice, fearing that the conscientious scruples of her subjects might, by chance, prove stronger than their prejudices, resorted to means, unheard of at the present day, to secure verdicts in accordance with her own relentless disposition. Sheriffs had general orders to select such jurors as they believed favorable to the Queen's views; but when this expedient occasionally failed, whole juries have been fined and imprisoned for daring to return verdicts in known opposition to her wishes. Such were the machinations against the oppressed Catholics, and such the remorseless bigotry of the Queen, that even this semblance of doing them justice, according to the Common Law of England, became a heartless mockery.

The Archbishops, under Elizabeth, enabled by the boundless authority of the Court of High Commission rigidly to enforce the Acts of Supremacy, of Uniformity, and others, enacted by debased Parliaments for the entire extirpation of Popery, readily won for themselves a notoriety worthy of the Inquisition in its blackest days. The eagerness they displayed in their too ready obedience to these nefarious enactments, by pursuing unoffending Catholics, might, in the eyes of bigoted high-churchmen, justly entitle them to be considered ornaments of the new religion, which, avowedly, had been purged of all the superstition and intolerance of the old. But could this intemperate zeal, whose end was blood, obtain the approbation of our God, who commands to forgive our enemies, and to pray for those who despitefully use us? And yet such holy hypocrites as Parker and Whitgift, who professed, in opposition to the Pope, to take the Bible as their guide, could employ such degraded emissaries as Topcliffe to dog the footsteps of their pretended enemies, to pervert their confidential discourses into treasonable threats, and to search the most private places of their homes for hidden evidences of Popery; when all Catholic ceremonies in public had been suppressed; when priests were prohibited to enter the kingdom on pain of death; when Catholics were compelled to attend Protestant churches, and assist in the performance of rites as repugnant to their consciences as Christians, as their independence as men. Yet these modern Pharisees, arrayed in lawn and hypocrisy, with prayer on their lips and murder in their hearts, would dare to kneel before the altar and implore God to deliver them "from envy, hatred, and malice, and all uncharitableness." Did God or mammon, respect for Holy Writ or lust of power, urge them on in these unhallowed courses? When the religion that they, at the same time, professed and disgraced, breathes peace on earth and good will to men, what Christian could regard such bitter intolerance as an evidence of sincerity? What portion of the Scriptures, that they professed to obey, had taught them to drink in, as music, the cries of their victims stretched on the rack? What feeling of humanity could prompt them to watch, with delight, their quivering limbs whilst being drawn and quartered by the hangman? Their unnecessary zeal in obeying those cruel edicts, was revolting alike to the charity of Christians and humanity of men!

Sophists, in attempting to extenuate the conduct of the Archbishops, might advance three plausible apologies for their insane bigotry. They might pretend that, actuated by profound principles of state policy, Whitgift had sacrificed to a sense of duty, his charity as a Christian. They might declare that according to the more than doubtful morality of "expediency," both he and Parker were justifiable in their persecutions, in order to retain their positions and influence at court, by yielding to the prejudices of the Queen. Or, lastly, they might tell us that they were influenced by the uncontrollable hatred, incident to the jealousy between rival churches. But I feel confident that I can show that each of these positions is untenable. I think I can prove that the persecutions, under these distinguished primates, sprung from, and were nurtured by, the malevolent intolerance that has always characterized the Established Church of England.

State policy has always been made, in despotic governments, the cloak for countless severities and many crimes. Ministers may be vile, the king tyrannical, and the church corrupt; yet historians, professing to preserve the records of truth, have always been found blandly to attribute their atrocities to the imperious necessity of "State policy." But this flattering vindication cannot be applied to the conduct of the Archbishops. They stood alone among the advisers of the crown in their unrelenting hostility to dissenters of every denomination; they surpassed the Queen herself in their rancor. Sympathy with public grievances and individual suffering, is not ordinarily of the keenest nature in the hearts of ambitious statesmen. They often correct abuses and submit to reforms, 'tis true, but they are rather driven by the force of public opinion, than actuated by compassion for the wrongs of the oppressed people. Yet those in the cabinet of Elizabeth, who were the bitterest enemies of the Catholics, shrunk back appalled by the bloody zeal of Whitgift and Parker, though a majority of the nation approved the exterminating edicts against popery. Lord Burleigh, and Sir Christopher Hatton, indignant at the unnecessary cruelty with which Catholics were pursued, boldly remonstrated with the Queen against the unseemly excess of her Archbishops. But their revengeful bigotry was too much in accordance with Elizabeth's own gloomy temper, to allow her to listen to the counsels of her more reasonable advisers.

Admitting that the interests of church and state were so intimately allied, as to make it necessary to restrain the open exercise of the Romish rites, how can their admirers palliate the conduct of the Archbishops, after the most private indulgence of these forbidden ceremonies had been suppressed, and the persecuted Papists compelled to attend the Protestant churches? Their terrified imaginations, haunted by the consciousness of cruelty, might on the slightest provocation have conjured up plots to overturn the state, and conspiracies to murder the Queen. But there were no grounds of fear, except of those air-drawn daggers that always shake the souls of tyrants. The Roman Catholics, though deprived of every civil and religious right, had never manifested a disposition to rebel against the government. Helpless in their sufferings, unarmed and unmurmuring, it seems to me that the Christian meekness of their resignation should have excited something like forbearance in the souls of their oppressors. But submission in their victims seemed but more fiercely to excite the ire of these insatiable churchmen. Even when all causes of animosity had been removed, and every object of persecution suppressed—when their foes had nothing more left of which they could rob them, and not even a murmur against their cruelty could be heard to excite their indignation, they played the part of the wolf in the fable towards the lamb: they accused the downtrodden Catholics of stirring the fierce stream of persecution that poured from the Protestant church, and still farther punished them for evils that they themselves had inflicted on the land.

So far were the Catholics from resisting the government, that the united efforts of the Parliament, the Queen, and her pet churchmen, were unable to drive them into rebellion, though their barbarities seemed perpetrated with that intention. They remained unshaken in their allegiance, though the whole Catholic world stood ready to avenge their wrongs. The Pope thundered forth his bulls. France and Spain sent emissaries and distributed money, with the vain hope of exciting a revolt, that they were most anxious to assist. These two nations then wished to aid them, in spite of themselves; and only demanded, in case of an invasion, their passive neutrality. But these despised Papists, deprived of every privilege that made the name of Englishman tolerable, so loved England and her Queen, that they were unwilling to receive their rights from strangers, when the price demanded for them was the Constitution of their country.

When a powerful armament of the then mightiest kingdom of the universe, threatened the entire subjugation of Great Britain; when the Spanish Armada, freighted with the picked men of Castilian chivalry, was hovering near the coast, and every English heart, from the Queen to the humblest peasant, quaked with terror—the persecuted Papists, instead of quietly awaiting the deliverance promised them by these Spanish invaders, rushed to their standards, and the Catholic gentry were the first to appear in the field, with volunteers for the defence of the Queen. All history cannot afford another such example of heroic disinterestedness. Poets love to sing the praises of patriotism; historians delight to immortalize its possessors; but the eulogy of a self-sacrificing patriotism like this should not be pronounced by poets and historians alone. It should not be confined to a single nation; it should be sounded in every land—it should find an echo in every heart. Patriotism, though so noble, so exalted, is but too often the result of the blessings of a government, or the delights of a home. But these Catholic gentlemen, in coming to the aid of the Queen, were sacrificing position, wealth, religion, and life itself to an ungrateful country. What more glorious evidence could be adduced that the spies and the rack, the fires and the gallows of their persecutors were not necessary to teach them their duties as Englishmen? What better proof could be required, that no considerations of State policy could dictate the destruction of men so ready to brave danger, in defence of their oppressors?

Passive obedience is too often demanded by monarchs from ambitious subjects, as the price of royal favor. And such is the tenacity with which men cling to power, that even honorable minds will frequently sink to the commission of mean, and sometimes guilty deeds, in order to retain it. Had the Archbishops held their sees, as the Ministers of State their places, by the frail tenure of a tyrant's will, selfishness might have afforded them, in the eyes of the worldly, a mean excuse for their conduct. But even this miserable pretext was denied them. They held their positions for life. In assuming the Archbishop's mitre they had been emancipated from the authority of the sovereign herself. They had no court favor to sacrifice—no places to lose. Thenceforth their lives were to be dedicated to Heaven alone. As the heads of the Church, their allegiance was due to God—not to the Queen. His commands—not her whims—they had solemnly sworn to obey.

During great revolutions, whether in Church or State, the opposing parties imbibe a bitterness for each other, which, however inconsistent it may be with their professions as Christians, is but natural to their feelings as men. Not a half a century previous to the epoch in English history at which we have arrived, the mighty reformation of the religious opinions of the world had taken place. The separation of the Reformers from the Catholic Church had been so recent, such startling changes had been effected, that the deadliest animosity still rankled in the hearts of both. They not only experienced the hostility incident to such occasions, but it became an object of the highest importance to the infallibility of each one, to prove the outrages against God and man of the other. And if we implicitly believe the different partisans, both Catholics and heretics were as certainly deserving of the gallows as they were declared to be of hell-fire. Every article of faith had been discussed—the propriety of every ceremony disputed. Questions of temporal authority and State rights, were so industriously mixed up in these spiritual wranglings, that each side learned to consider it as sacred a duty to hate the other, as to go to church. It was no isolated doctrine that was to be argued—no single alteration of forms that was demanded. The entire religious structure was to be overthrown, and a new fabric built up.

But, unfortunately for the fame of the ghostly advisers of Elizabeth, Protestant dissenters shared the aversion they had so fearfully manifested towards the Catholics. Puritans and Catholics, bitterly as they were opposed to each other in religion and politics, suffered in common. Without a single tie of sympathy—farther removed from each other than either was from their mutual enemy—they were yet united in being martyrs to the same insane malevolence. So large a proportion of the ministers, officiating in the Established Church at the beginning of Elizabeth's reign, being in favor of the dissenting doctrines, their opinions should have commanded more consideration than they received. Simple, even to austerity, in their notions of religion, they could not silently endure those ceremonies of the Established Church which had been borrowed from the splendid superstitions of Rome. The tippet and the surplice, the sign of the cross, and the crucifix, were to them the shameful badges of allegiance to the Pope. They contended that these rites, transferred from the old church to the new, were calculated to keep alive in the minds of the people the recollection of the captivating religion they had abandoned. With them these ceremonies were matters of conscience; their presence violated the sacred tenets of their faith. The Queen being far too shrewd in judgment to regard them otherwise than as mere forms, wholly unimportant in the great scheme of salvation, worldly considerations should have restrained her from the attempt to force them on her dissenting subjects, when they so sincerely believed their primitive form of worship to be outraged by such idle exhibitions. The jealous care with which she guarded her prerogative, caused this most grievous error of her life. It was not that she deemed the surplice and the sign of the cross essential to the purity of her faith, that she insisted on their adoption; it was because she considered the discontented murmurs of the Dissenters disrespectful to herself. By the laws of the land she was the "supreme head of the church," and she was unwilling to abate her authority even in trifles.

No one can pretend that the laws which created the High Church of England did not confer upon the Queen the right to govern her own spiritual servants in her own way. And when the ministers of the Presbyterian persuasion broke into open rebellion against her authority, by refusing to sign the Thirty-nine Articles, I think the Archbishop did but consult the interests of his Church, when he ejected them from their livings. But, after having deprived them of all temporal advantages, it seems to me it would have been the part alike of the Christian and the statesman, to have left them in the secret enjoyment of their humble worship, without plunging into those wild excesses of persecution, which, commencing in 1567 with the dispersion of the conventicle in Plummer's Hall and the arrest of its principal members, resulted in a revolution, fatal to England, as to her Church.

The fact that the Independents, in their wild fanaticism, having manifested, even at that early period, as ferocious an animosity to the Queen and her government as to her church, might justify the enactment of those laws, executing their ringleaders, and compelling thousands of the sect to fly the kingdom. But the Puritan ministers, not originally denying the lawfulness of the High Church government, and only demanding certain reforms in her discipline, might have been easily reconciled by the abolition of the obnoxious ceremonies,—by restraining the plurality of benefices, and correcting certain other abuses, that had already crept into the Church. 'Tis true, that as early as 1570, Thomas Cartwright had promulgated the doctrine that all church government was unlawful, except that taught by the Apostles, which was the Presbyterian; yet a few timely concessions from the Queen would have prevented its after agitation by the five famous commoners, and its final triumph, in the downfall of the hierarchy, and the establishment of Presbyterian Synods, by Cromwell and his military companions.

The Queen and her Archbishops, blinded by the vindictive violence of their bigotry, were not satisfied with dismissing the dissenting ministers from their benefices,—with venting their fury on private conventicles, and forcing all persons over sixteen years of age to attend some church of the Established order, on pain of banishment; they were not contented with subjecting the hated Puritans to the inquisitorial oath ex officio, which violated that cherished maxim of common law, that no one could be compelled to criminate himself; but the Archbishop directed all pastors, not only to encourage, but positively to enjoin sports and pastimes on the Sabbath. This was a blow aimed directly at the Puritans. The Judaical strictness with which they kept holy this seventh day,—the severity with which they regarded the frivolities of the gay and the young, were the distinguishing features of their worship. Grave in their deportment, stern in all that regarded their religion, these hardy Dissenters could but ill brook this last insult to the peculiar tenets of their faith. They were not prone to anger, but in sullen silence they brooded over their injuries, till the demon of resistance was aroused among them, which only slept when their king was beheaded, and the constitution overthrown.

The only apology that even their eulogists attempt to offer for the short-sighted policy—to give it no harsher name—of the Queen's primates, is, that the safety of the Established Church depended on the total destruction of every denomination of Dissenters. Surely, worldly wisdom, unaided by the feelings of the Christian, should have taught these imperious advisers of the Queen in religions affairs, that the obstinacy of bold and sincere men was not to be quelled by punishment; that the intrepidity with which the leaders suffered, did but teach their followers their duty to God and their religion. Persecution has never failed to make proselytes, and, after the forty years of uninterrupted molestation, during the reign of Elizabeth, the number of the Dissenters had greatly increased, their popularity had become more deeply rooted, and their enmity to the established order more irreconcilable.

The first James was a willing, but not a daring tyrant. Had his courage been commensurate with his cruelty, the long and systematic persecutions of every denomination of Dissenters, under Elizabeth, would have appeared mild, compared with those under him. But the Puritans, having grown too strong to be zealously assailed by so timid a despot as James, enjoyed, during his whole reign, a respite from the active malevolence of his predecessor. The Catholics, too weak to be dangerous, became the especial objects of his malignity. Upon them he vented all the virulence of a disposition, which only wanted courage to render it truly dangerous. In persecuting Papists, he indulged in the luxury of being cruel, without any uncomfortable fears of resistance or retaliation.

The austere piety of James's unfortunate son and successor, exerted an immediate and powerful influence upon the character of the church. Charles's sullen resolution inspired his Primates with the requisite boldness to indulge their natural propensities for intolerance. The vindictive spirit of other days was kindled into a blaze, and Puritans and Catholics became once more fellow-sufferers. It was during the zealous revival of persecution, that the Established Church so startlingly manifested the feline fondness for toying with the victims of its tortures. Had it been simply fear or hatred of the growing sects of Protestant Dissenters which urged them to such extreme severities, the safest and most complete gratification of both feelings would have been effectually to get rid of them. But permission to leave the kingdom was refused to Lord Say, Hamden, Cromwell, and their followers, by Archbishop's advice to the king. Though the hatred of these so-called "bold bad men" would have been gratified, and all fear of their machinations removed by their self-inflicted banishment to the wild shores of New England; yet the Church would have lost half of its sweetest occupation, by allowing them to escape her. She would have henceforth been compelled to confine her gentle attentions to the Catholics, who presented much too narrow a field for the genius of Laud and his associates. And of course the king, who regarded the delight his church derived from the lingering torments of her victims as an innocent relaxation after her more serious duties were over, was much too pious to circumscribe her pleasures, by permitting one half of his best subjects to escape to America.

The Puritans, surrounded, and pressed upon, without hope of escape, took redress into their own hands, and taught the

Established Church, when too late, to dread the power they had trampled upon. But the poor Catholics, always unfortunate, continued to endure the bitterness of public persecution, in addition to all those domestic sufferings, which the unsuccessful party in a civil war must always submit to. Adhering to Charles throughout his disastrous campaigns, their very virtue, in loyally defending the constitution against the encroachments of Parliament, became to them a new source of evil. Yet where are the eulogists of their devotion; what applause has ever been awarded them for their heroic stand in favor of the constitution of England? But we need not search far to find those who will tell us that the Primates of England, at this epoch, were the properest and most godly of men. They, beyond doubt, continued the formal routine of their duties, complacently pocketing the immense revenues arising from their sees, and saying a lengthy grace before every meal. But the strict performance of these ghostly duties is not all that England has to be grateful for. They reduced the Catholic population to the lowest depths of misery. They pursued the Protestant Dissenters with every species of atrocity. In their holy zeal, they brought sorrow and ruin to one half the hearths of Great Britain, and finally plunged the nation into the bloody horrors of a civil war. Yet whilst performing these eminent services to the state they never omitted their weekly duty of praying to Heaven that it might please God "to keep *all* nations in *unity*, *peace* and *concord*."

All persecution of dissenting Protestants ceased, of course, with the commencement of the civil war, and was never afterwards extensively revived. But the favor with which Charles II., on his restoration, regarded the unlucky Catholics, was sufficiently evident to make them the special objects of the suspicion and hatred of the public, without being strong enough to protect them from the consequences. In the opinion of the multitude there was no crime too heinous for them to be guilty of, there was no evidence too trivial to convict them. They were even accused and believed guilty of the great fire of London, as the early Christians had been accused of the conflagration of Rome. Plots, murders, and conspiracies, were arrayed with fearful rapidity against them. Rye-houses and meal-tubs were alleged to be the extraordinary scenes of their plottings. The trade of public informer was then first known in England, and in falsely swearing the destruction of the innocent Catholics, such wretches as Oates and Bedloe became the petted favorites of the English public.

For rather more than a century the interdicted Papists had known little else than a series of persecution, confiscation, test-oaths and public executions. The privacy of their homes had constantly been invaded by spies; and fear and suspicion had broken up the little circles of social enjoyments. Their brief public careers had been run in rebellions and civil war. Public tranquillity and domestic quiet had been equally denied to them. For a century more they continued the doomed objects of an implacable intolerance, when at the end of the reign of George II. religious commotions ceased. Jacobitism was only known in name, and the Catholics at last found peace in practical toleration.

CHAPTER XI.

PRESENT STATE OF THE ESTABLISHED CHURCH OF ENGLAND.

THE present Church of England does no discredit to its origin and past career. It is what might have been expected from the violence with which it was established, and the persecution with which it was sustained. It is a bloated, unsightly mass of formalities, hypocrisy, bigotry and selfishness, without a single charitable impulse, or pious aspiration. It is a magnificent establishment, abounding in wealth and worldliness, oppression to the poor, and of no great spiritual service to the rich, which is maintained by government, and patronized by the aristocracy, as the convenient means of disposing of spendthrift "younger sons," and accommodating aspiring parvenues, who have money to exchange for position. Ministers are universally regarded as *gentlemen* in England, and people of obscure birth or ignoble occupations may acquire easy access to gentility by purchasing a place in the church.

That the Church of England numbers among its members many sincere and devout Christians I pretend not to deny, but I do assert that the system which has been adopted for its regulation precludes the possibility of its ministers being actuated by those exalted feelings which should always animate the teachers of God's holy word. The fact of all the church livings being regarded as property, must continue to provide ministers of the gospel only acquainted with the forms of religion: having no piety but their prayer-books, no morals but their black coats. According to the English notions of the duties of clergymen, they may be the properest and most exemplary men. They all wear white cravats, hate beggars, and collect their tithes with the most commendable regularity. They are united in their resistance to every attempt at reform, and are untiring in their exertions to render inviolable the antiquated abuses of the church; they manifest their zeal by persecuting Catholics and cordially hating dissenters of every denomination; they toadyize their patrons with the most Christian meekness, and display their regard for the honor of "the cloth," by begging or buying favor sufficient to unite in their own persons as many profitable livings as possible. Being conscious that a minister, like every other man in England, is respectable in proportion to his income, they show their zeal for the dignity of the church by violating its most sacred laws against Simony, in order to become rich by becoming pluralists. The Christian piety of these holy men, who exhibit their zeal by persecuting Catholics, and reviling dissenters, whilst they themselves indulge in the worst species of worldliness, calls to mind the delicate conscience of the corpulent founder of their church, who was too God-serving a man to commit adultery, but could piously cut off the head of an innocent wife in order to make way for a lust of more recent origin. I am not so visionary as to entertain a hope of rendering them immaculate, but I would have them Christians in action as in name. I am too thoroughly acquainted with the intense selfishness of an Englishman's nature to suppose that his duties to Heaven could induce him to sacrifice the advantages of worldly position, or that a feeling of piety could produce even momentary forgetfulness of the fascinations of "belly-cheer," but I would have these appointed preachers of the gospel approach, in distant imitation at least, the self-sacrificing devotion of the Apostles, who went forth without scrip and without shoes to preach Christianity to the world. Their hearts and souls are absorbed in calculations of tithes, and struggles for richer livings, but they consider themselves acquitted of all they owe to God by the observance of a few empty forms. The specious hypocrites carefully envelop themselves in surplices, but manifest their worldliness by hankering after fat livings, instead of doing good works, as Achilles betrayed his sex, when disguised among the daughters of Lycomedes, by his preference for arms to jewels.

These heartless worldlings are not only guilty of the deepest injustice to the members of the Established Church in monopolizing the benefices, by paying obsequious court to their owners, to the exclusion of abler and more pious teachers whom the people might select, but they insult their helplessness by pocketing their money without pretending to observe those duties they are so well paid to perform. If they were contented with receiving an enormous salary for mechanically drawling through the morning and evening prayers, and indolently reading once a week a stupid sermon of fifteen minutes' length, without being animated by a single feeling that should influence a preacher, the injustice would be less glaring. If they were simply avaricious, the wrong would be less outrageous; but they are energetically grasping. To become gay non-residents, and rich pluralists, they contemptuously discard even the semblance of those duties, which honor if not religion should demand from them for their flocks. The following startling abuses in the Church of England were exposed by returns recently made to Parliament.

Number of benefices	10,987
Resident incumbents	6,699

Non-resident incumbents	3,736
Vacancies and recent institutions	199
Sequestrations	37
No returns	316

"The number of curates serving benefices on which the incumbents are non-residents is 2,711. The number of curates assistant to resident incumbents is 2,032, total number of curates 4,743." Here it is seen that a third of the entire number of clergymen of the Established Church do not even reside in the parishes, over which they profess to preside, but leave the labor of their duties to starving curates, 2,521 of whom receive less than £100 a year. By deducting the number of curates employed in the benefices of non-resident incumbents, from the number of the non-residents themselves, it will be found that in more than a thousand benefices no religious service is performed, although their respective pastors are regularly pocketing their share of the $50,000,000, annually expended for the support of the Church of England. The monstrous fraud and injustice of such a system are too glaring to require comment. The facts themselves are their most eloquent condemnation.

The nobility have so many extravagant younger sons, and dissipated poor relations to establish in life, who would degrade their families by engaging in any active pursuit; there are so many of the young gentry, too proud to work, and yet not rich enough to be idle, for whom some lazy, honorable occupation must be provided, that the army, the navy, the public offices, and the colonies are insufficient to accommodate them all. The church, with its monstrous mass of impiety and injustice, must be retained, like the East India Board, as a more extended means of accommodation for the youthful drones, whom the aristocracy have thrown for support upon the hands of the people. But besides the assistance extended to the aristocracy, the government itself derives great power and profit from the patronage afforded by the church. And when we remember that it is composed of Englishmen, it would be madness to suppose that they would sacrifice such advantages to any conscientious scruples. It is true that those who purchase, or accept the livings, are influenced by worldly rather than religious considerations; it is certain that the opportunity to enjoy an easy, indolent sort of existence, rather than a pious wish to dedicate their lives to Heaven, induces them to enter the church. But what is it to the government, though the religious instruction of the nation be intrusted to the worldliest of the worldly? What is it to them that the ministers, whose example is to influence, and piety direct their flocks, must perjure themselves by solemnly swearing when they are ordained, that they are moved to take orders by the Holy Ghost? What matters it though the vilest hypocrites occupy the holiest places, if their ends are accomplished, and their aristocracy sustained? The prayers are generally read by somebody, and the responses attended to. Could more be expected from an established church? What must we think of the policy of an enlightened government, which could deliberately perpetrate such an outrage against the religious feelings of its subjects? What opinion must we entertain of the piety of subjects, who could submit to it? If there be a crime on earth, for which even governments are amenable to Heaven, it is assembling on the hallowed Sabbath these mocking hypocrites before the altar of God. If there be sacrilege, which must sooner or later call down the wrath of an offended God, it is prostituting the holy offices of religion to the support of an order.

One of the most active causes of the success of the Reformation in England was the desire in the nation at large, to be freed from the domineering control and oppressive incomes of the priesthood. The great changes in the forms of religion were not so much the result of reasoning on theological subjects, as a conviction of the fraud and corruption existing in the Romish Church. The covetous and arrogant dispositions of the priests, and their vast temporal power, was what most disgusted the people, and made them eager for any revolution which promised a reform of those abuses. But what did they gain by the change? It was but a simple alteration of names; a mere transfer of authority from the Catholic priesthood to the Reformed clergy. The sceptre of the king was substituted for the keys of St. Peter. The crown usurped the place of the tiara. The patronage of the livings belonging to the Pope fell to the share of Henry VIII; those benefices which had been claimed by the Abbots and Priors were transferred to the Bishops, and those of the Catholic nobility to the greedy favorites of the fat king. An enormous amount of money was appropriated to give grandeur and magnificence to the new establishment. The value of church property has been estimated at the almost incredible sum of $900,000,000. Bishops were lodged and supported like princes, and ordinary pastors like nobles. Mr. Baring many years ago stated in the House of Commons, that the income of the Bishop of London amounted to the astounding sum of $500,000. Great pomp and ceremony were preserved in order to render the services imposing in the eyes of the multitude. No pains were spared to make the offices of the Reformed church respectable among all classes, and the immense expense incurred in their endowment caused them to be eagerly sought for by the aristocracy. In this gorgeous worship, religion lacks nothing but its devotion, the creed is only deficient in sincerity. It is maintained at an expense equal to that of all the other Christian denominations in the world. It is supposed that the support of the Church of England annually costs the government £9,459,565, whilst all the Christians of the rest of the world pay to their ministers but £9,949,000. It seems, therefore, that the High Church of England, with 6,500,000 hearers, requires for its maintenance as great an expense as all the other forms of Christianity in the universe, with 203,728,000 hearers. It is a favorite theme with High-churchmen to descant upon the splendid displays and absurd extravagance in the administration of the Catholic church, but on examination it will be found that the Reformed Church of England costs the people 40 times as much to every million of hearers, as the administration of Papacy in France, to the same number of hearers. The monstrous excess in the pay of the English clergy appears from comparing their incomes with those of dignitaries of corresponding rank in other countries. The pay of a Bishop in France is $3,125, and that of a rector is $250. In Rome the income of a Cardinal, next in dignity to the Pope, $2,500; that of a rector of a parish $150. But in England many of the Bishops have been receiving over $100,000, whilst we have seen that the income of one amounted to half a million; and there are rectories in that country valued at $40,000 and $50,000. We very naturally suppose that extraordinary devotion among the people, or the vastly superior religious instruction afforded by their pastors, must demand this amazing preponderance in the pay of the English clergy. But we have already seen that there are more than one thousand benefices, in which religious services are utterly neglected, and we can entertain no very high opinion of the pious solicitude of the people, who submit to the appointment of their pastor by the owner of the manor, with the same indifference they might be supposed to feel about his selection of a horse for a fox-hunt.

I contend that this outrageously wasteful extravagance in the church establishment, is not simply an oppression to an already overloaded people, but that it deprives them of proper religious teaching, by inducing ambitious worldlings to sue for the positions which Heaven intended for the pious and lowly. But we are informed that this enormous outlay is essential to the dignity of the church. If the simple majesty of Christianity had been insufficient to impress the hearts of men, it would have proved somewhat difficult for its humble founder, born in a stable, to establish its tenets. What wealth, what pomp, what magnificence, did the apostles carry into strange lands to dazzle converts to the new faith? The glare and glitter of show and parade are not more important now than they were then. The unaffected devotion and active zeal of one devoutly pious pastor, would command more real respect than the ostentatious profusion of all the pluralists and non-residents in the kingdom. It is the cause of the aristocracy, not that of Heaven, which is promoted by this vast expenditure in support of the Established Church. But the advocates of this ruinous system pretend to deem parks, palaces, plate, and equipages indispensable to the dignity of these magnificent prelates, whose divine Master made his entry into Jerusalem on the colt of an ass. Mansions, villas, warrens, and manorial rights are thought necessary for their amusement, whilst "the Son of man had not where to lay his head." Is it strange that in giving to the bishops the wealth and position, the government should also give them the worldliness of nobles? In becoming rivals of the aristocracy in fortune, is it not natural that they should become their rivals in extravagance and dissipation?

A bishop, "being a man, must feel like one." When he finds himself surrounded by every refined enjoyment that luxury can invent or wealth afford, and feels compelled by his position to vie in sumptuousness with the proudest of the land, it is but natural that his thoughts should turn from heaven to earth. When he feels that his money, not his piety, gives him consideration among his fellows, he must be more or less than man, if he does not soon learn to exult more in his magnificence than his lowliness. When he discovers that profusion more than charity purchases the applause of men, when he feels convinced that the grandeur of a spiritual lord rather than the devotion of the preacher of the gospel commands their respect, it would be strange indeed if his heart did not sink from God to mammon. Worldly affluence soon bounds all his hopes. Fashionable pre-eminence becomes his highest ambition, parade his chief delight. Such would be the result even if these holy men had been originally actuated by sincere feelings of piety. Remember the author of the proverb, that "it is easier for a camel to pass through the eye of a needle, than for a rich man to enter the kingdom of heaven." But I feel confident of being able to prove, before the end of this chapter, that the clergy enter the church as they would pursue any other profession which promised success to an ambitious man.

These worthy bishops piously exhort their followers to "take no heed of what ye shall eat, nor what ye shall drink, nor for your bodies, what ye shall put on," whilst they load their own sumptuous tables with every delicacy that the country can afford, stock their cellars with the rarest wines, and array themselves in the costliest importations from France. In their lazy dreams of sensual enjoyment, they seem wholly oblivious of the scriptural injunction to "take care that your hearts be not charged with surfeiting and drunkenness, and the cares of this life." But though they annually squander millions of the people's money, in sustaining the "pride, pomp, and circumstance" of their positions, yet I must confess, strange as it may seem, that in obedience to the command "distribute to the poor, and seek treasures in heaven," they still find the means generously to feed the hungry with religious tracts, and to relieve the wretched by praying for them. Who can henceforward impugn the piety of a Bishop?

He should be named a fountain of charity as of grace in England. Who can now pretend that when the poor beg for bread, he gives them a stone? If a haggard victim of disease appeals to his sympathies in behalf of a starving family at home, he unhesitatingly presents him a tract, ingeniously illustrating the beauties of faith, in the touching incident of Elijah and the poor widow, with the handful of meal, and a little oil in the cruse. Should a helpless mother implore his assistance to bury one child already dead, among her others who are slowly dying of the typhus fever, he piously assures her that she shall be remembered in his prayers. The magnanimity of such self-sacrificing charity will be better appreciated, when it is remembered that the tracts are gratuitously furnished him by the religious societies, and that even decency demands that he should occasionally pray for the health and prosperity of the kingdom. The poor mother is probably included in this general prayer, if he does not entirely forget her application a half an hour after she quitted his door. As an evidence that the cases in which the charities of the bishops might relieve starvation are not altogether imaginary, I give the following extract from the London Observer, made during my visit to England last summer.

Death from Starvation.—Last night Mr. Brent held an inquest upon Jonathan Nicholls, aged 51. Deceased, whose body was a mere skeleton, had been formerly a schoolmaster, but was latterly so reduced as to be compelled to earn his livelihood by writing window bills for tradesmen, and with all his industry sometimes only realized a few pence a-week. The parish allowed a loaf a-week for the support of himself and his wife, who is paralyzed. During the last twelve months deceased was daily sinking from sheer starvation, but still buoyed up with the hope of getting some property to which he was entitled. On Monday morning his wife found him dead in bed at her side. The following day he became entitled to £120 cash, and £60 a-year. Mr. Lutheron, surgeon, deposed that death resulted from want and disease of the lungs. The foreman, on behalf of the jury, expressed their horror and disgust at the parochial authorities limiting the support of deceased and his paralyzed wife to a solitary loaf of bread a-week, instead of inquiring into their wants, and contributing a sufficient quantity of food for their support. The coroner summed up, and the jury returned a verdict in accordance with the medical evidence.

If a man in the position that this one evidently had been, could die so terrible a death, how appalling must be the condition of the millions, born in degradation, and reared in ignorance.

I wish not to intimate that the mean privations of the ascetic constitute my ideas of Christian humility. The terrible lacerations, to which the solitary enthusiasts of early times subjected their weak frames, are revolting alike to my ideas of religion and humanity. I cannot believe that corporeal punishment prepares a man's soul for heaven, though inflicted by his own hands. We all know that so intimately are man's physical and intellectual natures interwoven,—so nicely are they dependent on each other, that intense corporeal suffering will turn the firmest mind from undisturbed thoughts of heaven itself. But leaving the excruciating agonies endured by the mad devotees of the desert out of the question—simple want will fill the most magnanimous soul with its own selfish repinings. The cries of nature must be heard. *Comfort* is not only the basis of all happiness, but it is absolutely indispensable to any concentrated action of the mind; and so far from those numberless little enjoyments which civilization has rendered essential to comfort being inconsistent with the beautiful simplicity of the faith taught by our Saviour, I think that a certain degree of intellectual pleasure, and even elegant luxury, greatly increases that contemplative fervor, which every minister should bring to his profession. I cannot think that any pastor could faithfully discharge his duties, who does not enjoy not only the mere necessaries of life, but many of its more refined indulgences. The mind must borrow healthy vigor from the body. But, surely, the clergy of England exceed those rational pleasures, so necessary to social contentment, when they surpass the richest citizens of the richest country upon earth in luxurious splendor, and vie with the proudest nobles in gorgeous displays. The mind, even of the most pious, when constantly dwelling on gilded trifles, and eternally occupied with thoughts of pomp, parade and position, must sooner or later, in spite of itself, imbibe a worldly pride and ostentation, little becoming the leaders of a great church. It seems to me that the Archbishop should teach every member of the Established Church his duty to his Maker, not only by his precepts, but his example. He should remember the advice of Jesus to the rich young man, to give all he had to the poor, and forsaking all things to follow him. Notwithstanding their princely incomes, the Bishops, in becoming ambitious of rivalling the richest and most dissipated, in their Bacchanalian revels, deprive themselves of the means, even if they retained the inclination, to perform the charities which their exalted rank in the church and enormous wealth give the world a right to expect from them.

I would have a clergyman live and dress like a gentleman, without committing any of the absurd excesses peculiar to that caricature upon the species, known as a dandy. I would have him indulge in all the innocent gayeties of the social circle. I never could understand the gloomy fanaticism of those who would have religion banish every thing like mirth from the human heart, who would fain make a smile a misdemeanor, and a laugh a crime. I could never satisfactorily determine why a sorrowful expression of countenance should indicate a pious mind, or a ragged coat be considered an evidence of a holy state of feeling.

And those who would make the Sabbath a day of mourning instead of rest and cheerful relaxation, it seems to me have strangely misconstrued the spirit of the Scriptures.

There is nothing morose about Christianity. The hearts of those who profess it should be filled with rejoicing and good will towards men. Thrice blessed is he whose soul is gladdened by feelings of true religion; for it is, after all, the only unalloyed pleasure enjoyed in this world. Success brings satiety, excitement is followed by reaction, but the happiness of sincere piety charms, when "pleasures cease to please." It but beams the brighter in misfortune, and will throw a halo of ineffable contentment around the saddest soul. Joy as naturally springs from religion, as his matinal carol from the lark. At the birth of our Saviour they came into the world together, "when the good tidings of great joy" were announced to the shepherds in the witching minstrelsy of rejoicing angels. The doleful looks and dismal groans of the mistaken zealots, who delight, in professing religion, to play the profound mummery of woe, have always seemed to me as absurd as unnatural.

The twenty-four Bishops and two Archbishops of England are a burden, as oppressive as unnecessary to the people. How have they changed the simple form of worship, preached by the followers of our Saviour! They have substituted ostentation for humility, worldliness for devotion. They promise vile lucre, rather than heavenly glory, as a reward to the faithful servants of the church. They have made religion a burden, instead of a blessing, to the people. What opinion must we entertain of the usefulness of a church, whose principle is avarice, and whose practice is tyranny? Selfishness, not charity, animates the bosoms of the Bishops. They persist in defending the hoary abuses of the church, for the worldly advantage of themselves and their relations, though they fall with crushing weight on the widow and the orphan. They are the modern Scribes and Pharisees, loving the high places at feasts and in the synagogue. The applause of men, rather than the silent approbation of God, animates them to do good deeds. They delight to pray aloud, and to do their alms before men. Their souls are absorbed in the accumulation of wealth, and their minds busied in providing rich livings for their relatives and friends. Their dioceses should be abolished, and their mitres broken. They should be driven from the church, as the money-changers and those who sold doves were expelled from the Temple by our Saviour; for they have filled the house of God with the tumult of traffic, and made the sacred offices of religion a trade.

What are the duties of the Bishops and Archbishops, that they should be so liberally pensioned from the pockets of the people? The Bishops do not preach. They never see the clergymen over whom they are appointed oftener than once in three years, when they make a hurried visit to the principal towns of their dioceses. But, even if they were most inclined conscientiously to fulfil the duties of their stations, they are compelled to be absent from their dioceses at least five months of every year, to occupy their seats among the hereditary lawgivers of the land in the House of Lords. They have no real authority to correct the abuses of the parochial clergy. Indeed, they rather encourage, by their own appointments, the fatal practice of non-residence and pluralities, which last the canons of the church denounce as "execrable before God." Should a Bishop bring a delinquent minister before his court, and convict him, the minister snaps his fingers at the decree, and claims his living as his freehold—too often a purchased one. If an effort is made to carry the sentence into effect, the guilty clergyman appeals from court to court, till at last he casts the charges on the Bishop, when they have been swelled to such an amount, as effectually to prevent the Right Reverend Gentleman's trying so expensive an experiment for the future. The Archbishops are still more useless. They do not appoint the Bishops, nor can they remove them. They cannot even call them together in convocation, without the sovereign's concurrence. It is true that the Archbishop of Canterbury is called upon to anoint the monarch, should a coronation occur, and that he is expected to christen the royal offspring. But, surely, one coronation during his incumbency, and a christening every year, which sometimes happens, ought scarcely to entitle his Grace of Canterbury to the luxury of Lambeth Palace, and an income of $75,000 a year. But the performance of religious duties seems to be as little looked for, as piety in the twenty-six spiritual Lords of Great Britain. Pelf and power engross all their solicitude. They count their enormous revenues, dispense rich livings and fat sinecures to their relations and dependants,—silently vote, in their places in Parliament, for every oppressive measure proposed by the existing government, and their duty is done.

To illustrate the tender consideration of the Bishops for the members of their own families, in generously bestowing on them rich livings and sinecures, in defiance of the stringent laws of the Church against non-residents and pluralists, I beg to call the attention of my readers to the case of the Right Rev. Mr. Sparke, Bishop of Ely. By a series of forced resignations and translations, it was finally arranged so that "the Rev. J. Henry Sparke held at the same time the living of Leverington, the sinecure rectory of Littleburg, the living of Bexwell, and a prebendal stall in the Cathedral of Ely: he was, besides, steward of all his father's manorial courts, and Chancellor of the diocese. The estimated annual value of the whole, $22,500."

"The Rev. Henry Fardell, the Bishop's son-in-law, held

the living of Waterbeach, the vicarage of Wisbech, and a prebendal stall in Ely Cathedral. The estimated annual value of his preferments $18,500."

"The Rev. Edward Sparke held the consolidated livings of St. May and St. Nicholas, Feltwell, the vicarage of Littleport and a prebendal stall in Ely; he was Register of the diocese and Examining Chaplain to his father. The estimated annual value of his appointments not less than $20,000."

"The Bishop's see of Ely and dependencies—$138,710. Total income of the Sparke family—$199,710."

Quite a comfortable little family arrangement. We shall give Prettyman, Bishop of Winchester, as another instance of this charming system. It could never be objected to him, as will be seen from the following list, that his children were left destitute in the world.

"G. T. PRETTYMAN;
Chancellor and Canon Residentiary of Lincoln;
Prebendary of Winchester;
Rector of St. Giles, Chalfont;
Rector of Wheat-Hampstead;
Rector of Harpendon."

"RICHARD PRETTYMAN;
Precentor and Canon Residentiary of Lincoln;
Rector of Middleton, Stoney;
Rector of Walgrave;
Vicar of Hannington;
Rector of Wroughton."

"JOHN PRETTYMAN;
Prebendary of Lincoln;
Rector of Sherrington;
Rector of Winwick."

The profuse liberality of these Reverend prelates will be properly appreciated, when it is remembered at what sacrifices it was indulged. The oaths that were violated, and the pangs of conscience that were braved, in order to make these hopeful young sons rich, should render the conduct of their pious fathers doubly praiseworthy. It is a man's first duty to provide for his family. The Bishop's "charity has improved on the proverb, and ended where it began." I give these two instances of a practice, universal among the Bishops, of concentrating in the persons of their immediate relations the most valuable livings in the church. How lenient ought we to be to the peccadilloes of the subordinate clergy of a church, whose heads so unhesitatingly violate its most solemn edicts against non-residence and pluralities.

The inequality in the value of the sees is another fruitful source of abuses in the church. It is an ingenious contrivance of the government to support that huge fabric of corruption. Though certain of finding these churchmen the most active enemies to reform, as they have ever been the ablest supporters of oppression, bigotry and persecution, yet unwilling to confide wholly in the power of depraved dispositions, the government has united the interest of the Bishops to their natural proneness to evil, and holds out the promotion to the wealthier sees, as an enticing reward for their treachery to the people, and apostacy to God. A Bishop never feels fixed till he has obtained one of the richer prizes of Canterbury, Winchester, London or Ely. The exciting hopes and fears, the eternal intrigues and worldly coalitions, which must be resorted to in order to run the scale of church preferments, are but little in accordance with the quiet devotion and humility of a devout Christian. The power which the government possesses of translating Bishops from one see to another, makes them the most servile of legislators. Their anxiety to curry court favor, sufficient to promote their ambitious views, unfits them for their secular duties. They and their clergy have always been hostile to the rights of the people; they have always been opposed to progress and reform; and have ever been the zealous supporters of every tyrannical measure, proposed by the government. From the year 1778, when the first tardy step was taken towards the amelioration of English Catholics, to the final passage of the Catholic Relief Bill in 1829, the opposition of the Spiritual Lords was united, and unwavering. From those earliest bills, introduced by Edmund Burke and supported by Mr. Fox, for repealing particular statutes, which chiefly prevented the English Roman Catholics from safely and quietly enjoying their landed property; and those other bills advocated by Mr. Pitt, in which the free exercise of their religion was, to a considerable extent, secured to them, and several penalties and disabilities, under which they had labored, were removed; through all the efforts of Mr. Grattan to obtain for them their elective franchise, and their right to hold seats in Parliament, to the final passage of the Reform Bill, 10th April, 1829, the Bishops were distinguished by the bitterest hostility. A law which increases the social or religious freedom of the people, is as certain to be opposed by the Bishops, as one which confers new rights and greater power on the aristocracy is sure to be supported by them. Their position enables them to do much evil, though their undisguised worldliness deprives them of the power of doing much good in the community. The advantages of wealth and education, which they enjoy, secure for them a dangerous influence in a country where gold is so much worshipped, and education so little known as in England. Their superior intelligence enables the clergy to reconcile the people to the most ruinous measures of oppression, though their evident want of piety makes their religious instruction fall on unheeding ears. They are the servants of the aristocracy, and the representatives of the worldliness, and can therefore have but few feelings in common with the people and devotion. Instead of the most affectionate confidence between the pastor and his flock, there always exists an ill-concealed distrust of each other. There can be no sympathy between them, and therefore no confidence.

When a Bishop's mind is absorbed by the assiduous attentions and servile compliance, with which he must pursue some noble patron, who is to recommend him to the notice of government but few of his thoughts can be reserved for heaven. No man can serve two masters. And when it is remembered with what tenacious fondness the Bishops cling to the emoluments of their offices; when it is remembered with what reluctance they have given even the vaguest information as to the profits of their sees; when we call to mind the frauds in which they have been detected by the commissioners appointed to ascertain the amount of their incomes, it will not be difficult to determine whether God or mammon reigns in their bosoms. The course of the Bishops was as much opposed to the conduct of men of honor as of Christians. Their practices were as dishonest as unholy. In the year 1830, the Archbishop of Canterbury's income was stated by his advocate, Dr. Lushington, to be $160,000. The very next year the return made to the commissioners was, gross $110,000, net $95,910, and on the ground of prospective diminution, it was written down $85,000. Yet during the seven years ending 1843, the Archbishop received, with the knowledge of the commissioners, an average income of $105,000. Such a proceeding on the part of an ordinary individual would have insured his transportation to Botany Bay, but in an Archbishop it passed over without punishment, and almost without comment. But this fraud, stupendous as it seems, is far surpassed in enormity by that practised by the Bishop of London. In 1831 the Bishop's income was given at $69,645. Between that year and 1843 a small city of elegant mansions arose on the Bishop's Paddington estate, calculated to produce in rents to the future Bishops of London $500,000 per annum. During this period this prelate had granted about two thousand leases, and yet his Lordship's income was given in by himself, in the year 1843, at $62,000, which was $7,645 less than it was in 1831, before a stone of the new houses on the property had been laid. Surely a surplice does cover a multitude of sins. A Bishop is evidently a privileged personage in England. "Such are the effects of a State-Church on those, who, before they suffered the moral paralysis of ordination and consecration, were probably men of average virtue and honor."

The Bishops, instead of being distinguished by that zealous independence of spirit which characterized the conduct of John Knox, even in the presence of his sovereign, and which should animate every Christian endued with a proper sense of his duty, are always found the fawning flatterers of power. "Sufferance is the badge of all their tribe." But these aspiring sycophants certainly receive their rewards in this world, and may possibly get their deserts in the next. They seem to be well aware that merit is rarely considered in the distribution of church preferments, and therefore pay their court to nobles with votes and influence to give the government, who are to advance their spiritual interests. From the following list it will be seen how successfully they have exerted their genius for servility. "Lowliness is young ambition's ladder." How many men, from the humble pedagogues to youthful peers, have climbed into being their mitred equals, in the House of Lords. At the same period we find

TOMLINE, Bishop of Winchester, tutor to Pitt.

Bethel, Bishop of Gloucester, tutor to the Duke of Northumberland.

Bloomfield, Bishop of Chester, married into the Harvey family.

Sharpe, Bishop of Ely, tutor to the Duke of Rutland.

Pelham, Bishop of Lincoln, brother to the Earl of Chichester.

Huntingdon, Bishop of Hereford, tutor to Lord Sidmouth.

Howley, Bishop of London, tutor to the Prince of Orange.

Law, Bishop of Bath and Wells, brother to Lord Ellenborough.

To these may be added a list of holy gentlemen who owed their advancement wholly to family interest.

Grey, Bishop of Hereford, brother of Lord Grey.

Poynton, Bishop of Derry, brother-in-law of Lord Grey.

Ryder, Bishop of Lichfield, brother of Lord Harroby.

Bagot, Bishop of Oxford, brother of Lord Bagot.

Vernon, Archbishop of York, brother of the late Lord Vernon.

If the trouble should be taken to examine any other period of church history, the same senseless favoritism or unscrupulous family pride will be found to have caused the advancement of most of the higher ecclesiastics of the land.

It is true that the former unlimited and exorbitant incomes of the Bishops have been restrained by Parliament within established limits; Canterbury and the larger sees being fixed at the moderate sum of $75,000. But when such shameless abuses have been exposed and are daily being brought to light, what assurance can the government give the people that the same disreputable practices do not exist in all the sees? Read the following extract from the London Daily News, made during my visit to England:

OVERPAID BISHOPS.—*Durham.—Salisbury.—Worcester.*—It appears, from a parliamentary paper issued since the dissolution, that in the sixteen years during which the Right Rev. Dr. Maltby has been Bishop of Durham, the net receipts of his episcopal revenues have been £342, 143, and that, during this period, he has paid to the Ecclesiastical Commissioners the sum of £180,127. Deducting, then, the payment from receipts, the Bishop has, it is clear, enjoyed an episcopal income of upwards of £10,000 a-year since the year 1836. But in another parliamentary paper, issued in 1851, may be found the opinion of the law officers of the crown given in 1836—the present Chief Justice of England having been one of them—that "the *distinct object* of the legislature appears to us to have been, that the sum payable *by* the Bishop of Durham should be fixed in the first instance at an amount calculated in the judgment of the Commissioners *to leave him a net revenue of* £8,000, and that this income should remain fixed during his incumbency." Now, this interpretation of the act has never been impeached or doubted by Dr. Maltby. It follows, therefore, that that right reverend prelate has, in the last sixteen years, received from the see of Durham at least £32,000 more than it was "the distinct object of the legislature" he should receive. From the same paper, it appears, that in the first fifteen years' incumbency of the see of Salisbury by Dr. Denison, he has received the net sum of £93,954, or about £6,263 a year. Now, in the Blue Book issued last year, may also be found an opinion given by the present Chief Justice Campbell, Lord Justice Lord Cranworth, and the Judge of the Court of Arches, in which it is stated that, from the plain intent of the legislature, it was competent to the Ecclesiastical Commissioners "to charge the Bishop of Salisbury with a contribution, if it appears that the annual revenue of that see exceeds £5000." In 1837, after this opinion was given, Dr. Denison was skilful enough to induce the Commissioners to come to the opinion that the average income of the see of Salisbury did not exceed £5,500; and therefore the Commissioners did "not think it right to recommend any diminution of it;" whereupon this fortunate prelate "expressed his sense of the Commissioners' attention," and from that day down to the beginning of 1852, has not paid one penny by way of contribution. As, however, in the opinion of the three great and eminent lawyers and judges we have mentioned, his income during those fifteen years ought only to have been £5,000—equal in the aggregate to £60,000—it follows that the excess received by Dr. Denison beyond that handsome amount has, morally and arithmetically, been overpaid him. Now his actual receipts have been £93,959, whereas they ought only to have been £60,000. Clearly, then, on every principle that ought to regulate a Christian, Dr. Denison now stands indebted to the Ecclesiastical Commissioners of England and Wales in the sum of £33,959,—without charging him any interest for the time he has had that amount in his safe keeping. Proceeding from Salisbury to Worcester, we find that Dr. Pepys has been Bishop thereof for nearly 12 years. In the first ten of those years, his net receipts reached £79,418; and of them he paid over to the Ecclesiastical Commission £23,443; leaving him £55,975 for himself. But as the amount of income contemplated by the Act, for the See of Worcester, was only £5,000, or £50,000 in ten years; Dr. Pepys has, it is clear, received £5,975 more than the legislature intended. His duty, under such circumstances, is plain and clear; he ought to make restitution of that balance to the Ecclesiastical Commission. And we make this suggestion, and request that Dr. Maltby should refund the £32,000, Dr. Denison the £33,959, and Dr. Pepys the £5,975, which they have received above their fixed income.

Much relief was to have been afforded the people by the act of parliament, fixing the incomes of the Bishops. Indeed a great hubbub about the reformation of the abuses of Church and State is a periodical occurrence in England. Meetings are held, addresess are made, petitions drawn up, and reform! reform! echoes through the country. Parliament opens with a set speech by some patriotic member, who in touching strains lays the subject before "the House." Resolutions are passed, commissioners are appointed, reports made, and a bill passed, which is altogether to abolish the doomed nuisance. The expectations of the people are naturally high, their rejoicings exulting. The Relief Bill promises every thing; it accomplishes nothing. One-half of the amount, received under the new law by the commissioners, has been generously appropriated to the palaces and estates of the Bishops. The other half is consumed in the repairs of cathedrals and parsonages, and in the salaries of the commissioners themselves, and their swarm of satellites, without whom it would be impossible for any commission to exist in England. How much better would it have been when it was determined not to lessen the burdens of the people, to have appropriated the accumulated fund for the increase of the livings of the poor clergy, instead of squandering it on the Bishops, who not only receive enormous incomes, and have palaces furnished for their convenience, but they must have vast sums for beautifying these palaces, in which they live rent-free. In the eight dioceses given in the list below, which have profited by the commissioners' fund there were 502 benefices worth less than $500 a year, and 85 under $250, whilst many of the Bishops are in the annual receipt of $75,000, with their magnificent palaces, and estates in addition, and there are some rectors whose livings bring them $40,000 and $50,000 per annum. These Bishops are as fatal to the church, as ruinous to the people. They are like the mistletoe, which saps and destroys the tree it seems to adorn.

In 1847 the commissioners had received $1,755,000, of which $715,000 were lavished on the palaces and estates of Bishops in the following proportions:

Lincoln,	$263,520
Rochester,	127,635
Gloucester,	114,485
Ripon,	68,435
Worcester,	35,000
Oxford,	32,345
Exeter,	17,500
Bath and Wells,	20,000

After such an exposition, it seems to me the people would cease to be gulled by these mockeries of reform. By this wonderful Bill of Relief nobody was benefited but the commissioners. The people had the same taxes to pay; and the Bishops were not allowed to dispose of their former incomes as they pleased, but must take part of them in the form of repairs to palaces, and improvements on estates. But such is always the game played by the government when acting in obedience to the cries of "reform." The new statutes merely change the destination of the amounts raised by taxes, instead of removing them altogether. The same oppression continues to exist, but is considerately disguised under a new name. Reform measures are held out as a blind to amuse the people, as the crimson flags in bull-fighting are presented to distract the attention of the bull from the armed man behind.

The Bishops' antipathy to beggars probably arises from professional jealousy. Having discovered the advantages of the pursuit, they are reluctant to have it crowded by too large a number of professors. If these helpless prelates could be tempted to preach at all, it would be to utter a tirade against the vagrants who piteously plead for a penny in the streets; whilst they themselves complacently pocket a couple of hundred thousand dollars, which they have succeeded in begging for beautifying their palaces. The different manner of receiving these two classes of beggars satisfactorily exhibits a strange contradiction in England, which prompts the nation to assist the strong, and abuse the weak. The idolatry displayed in England for every thing like greatness, is amazing. A great scoundrel receives a sympathy which a petty one could never hope to obtain. A mendicant Bishop, with palaces, estates, and a vast income provided for his support, pursues his avocation of begging with honor and success; whilst the starving Lazarus, imploring the crumbs that fall from the rich man's table, is scorned, reviled, and even punished for daring to ask for bread. The rosy, reverend gentleman of the Church, whose magnificent provision should place him above the degradation of alms-asking, is lodged in a palace; but the wretched pauper, who supplicates charity in the form of half-pence, is lodged in the house of correction. One begs from a naturally grovelling disposition, and is rewarded with distinction; the other begs from necessity, and is punished with infamy. The Bishops hate beggars, because they must share with them the mite of public charity, which would otherwise fall undivided to their lot. The fortunate recipients of thousands of pounds in the shape of *charity*, they are too greedy to abandon a few paltry half-pence to the wretches they themselves have assisted to make. In the collection of tithes, what orphan was ever spared, or widow respected? "Woe unto you, Scribes and Pharisees, hypocrites! for ye devour widows' houses, and for a pretence make long prayers: therefore ye shall receive the greater damnation!"

But when we remember the extremes which each worthy Bishop attempts to reconcile in his own disposition, it no longer seems wonderful that he needs the charitable assistance of government, to keep his dwelling in repair. A Bishop would be ostentatious, and at the same time economical; he would fain be lavish and saving, would appear profuse in expenditure whilst he is sordid in practice. I know of no two qualities more difficult to sustain without vast sums of money. A prelate has certainly a most troublesome task to accomplish. To sustain the dignity of the Church he must vie in splendor and parade with his wealthy rivals among the temporal Lords, at the same time that he secures consideration for himself and provides for his family by hoarding an immense fortune. With two objects, so expensive to attain, 'tis not surprising that the Bishops should be destitute of the means of indulging in charity, or repairing their palaces. Gentlemen oppressed by burdens so onerous, and so unusual, as their own dignity and their own family, could scarcely be expected to do any thing so extraordinary as repair their own houses. But difficult as it is for the same individual to maintain the magnificence of an

English prelate and the economy of a prudent father of a family, the Bishops, assisted by the alms of the government, appear to manage it. Sir John Newport stated in Parliament, that three Bishops during the fifteen previous years had died, leaving $3,500,000 each to their families. How little this looks like dispensing their salaries in charity. How poorly it accords with their weekly exhortations—"to lay up treasures in heaven, where rust doth not corrupt, nor thieves break through and steal."

It would be evincing an unbecoming disrespect for the illustrious example of their superiors, if sleek incumbents and sapient deans did not display the same grasping greediness which characterizes the higher dignitaries of the Church. The High Church principle is so happily illustrated in the following extract and table, that I cannot forego the gratification of giving them.

The frauds committed by deans and chapters have recently been shown, at least, to equal in flagrancy, those of which the bishops stand convicted on the evidence adduced before the Ecclesiastical Commission. The property bequeathed to cathedral churches was originally distributed by the donor's will, in certain exact proportions, to the various officers of the cathedral, to grammar boys to be boarded and educated, and to other poor beneficiaries. This proportionate annual distribution was devised in perpetuity, and all deans and chapters to this day bind themselves individually by oaths of awful solemnity, faithfully to perform the duties of their trust. Instead of keeping these oaths, the dean and prebendaries now divide vastly-augmented revenues intrusted to them chiefly among themselves, leaving their weaker and more dependent fellow-beneficiaries profited but slightly, and in many cases not at all, by the enormous increase of the property in which they have a joint interest. This shameless dishonesty will appear from the following table, which shows the original as compared with the present stipend of various cathedral functionaries, in different dioceses. The extension of the table to, at least, twelve of the richest cathedrals, would give a similar result in all—

CANTERBURY.

	1542. £ s. d.	1831 and 1849. £ s. d.
Dean	300 0 0	2,050 0 0
Prebendaries, each . .	40 2 11	1,010 0 0
Minor Canons, each .	10 0 0	80 0 0
Grammar boys, each .	4 0 0	1 8 4
Bedesmen, each . .	6 13 4	6 13 4

ROCHESTER.

	1542. £ s. d.	1840. £ s. d.
Dean	100 0 0	1,426 0 0
Prebendaries, each .	20 0 0	680 19 0
Minor Canons, each .	10 0 0	30 0 0
Grammar boys, each	2 13 4	2 13 4
Bedesmen, each . .	6 13 4	*Nil.*

WORCESTER.

	1542. £ s. d.	1840. £ s. d.
Dean	133 6 8	1,486 0 0
Prebendaries, each .	20 0 0	626 0 0
Minor Canons, each .	10 0 0	36 0 0
Grammar boys, each .	2 13 4	0 5 10
Bedesmen, each . .	5 0 0	5 0 0

ELY.

	1542. £ s. d.	1840. £ s. d.
Dean	120 7 6	1,357 0 0
Prebendaries, each .	20 0 0	632 0 0
Minor Canons, each .	10 0 0	22 10 0
Grammar boys, (24 at)	3 6 8	(7 at) 3 6 8
Bedesmen, each . .	6 13 4	6 13 4

Such is a specimen of the unprincipled rapacity of this branch of the Anglican clergy, and of the corrupting tendency of our State-church system. It is melancholy to reflect, how many men have been hanged within the last forty years for less flagrant delinquencies!

Whenever the friends of freedom and reform had dared to assail the holy monster, its sordid worshippers have never failed to plead its antiquity, as its protection. But can age make abuses tolerable? Can long endurance rob oppression of its sting? This pious horror in Churchmen of disturbing existing forms, has no doubt preserved unaltered the pittance originally doled out to Grammar boys and Bedesmen, though it was not strong enough to retain the same exactness with regard to the salaries of the Deans themselves. If the poor boys, for whose benefit the charities were originally established, are not to be allowed to receive more than their original stipend, the surplus revenues would have been better employed in alms to England's three millions of paupers, than in increasing the salaries of these lazy churchmen, who apparently have more belly than conscience. But it seems that these antiquated forms of the church are only inviolable, when they minister to the selfishness of its votaries. The church itself is only maintained as a convenient and respectable hiding-place, where churchmen may nestle in corruption.

The delegation of political power to the priesthood has always produced, in every country where it has occurred, bigotry in the church and tyranny in the government. It leagues together two powerful accomplices for the oppression of the people. It is destructive to all civil and religious liberty. The clergy are denied by our government all participation in political power; and wisely has it been done. There can be no liberty where there is not freedom of conscience. To restrain the free intercourse between man and man is tyranny. What shall we call the attempt to coerce a man's communion with his God? A man's conscience is too sacred—religion is too holy to be subjected to the control of human institutions. To declare by law the manner in which a man must approach in prayer the throne of his Maker, is sacrilege. It is exalting earthly things above divine.

The unhallowed connection between Church and State,

as unnatural as Pasiphae's amour with the bull, has produced in England a monstrosity, with all the hideousness, and more than the voracity of the Minotaur. What can be more hideous to a pious mind than making a trade of religion? What can be more revolting even to a worldling than the idea of serving God as a shopman serves his customers, for a living? The church, not satisfied with the tithes of England, which are annually offered up like the seven chosen youths of Athens to appease the voracity of the Minotaur, extends her devouring appetites to poor famished Ireland. She greedily gleans amidst the ruins that famine and misrule have made, the tear-stained means to support her bloated opulence. She wrings from misery reluctant contributions, which she only needs to minister to her luxury.

Why is not Scotland too made to contribute to the support of this magnificent establishment? Why is she not called upon to assist in filling the gaping coffers of the English church? Rich and prosperous, she is much better able, it seems to me, to bear such exorbitant demands, than the land of suffering Erin. But no. The holy fathers of the church seem endued with discretion not inferior to their voracity. It is easy work, worthy of unwarlike churchmen, to despoil poor prostrate Ireland; but Scotland has alike the will and the power to resist oppression. Her strength is her protection. With Christian forbearance the Bishops

"Trample on the worm, but pause e'er they wake
The slumbering venom of the folded snake."

In Ireland the natural order of things is reversed. The people exist for the benefit of the government, and not the government for the sake of the people. This unhappy country has ever been regarded as a safe and convenient place to quarter needy court favorites, and useful creatures of the crown. Clergymen take benefices in Ireland as bankrupt noblemen make tours on the continent, to recruit their exhausted finances. Absenteeism is even more fashionable among them than the landlords of the country. The Earl of Bristol, Bishop of Derry, spent twenty years in Italy, and during that time received $1,200,000.

There are in Ireland but half a million of Protestants, yet previous to the passage of the reform bill an establishment of twenty-two Bishops were sumptuously supported, although what all of them pretended to superintend one Bishop in England would do. It is true that the number of high dignitaries in Ireland is now reduced to two Archbishops and twelve Bishops; but what enormous disproportion between the extent of the church establishment, and the number of church members in the two countries! What monstrous injustice!

The value of the ecclesiastical revenue of Ireland was, in 1834, over $7,000,000. There were 3,195 places, divided among 850 persons, giving to each an average of more than $8,000. Thus we have an example of the Established Church in Ireland, claiming, in order to minister to the religious comfort of one-fourteenth of the population, one-tenth of the entire produce of the soil for the support of eight millions of people, in addition to her own vast revenues. Yet England professes to wonder that the people are starving, and the country is depopulated. The attempt to force the Established Church on Ireland has brought misery on a brave nation. What change have centuries of oppression effected in the religious opinions of the country? Ireland now presents the strange scene of tithe-fed clergymen without parishes, parishes without churches, and churches without people. Of her 2,394 parishes, 155 have no church, and not a single Protestant inhabitant, and there are 895 parishes with less than 50 Protestant inhabitants, including men, women and children. But the payment of the pastor is as compulsorily exacted in these parishes as in any others. The following table presents a glimpse of the strange state of things in Ireland.

Parishes.	Members of the State Church.	Tithe Composition.
Kilkalty	13	£400
Ballyhea	15	400
Templeracarigy	27	498
Ballyvourney	30	500
Ardagh	14	600
Whitechurch	20	784
Mogeesha	19	809
Clonfriest	35	869
	173	£4,860 or $24,300

That there is as much difference in the amount of duty as in the pay of the Catholic priesthood and the clergy of the Established Church, I beg leave to call attention to the following facts. In the district of New Erin there are 4,500 Catholics, and 30 Protestants; in Donnes Keath, there are 5,700 Catholics, and 90 Protestants. But, in both these, as in Kilcummin and Tollamore, where there was not a single member of the Established Church, there were four or five clergymen, and but one priest.

It is singular that in a nation professing to be so nervously proper as the English, among a people so nervously tenacious of every imagined right, the present system of appointing clergymen should, for a day, be permitted to prevail. It is the boast of Englishmen that the accused in England enjoy the privilege of being tried by their peers; in legal questions, touching the rights of property, every man is allowed to select his own advocate; in Parliamentary and other elections, every voter can freely exercise the right of suffrage; but in the question of salvation, the people have no voice at all. With regard to life, property and franchise, they have rights, and can maintain them ; but the privilege of selecting their own ministers of religion is denied this self-styled "freest nation upon earth." "What shall it profit a man, if he shall gain the whole world, and lose his own soul?" But the souls of the populace in England weigh but little in the scales against the rights of the aristocracy. Their church-livings are the most profitable portion of their personal possessions. The order must be sustained, though heaven itself be forfeited. For the most ordinary duty men are generally selected whose zeal and whose talents best fit them for its performance. And the reward for its execution should remain in the power of the employers, as a guarantee of good faith on the part of him who undertakes it. These are simple precepts, recognized in the least important of worldly transactions ; but in ministering the holy offices of religion, they are scornfully disregarded. Court favor, family interest, or the sordid disposition of the owner of the living, regulates the appointment of every minister of the Established Church in England. The arrogant proprietor of a benefice presents it to him who fawns most, or pays highest, without the slightest regard to his qualifications. He may be ignorant, immoral, and, in every respect, repulsive to his congregation, but the laws are inexorable : he must not only preside at the desk of the church to which he has been so arbitrarily appointed, but he must be handsomely supported by its members. There is no power of appeal in the people. The unwelcome intruder must continue a life-long burden to any parish on which his wealthy patron has been pleased to impose him. Should such an unwarrantable interference with the pettiest bargains of the people be attempted by the government, it would be denounced in all parts of the kingdom, as a heinous offence against the liberties of the subject. But, as only religion, and not money, is involved in the outrages perpetrated by the owners of church-livings, they not only pass without censure, but without comment. The relative value of salvation and lucre is reversed in Great Britain. Though the aristocracy boldly endanger the first, they have not the moral courage to give up the last. The patronage of church-livings is a very profitable source of revenue. What considerations, then, earthly or divine, could induce its surrender?

The titles which subject church-livings to the same laws of sale and transfer as any other personal property are founded in superstition or corruption, and should not therefore be sustained. Robber Barons, haunted on their death-beds by the fearful memories of a life of bloodshed and crime, had, in making rich bequests to the church, prayed that some favorite might be remembered in the appointment of parish priests. Or intriguing worldings had boldly bargained with unscrupulous monks for the rights of presentation to certain livings in the church, in exchange for land and money, which were far dearer to the priesthood, than the proper administration of religion to the people. The acquired privileges were handed from father to son till the Reformation, when this glaring abuse should have been earliest abolished. But the traffic was too much in accordance with the social principles of the people seriously to offend their religion. The church-livings were still considered *property*, but the titles were piously transferred to the supporters of the new form of religion, and are still acknowledged to the shame of the Established Church of England. The English, with their idolatrous respect for birth, could not be expected to interfere even with abuses made sacred by so holy an origin.

The church-livings continue therefore a fruitful source of corruption in the government, and moral debasement in the people. Of the benefices of England 1301 are assigned to the Bishops, as if purposely to tempt them to make pluralists and non-residents of their relations and favorites, to the great scandal of that church of whose piety and purity they are the responsible representatives: 1048 of them belong to the crown, to be judiciously divided among the properest tools of despotism, who are required to propound doctrines of abject submission and slavish compliance, instead of making the pulpit, as it was during our own glorious revolution, the fountain of liberty as well as religion. The 6,619 livings owned by private individuals are the cause of degradation to their owners, and debasement to the people. The conscience of their proprietors is seared, and their hearts hardened in this fearful traffic of human souls, whilst the moral character of the nation is debased by the appointment of unworthy persons as clergymen, whose example and precepts are to direct their religious aspirations. To complete the list of benefices, 982 belong to Deans and Chapters, and 743 to the Universities. As an example of the manner in which they are divided: the Archbishop of Canterbury alone is patron of 149 livings. The Duke of Beaufort has 26, and the Duke of Devonshire 31 shares in these holy stocks, whilst His Grace of Bedford possesses 32, probably in consideration of his being descended from the *virtuous* Duke of Bedford to whom Junius addressed his famous letter.

Before it is decided by the parents of a boy whether he shall become a lawyer, a physician, an officer in the army, or a member of some useful mechanical trade, it is always determined whether he is qualified for the position. But the dunce of the family, in England is too often made a minister merely because his stupidity unfits him for every thing else, and because his family happens to possess the necessary influence to procure for him this easy mode of making a comfortable living. Piety is the first requisite in a clergyman, but even when accompanied with the most brilliant talents it has but little chance of preferment in the Established

Church of England unless backed by fortune and friends. Genius is altogether unnecessary, and piety is not expected in her ministers. Not the religious instruction of the people but the pockets of the owners are the primary object of the presentations to church-livings.

But the incompetency of the clergy which must inevitably result from this faulty mode of presentation, serious as it is, is not the most monstrous of the abuses to which the system is subject. If those who have livings in their gift would confine themselves to the appointment of incompetent relations and dependants, the church might escape without more serious hurt, than having its sacred offices ministered by silly but inoffensive people. But the venal instincts of the nation prompt the lucky proprietors of these church-livings shamelessly to dispose of them to the highest bidder. Who can wonder that the church is disgraced by improper persons as its ministers? Though Englishmen might deal in all else; though they might sell country, honor and friends, it seems to me that even their hardened hearts ought to be appalled by the thought of making a traffic of religion. They profess to despise those engaged in ordinary commerce, but their delicate natures are not at all shocked by this sacrilegious commerce in the souls of men. The value of the article dealt in probably elevates it in their estimation above the sordid nature of other branches of trade. A banker is more respected than a merchant in England; and I suppose on the same principle a dealer in salvation is deemed a much more honorable sort of personage than a dealer in codfish. How can the people reverence religion with the pious adoration becoming in Christians, when they see its holy offices bartered for, as any other kind of merchandise? With a vicious worldling as their minister is it strange that they should falter in their respect for the church? When they see everywhere the forms, but seek in vain for the spirit of religion, is it not natural that they should learn to think that their duty to heaven was accomplished by going to church? Is it surprising that with them piety should mean a gilded prayer-book, and well-cushioned pew? that religion should consist in kneeling, and charity in loud-uttered responses? Is it remarkable that they should serve God by subscribing for a finer church than their neighbors, and think they obey all the admonitions of heaven in taking the sacrament from a costly service of silver plate?

But when once ordained the ministers of the Established Church of England are fixtures for life. Blackwood's Magazine, the usual advocate of Tory and High Church principles, has candidly confessed that "a clergyman may be destitute of religious feeling; he may be grossly immoral; he may discharge his duties in the most incompetent manner and lose his flock; he may almost do any thing short of legal crime, and still he will neither forfeit his living nor draw upon himself any punishment."

We are assured that every precaution has been taken to suppress the scandalous sale of church-livings. But statutes have been multiplied and solemn oaths have been devised to very little purpose. It requires a cunning contrivance to restrain the avarice of an Englishman. Upon his institution a clergyman is compelled to swear that "he gave not the least consideration whatever either himself, directly or indirectly, nor any person for him with his privity, knowledge or consent." But oaths are not apt to be binding among a people where religion itself is so little respected. The fact of a man's being willing to purchase a living when he must do so in violation of so serious an oath, should be taken as convincing evidence of his being unworthy of the place. But what is his unworthiness to the owner of the benefice, if he pays well for it? It is his anxiety to realize the greatest amount of profit by the transaction, and one man's money is as good as another's.

It frequently happens that all decency in the arrangement is forgotten, and both seller and buyer are present at the bargain But a conscientious gentleman, whose mind, more timid, is still haunted by the spectres of the outward forms of propriety, will square accounts with his conscience by getting a friend to buy the living and present it to him. His own money makes the purchase, but he does not buy the benefice. What a silly contrivance to impose on sensible people! Yet it is sufficient to protect the offender from the rigors of the law. He pockets the fruits of his perjury but whispers to remorse, "Back—back, vile demon! thou canst not say that I did it." Under a system so vicious, men, the most depraved in their tastes and debauched in their habits, may become ministers of God's holy word. They have only to pay the price and swear that they did not pay it. And when we remember how sure, how profitable, and how respectable an investment a living in the church is, it is not at all remarkable that such disreputable members of society should be eager to become purchasers. It seems to me that prayers uttered by their vile breath could not ascend to heaven, but would hang over their congregations like a cloud between them and the glory of their Maker. This is not one of the Legendary abuses of the High Church system that modern progress and reform have long since corrected. This is not one of those crying sins which only exist now in memories of brawling dissenters and discontented radicals. It is an affair of every-day occurrence. Church-livings are as regularly advertised for sale in the public prints with a florid parade of their advantages, as we would advertise farms with their convenient appurtenances. In support of what I declare, I give the following extract from the London Times made during my recent visit to England.

Traffic in Advowsons.—We have received the following letter on this subject from "S. G. O." (the Rev. Mr. Osborn):—

Sir—your paper of August 5, contains an advertisement headed "Next Presentation to a valuable Living in Dorsetshire," "a most highly desirable living," situation "salubrious," "annual value upwards of £700 per annum, with a capital residence, garden and pleasure-grounds most tastefully laid out," "population 1000," *present incumbent* 80 *years of age.*" I must add to the above description, there are two churches, two dissenting places of worship, two resident Roman Catholic priests, and a very large nunnery. You have now before you the parish of Spetisbury-cum-Charlton. To any one with money to invest in a cure of souls, can a more tempting speculation be offered? By the bye, the advertisement adds, "the rent-charge is easily collected." I must, however, protest against the course which has been pursued to obtain grounds for this amount of temptation—*i. e.*, the putting in, a very short time since, the old man of 80, who for many years past, on his own petition to the bishop, was declared incapable of performing duty, had a dispensation from residence on his then living, and was not instituted to this living with the least expectation that he would reside on it. The patron, wise in his generation, has done the best the law allows him to do to make the article suddenly thrown on his hands of the utmost salable value; the Church, to her shame, has *per fas aut nefas* become a party consenting to the transaction. We have been lately cited with all due solemnity to the solemn (?) work of sending proctors to Convocation. I was not able to attend; had I done so—had I proposed the Rev. Mr. Baskett, the octogenarian incumbent of Spetisbury-cum-Charlton, on the grounds that he had been just instituted by my diocesan to one of the most important cures in the diocese, and therefore I had a right to presume had not only an experience from his age few possess, but also this recent public testimonial to his worth as a parochial minister—would any one member of that solemn conclave have ventured on the indecency of saying, "Sir, Mr. B. was appointed to this important cure not for his capacity, but being incapable; he was not chosen because his age gave him experience, but because 80 years of age in an advertisement, as the age of the present incumbent, makes the living more valuable in the market; he was too infirm to reside on his last living—he has no intention of residing on this one." From the presiding archdeacon to the apparitor in waiting the idea would have been scouted, and yet—so it is.

From the following advertisment of a church-living it might be reasonably supposed that there was an occasional Nimrod among the holy fathers of the church.

To be sold, the next presentation to a vicarage, in one of the midland counties, and in the immediate neighborhood of one or two of the *first packs of fox-hounds* in the kingdom. The present annual income about £580, subject to curate's salary. The incumbent in his 60th year.

Yet the pious gentlemen for whose avarice these advertisements are intended as a bait, are asked at their ordination, "whether they feel themselves moved by the Holy Ghost to take upon them the sacred office of the ministry?" Their answers are of course in the affirmative. But who can doubt that the emoluments of the living, and not the "Holy Ghost," had moved the zealous candidate for church-preferment? It would be sacrilege to treat the more serious concerns of human life with such solemn mockery, but the language has no term properly to describe the profanity of subjecting religion to such impious practices.

The Bishops are surrounded by a swarm of Deans, Archdeacons, Prebendaries, Chancellors, Commissaries, Surrogates, Registrars, Proctors, Apparitors, &c. &c., to the end of a long list, the only apparent object of whose maintenance at an enormous annual expense is to increase the pomp, and expose the follies of the Established Church. Cranmer has justly described them as "good vianders too much given to belly cheer." The Deans and Chapters nominally elect the Bishops. This is the most miserable of all bad farces. The Bishops are really appointed by the crown, and the Deans and Chapters hurry through a form of forced ratification. For this important duty they enjoy an income of about $2,500,000. But useless as these crowds of sinecures appear, it is evident to the close observer that their numbers, the absence of all duty, and the large salaries, make them eagerly sought by the younger sons and poor relations of nobles; they are essential to the prime object of government, the preservation of the order of nobility. They materially increase the number of lazy situations, with fat wages, adapted to the tastes and indolence of the younger sprigs of nobility who are habitually quartered on the people.

The Established Church is a double curse to the people of England. It assails their freedom and interferes with their religious instruction. The vast revenues of the church are monopolized by the Bishops, dignitaries, and aristocratic pluralists, whilst the curates, the real ministers to the religious wants of the people, are starving upon the miserable pittances doled out to them by their rich patrons. At a particular epoch in the history of the church there was one individual who united in his own person eleven livings. But here is a list of the pluralists.

Number of Individuals.	Livings held by each.
1	11
1	8
5	7
12	6
64	5
209	4
567	3
2027	2

Yet it was a violation alike of law and the canons of the church that any minister should hold more than *one* living. The outrage would be less flagrant if this "simony" was tolerated in order to relieve the holders of the poorer livings from almost penury by conferring several of them on one minister. But those places which are most greedily pounced upon by the aristocratic pluralists and non-residents are the richest benefices in the church, some of them being worth forty or fifty thousand dollars a year. Every pluralist must be a non-resident in some of his benefices, and the majority of them enjoy the profits of several livings without residing in any of them. Indeed it is their intention to accumulate the incomes of as many valuable livings as will enable them to leave their parishes and dash and dissipate in the fashionable circles of the metropolis. The nation are thus not only burdened with their enormous salaries, but are by them deprived of the advantages they might enjoy from their ministers not being rich enough to live much abroad. As an evidence that the English sense of right is not wholly dead with regard to the monstrous abuses of the church, I append the following extracts from the comments of the Times of August last on Mr. Robert Moore, who in his own person united the rich livings of Hunton, Latchington, Eynesford, and Hollingsbourne, besides a cathedral stall, and the principal registrarship of Doctors Commons.

A great deal, as might have been expected, has been written and said of the Rev. ROBERT MOORE and his emoluments. The discovery or rather the public announcement, that in the middle of this 19th century there still existed an individual possessing in private fee a sinecure office worth 9,000*l.* a year, a rectory worth 1000*l.*, a second rectory worth another 1000*l.*, a third producing 600*l.*, a fourth 150*l.*, and a cathedral stall of the most desirable fertility to boot, was an incident well calculated to arrest the attention of the public. Such visions are monsters of the old moral world, and are gazed upon like the gigantic fossils of a past creation. Mr. Moore, however, is pained at his own attractions, and feels hurt, as he expressed to ourselves, at the reflection that he "should have been held up more than others similarly circumstanced to public odium, and made the subject of misrepresentation and exaggeration." Now, though our first considerations are due to the inter ests of the community at large, we should but ill discharge our office if we rendered less than justice to any individual. Once more, therefore, with a confident expectation that we shall carry with us the opinions of the public, and with some hopes of extorting the assent even of Mr. Moore himself, we submit his case to a fair and comprehensive review.

The Times appears not so much surprised by the existence of so outrageous an abuse, as by its "public announcement." That the case should have been brought before the public does seem strange indeed, when so much pains is ordinarily taken to conceal the peculations of Church and State.

When the fact is notorious that the poor clergy and the curates perform all the clerical labors of the Established Church, what object is attained by supporting these wealthy pluralists who do no duty at all, unless it is to oppress the people and sustain the fictitious superiority of the aristocracy? This, however, is one of the worthy aims of the British government. If every congregation were permitted to select from free choice its own minister and compensate him with a reasonable salary, such clergymen only would officiate whose piety, whose talents, and the correctness of whose lives eminently fitted them for so responsible a position. Worldly and worthless characters would be no longer tempted by excessive pay to enter upon duties so holy and so little congenial to their dispositions. The people would be freed from the present crushing weight of the Church, and have their religious ceremonies performed by sincere and zealous Christians. Pluralists and non-residents would be unknown in the Church, for pious and not sordid considerations would then influence men to take holy orders. The people would be improved by the unaffected devotion of their pastors, instead of being corrupted by seeing how little regard for heaven they have, who have been called to preach it.

The High Church system is unjust and oppressive to its own members, but is cruel in the extreme to unfortunate dissenters. It impoverishes them by compelling them to contribute to its own support in addition to sustaining their own clergymen; and it outrages the pious feelings of conscientious Christians by forcing them to contribute to the maintenance of a form of religion which their hearts condemn as wrong. The dissenters of England form no inconsiderable remnant of the population whose voice is naturally lost amidst the joyful songs of the large majority. The government discourages every attempt to ascertain their true strength and respectability, and affects to regard and treat them as an obscure faction, the smallness of whose numbers renders them unworthy of being listened to when they complain. But those who have had an opportunity of judging them "by their works" must feel convinced, that if they are not more numerous they are much more active than the clergy and members of the Established Church. But take the county of Lancashire, from which returns have been made. It was found that there were 590 dissenting churches and 255,411 sectarians. There were 281 places of worship according to the Established Church, and the entire population of the county was 1,052,859 persons. Those who were numbered among the sectarians must of course have been active members of some congregation, whilst the census of the country included people of all ages and conditions; this could not therefore present a fair proportion between the churches. But a reasonable calculation would enable us to conclude, that under this iniquitous system nearly one-half of the people were taxed to build churches they never entered, and to support ministers they never heard. The number too of dissenters is daily increasing. Zeal and sincerity must eventually overcome formal hypocrisy. But even, when the religious opinions of the nation are wholly reformed, the wealth and selfishness of the stubborn aristocracy will still remain an insurmountable barrier to reformation in church government.

I have attempted to describe the results from the sordid system [illegible]le, prevailing among the pious proprietors of church[illegible]s. I shall give but one example of the abuses of [illegible]h favoritism, in the presentation to livings, is capable. It was the original intention of Cranmer, in his code, which the death of Edward VI. prevented from passing into a law, that bastards should "not be admitted to orders, or livings as a consequence, unless they had eminent qualities." "But the bastards of patrons were, *on no account*, to be inducted into preferments, if presented to them by their presumed parents." Had this provision taken effect, it would have been somewhat unfortunate for the Rev. Lord Augustus Fitzclarence, the natural son of William IV. by Mrs. Jordan, who has, since 1829, been the rector of Mapleduram, and is the private chaplain of Her Majesty Queen Victoria. His Reverend Lordship happily illustrates, in his own preferment, the rather loose code of morals acknowledged by the Church, as his only possible claim upon her munificence rests on the fact of his parents having outraged her most sacred rite. But the absurd superstition that "the king can do no wrong" may be incorporated in the religion, as well as the constitution of England, for aught I know; and there may be no particular indecency in rewarding the profligate bastard of a profligate king with the holy office of minister of God's word. Those who will call to mind the chaste vindictiveness with which Queen Victoria prosecuted the Lady Flora Hastings affair, must be somewhat surprised at the intimate spiritual relations which exist between Her Majesty and this reverend individual, merely because he chances to be the result of a caprice of a royal personage for an actress. But one might infer that Her Majesty entertained quite an affection for her accidental relations, as another of the Fitzclarences enjoys the honor of commanding the royal yacht.

But the legion of church abuses, which now make the wicked scoff and the pious grieve, must conti[illegible]o curse Great Britain, whilst money is regarded as th[illegible] blessing by the nation. Religion must always suffer u[illegible]sad disadvantages, when compelled to contend with avarice in the heart of an Englishman. Whilst the aristocracy have benefices to sell, and younger sons to provide for, the church will be retained as a cloak for their dishonorable practices.

CHAPTER XII.

HERALDRY.

THE mysterious mummery of Heraldry is one of those farcical superstitions, still tenderly cherished by the British aristocracy. The whole power of the English government is exerted to make this venerable absurdity respectable. A mighty nation unites in pronouncing its pedantic nonsense the wisdom of an oracle.

A college of thirteen persons is maintained, at the expense of the government, to practise this sacred hocus-pocus for the satisfaction of its subjects. Each member of this learned institution must graduate in gibberish, and a man must possess sheepskin authority for indulging in Heraldic slang. The highest importance is attached to the edicts of the Heralds. Their simplest fiat becomes supreme law. No court of justice can change, nor can the sovereign himself, modify their decisions. All classes look up to them with equal veneration. The low-born regard them with awe, for it is from their college that must issue every testimonial of gentility acknowledged in the kingdom. And they wield over the nobility, as keepers of their pedigrees, that sort of influence which a father confessor obtains over a man, in becoming keeper of his conscience.

The college has retained, with its defunct technicalities and outlandish phrases, something of the barbaric magnificence of chivalry. The three kings-at-arms, with their four

Heralds and six Pursuivants, still play a conspicuous part in all court ceremonies and state shows. Arrayed in the gorgeous costumes of their order, stiff with gold lace, and bedizened by the grotesque symbols of their science, they assume the stately strut, as well as the grandiloquent language, of the middle ages. And yet the multitude seem to discover nothing ludicrous about this masquerade of exploded fashions, in which the Heralds must perform the solemn farce allotted to them.

They profess to cling with fond tenacity to Heraldry, as a lingering remnant of chivalry. I delight in the days of love and lances; I love to dwell on the heroism and high-toned honor of the devoted knights. Embalmed in all the poetry of its nature, the tales of chivalry have always exercised over me a witching fascination, that no other portion of history possessed. The souls that could melt to tenderness in silent adoration of a ribbon, or a glove, and yet boldly break lances in the name of the fair givers of these holy relics, have always commanded my highest admiration. Devotion to a woman is the only feeling which does not become absurd when indulged to excess. But chivalry only lives when surrounded by the atmosphere of fancy. As the beauteous moth, which has existed for ages imbedded in amber, sickens and dies when its sparkling prison is broken, so the romantic deeds of chivalry become ridiculous when removed from the bright realms of imagination.

What a storm of derision would assail any modern Don Quixote, who would insert his head in an iron kettle, and wander about the country with sixty or a hundred pounds of pot-metal on his back, merely for the fun of bloody noses and broken heads. In these modern days of utilitarian doctrines, a broken head, in whatever cause it may have been acquired, is considered any thing but ornamental. And a dinner-pot is believed to be a much more appropriate receptacle of a Westphalia ham, than the cracked pate of its romantic owner. A man would justly be deemed a fool to risk his neck for a smile of his lady-love, in the noise, dust and discomfort of a tournament, when he might convince her of his unshaken devotion with so much less trouble. A lover will quaff several glasses of champagne to the health of his mistress, who has decorated his button-hole with the satin ribbon from her shoe, but he could scarcely be expected by the exacting damsel herself to shed a single drop of his blood, in appreciation of the honor. Why then, when the most beautiful portions of this romantic code appear so absurd when applied to modern actions, should a barbarous folly connected with it be retained, which chivalry itself only tolerated because it was necessary? For then the mailed hands of the thick-skulled Barons were much more cunning in the use of a lance than a pen, and their signet-rings, adorned with their peculiar coat of arms, were indispensable in signing important documents and holding secret communion with distant friends. But thanks to the enterprising efforts of the Dominie Samsons of England, the Nobility can now indite a scrawl, recognizable in the courts of law as their legal signatures, and raging bears and rampant lions have ceased to be necessary to represent the sign-manual of these respectable gentlemen.

Tilting is both dangerous and laborious. Platonic attachments have been found, upon experiment, a bore; and the English gentry have something else to do, besides wander about the country seeking whom they may devour. The romantic portion of Knight-errantry has been unanimously voted a nuisance, but Heraldry is retained to exalt the nation's vanity at the expense of its common sense. The aristocracy require the College of Heralds to assay the old nobility before declaring its worth, and by stamping the new, to give it currency. Although they themselves must feel that the coin is spurious, yet so long as the whole nation continue weak enough to receive it as genuine, they will, from feelings of self-interest, do all in their power to promote its circulation.

The fact of the Heralds' College being "incorporated and invested with many privileges and immunities," by the third Richard, forms a somewhat remarkable coincidence with the arbitrary exercise of authority by that institution. But though founded and professedly sustained to preserve intact the precious superiority of noble blood, over all other less pure sources; although its chief duty is to treasure those noble and generous qualities in which the nobility are said to excel, yet it happens, strangely enough, to furnish the most indubitable evidence of the omnipotence of money in Great Britain.

With regard to all "scutcheons of honor or pretence," the Heralds are absolute. They provide appropriate genealogies for newly created peers. They decide, without appeal, who is genteel. They furnish *for a compensation* ancestors and coats of arms to rich *parvenues*, whose families have hitherto been unfortunately innocent of such expensive appendages. In reference to all these matters no man dares question their decisions. "But the evidence of Heralds to support pedigrees is not received in courts of justice." Thus we see this sordid nation unhesitatingly trusting their noble titles, and what ought to be dearer than all titles of distinction, their honor, to the keeping of these bombastic numskulls, but when their fiats happen to involve something more substantial than the confirmation of a new title, or the arrangement of an imaginary line of ancestors, they are altogether disregarded. Their evidence is not received in courts of justice. The nobility deem the Heralds good enough guardians of titles, but their Lordships prefer taking care of their *purses* themselves. The shallowest researches of the College can legally enrich a man in all sorts of ancestral glory, but their most laborëd efforts, in establishing his descent, cannot confer upon him an acre of land. Its pedantic certificate may give or take away gentility, but its most solemn oath in a court of justice cannot interfere with the sacred inviolability of *cash*. This is something too precious to be tampered with by such empirics as the Heralds. An Englishman esteems his honor of so little value himself, that he is not at all apprehensive of being robbed of it by a neighbor. It may therefore be safely intrusted to a Herald. But money is of so delicate, so evanescent a nature, is so highly prized and eagerly sought for, that it is believed dangerous to confide it to such unscrupulous guardians as the College of Heralds. When questions of money are agitated, all the learning and experience of the most learned professors of the law are called in, though the Heraldic College is thought adequate to determining the doubtful quality of a man's blood. Perhaps the nation are right for being a little skittish of the most venerable college. The initiated are too familiar with the ready means of procuring for wealthy clients Heraldic evidence of, I care not what, willingly to confide to their decision so important a portion of themselves as their purses.

It is well known that any man is entitled to the Heraldic distinction of a coat of arms who can afford to live without occupation and to pay liberally for the honor. The king at arms may at any time create a *gentleman* by granting a crest. Indeed the Heralds' College may be described as a wholesale manufactory of gentlemen. Masses as incongruous as the contents of a *chiffonier's* rag-basket at Paris, may be thrown into the extraordinary Heraldic machine, and yet nothing but gentlemen are turned out, just as paper is produced from all sorts of rags. Gold is the principal ingredient used in this magical process. It is found to be an acid sufficiently powerful to reduce materials however rude and vulgar to the proper consistency for the manufacture of gentlemen. But unfortunately for the success of the makers the genuine article is so readily counterfeited that they are compelled to pin a label, in the shape of a coat of arms, on each gentleman's back, as the maker's name is pasted on a vial of Jule's hair tonic, to prevent impositions on the unsuspecting public.

If there be any thing really contaminating about industrial pursuits, it is worse than folly to pretend that the Queen, assisted by her Heralds, can remove the pollution. If there be any thing disreputable about the manufacture of soap, or the brewing of beer, what must we think of the understandings of people who profess to believe that the Queen, by pronouncing a few words of Heraldic jargon, and touching a shoulder with a sword, can miraculously purify blood which has been for centuries thickened by soft soap, or cleanse veins that have been for ages muddied by stale beer? The candidate for gentility, after passing through the hands of the Queen, is subjected to the legerdemain of the chief Herald, who gabbles some mysterious incantation, and, *presto*, the impure sources of his blood are magically made worthy to mingle with the Helicon streams of the aristocracy. Previous to this juggling lustration, the gentlemen of England would have felt contaminated by any association, however formal, with the vulgar tradesman; but the instant he has his card of variegated hieroglyphics hung about his neck by the Heralds, he is deemed no longer an improper companion for the aristocracy. If our transmuted brewer be ambitious of ancestral honors, he can be readily provided by the Heraldic College with a line of doughty forefathers, whose extent shall be warranted to bear a mathematical proportion to the length of his purse. If he is unfortunately troubled with some not very euphonic appellation, a sufficient outlay in the same quarter will readily relieve him of the incumbrance. Any name can be metamorphosed to suit any taste, whether it inclines to the heroic or the sentimental. Hodges, for instance, by an ingenious transposition and alteration of letters by the Heralds, may be changed into Hengist and Horsa; and the various corruptions by which the originally heroic name has degenerated into plebeian *Hodges* will be so minutely traced, and satisfactorily established, that no reasonable man can longer entertain a doubt that our plain Hodges is a veritable descendant from one of the northern demigods.

It is strange that the nation should continue to hearken to the senseless prate of the Heralds, when they are aware how easily wealth may procure its advantages. Vast revenues, judiciously invested, may not only ennoble their possessor, but procure for him, if desirable, new name, ancestors and position. The Heraldic College is certainly an inestimable blessing to the upstart wealth of Great Britain, since, by its alchemy, the sordid gains of a vulgar tradesman can be transformed into ample possessions of a proud noble. But, in providing an aspirant with pedigree and coat of arms, all metaphorical allusions even to the past pursuits of the new-made gentleman are studiously avoided. This is an egregious fault. The arms of the fresh aristocrat should possess some allegorical connection at least with his manner of acquiring money enough to purchase his distinction.

For an enriched and lately ennobled soapmaker, for instance, I would beg to suggest something like the following as an appropriate coat of arms: *Party per nebulé or* and *vert*. In the *sinister base* a huge caldron, *gules* and *azure*. At the *honor point*, an ass *rampant-regardant*, *attired* with bouquet and ribbons of azure. In the *dexter base*, a small patch of *trefoil*, having in its midst five peacocks *in full pride*. There's a touch of Heraldry for you! Looks knowing, does it not? But why display my treasured lore in this ancient and profound science, when nine-tenths of my democratic readers could not understand me if they would, and the other tenth wouldn't if they could; and yet I feel as much tickled by my self-concocted coat of arms as a child with a new drum, and, like the noisy urchin who drums everybody out of the house to convince them of the reality of the possession, I am going to incur the danger of being very absurd in order to show the genuineness of my pet patent in Heraldry. I know it is very stupid to explain a joke, and extremely pedantic to make a great display of knowing a little; but, as I am temporarily discoursing of asses and Englishmen, think I am excusable for indulging in a little folly and considerable ostentation. So ye learned and uninitiated, have at ye all: here goes. When *we* Heralds speak of *party per nebulé or* and *vert*, we intend to convey the idea of the field of the escutcheon being divided into two parts, by a wavy, irregular sort of line; one side is colored, or gold; the other *vert*, or green. The gold alludes to the riches of the new-made knight, and the green to the refreshing verdancy of every thing aristocratic. The *sinister* base is the left-hand corner of the shield; and the mammoth caldron, which occupies the identical corner of our coat of arms, is intended vaguely to intimate the origin of our ennobled soapmaker. *Gules and azure* mean red and blue, the colors the big kettle was painted, indicative of the fancy tendency of the manufacturer's notions as he grew rich. The *honor point* is a position in the upper portion of the dividing line. The ass *rampant-regardant*, is an ass mounted on his hind legs and complacently looking back at his tail, which appendage, in the case of our animal, is appropriately decorated with bouquet and blue ribbons, although somewhat singed and drooping on account of the recent exodus from the soap-boiler. Of course this principal figure on our escutcheon allegorically represents the plump citizen himself. The zig-zag lines above alluded to form the ladder by which the lucky ass has climbed from his humble beginning, through the medium of his wealth, to his present exalted position. From this happy half-way place, this highest point in the hedge, which excludes him from the Elysian fields of his aristocratic neighbors on the other side, he exultingly snuffs his coming triumphs, and brays an indignant adieu to all recollections of the past. It is scarcely necessary to explain that the patch of *trefoil* is nothing more than our common clover, and that the five peacocks *in full pride* are the five orders of nobility puffed up to the utmost extent of pomposity. In short, this *dexter* portion of our escutcheon is intended to intimate that our supremely happy ass, being let down from his dizzy elevation, will soon roll in clover with his noble betters.

The enormous profits of soap-making render it a favorite road to the peerage. Whether the English are the cleanest or the dirtiest people in the world does not appear from history, but certain it is that the consumption of soap in that country has been very extraordinary since its being first made in Bristol in 1524. Its lucrative advantages have tempted kings to become monopolists in this branch of trade, and many a greasy manufacturer has snugly floated down the sluggish but certain stream of soft soap into an aristocratic harbor. Indeed there is no one person or class to whom the nobility are so much indebted for increase as the soap-makers, if we except Charles II. and the brewers. Had the city fathers congratulated the merry monarch on being the father of the nobility, instead of the people, Rochester's reply would have been as true as it was witty, when he said there was no doubt of his being the father of a good many of them. For five of the twenty-two Dukes of England owe their titles to being direct descendants of the illegitimate children of Charles II. by his mistresses. But the soap-makers and brewers are the compounders of the great staple commodities of consumption in Great Britain, and therefore surpass even Charles himself in the number of their additions to the peerage.

It is with the sincerest regret that I see a growing disposition in my countrymen to rig themselves out in this cast-off tinsel finery in which the Heralds of England are authorized to array Englishmen. It is with the deepest mortification that I remember how eager Mr. Smith and Mr. Jones are on arriving in England to rush to some antiquarian bookstore, and, searching through the ponderous folios of Heraldry for the numerous families of Smiths and Joneses, to select that coat of arms which they think will look best on a carriage door, and adopt it as their own. I do not mean to blame them for consulting *the becoming* in their selections, more especially as they have about as much right to one crest as another. I am forced to confess that to see an honest Republican tricked out in the Heraldic motley, that aristocratic fools of Great Britain cut their antics in, is to me eminently ridiculous and disgusting. I could join, with heart and soul, the English press in lashing to threadbare confusion the absurdity of this harlequin masquerade. It evinces a weakness of character unworthy of American manhood.

Heraldry is absurd even in England; but still it is a legalized absurdity. They have a formula of folly, and have reduced nonsense to a science. The edicts of the Heralds' College are as solemn and as serious as any other legal proceedings, and their decisions are as binding as those of the courts of law. But here we have no such mummery. Coats of arms are not legally established, and there is no institution to give them validity. Every Smith and every Jones can select the style of arms most suited to their fancy from the numerous families of their names in England. The jackdaw in his borrowed plumes would be imposing compared with Smith strutting in those he has stolen. Where is the legal record in this country to determine which branch of the Smiths he is descended from? Even though such records might originally have been carefully preserved, they must have perished from ceasing to be useful, after the Revolution had made such things contemptible. He would have been a bold man to brave the storm of derision that must have assailed any individual boasting of being descended from a particular branch of the Smiths, because they happened to be richer than the rest; such miserable vanity, was opposed to the genius of the new-made Republic, and was not to be tolerated. A man would scarcely have incurred the scorn of his countrymen for the solitary gratification of a coat of arms. In abolishing titles our forefathers rightly abolished their trashy appendages. But if coats of arms be essential to our happiness and respectability, let us revive titles, and establish a Heralds' College of our own, not meanly pilfer gentility in pinches from England's scanty store. The nice young man who is guilty of such petty larceny should be smothered in a bandbox of musk, as the only punishment worthy of such a deed.

There is also an increasing anxiety, in our upper circles, as to what a man does—and who his father was. Provided his pursuit and his parents be *honest*, the man should be allowed to speak for himself. His possessing the manners and cultivation of a gentleman, and the means to support the appearance of one, should be a sufficient passport into any society, if there be nothing disreputable connected with him. The position of his father should no more be regarded as an apology for the blackguardism of the son, than the obscurity of that parent should interfere with his advancement. More honor is due the man who attains distinction in defiance of the obstacles of "low birth and iron fortune."

It is the man who ennobles the occupation, and not the occupation that ennobles the man. It is worse than ridiculous to exclude a man of intellect and acquirements from the higher circles of society because his father was a mechanic, or because he has been one himself. It is absurd to attempt to determine inexorably what occupations shall or shall not be admitted into society. Such things regulate themselves as naturally as water seeks a level. Men are unwilling to expose their own deficiencies by intruding into circles where they must suffer from contrast. And people are not going to force themselves into assemblies where the coarseness of their manners or dress would attract general observation. They could not be coaxed into such positions, and it therefore becomes unnecessary to pass laws for their exclusion. There is a decided inclination in many portions of our country to attach undue importance to the "learned professions," without regard to the individual qualifications of their members. And those professional gentlemen are most inclined to presume upon this importance whose claims are smallest. I have often felt amused by the airs of superiority which very young lawyers and doctors are inclined to assume. Although both professions are somewhat too much given to this sort of thing, it is especially observable in provincial "members of the bar." The time required by most men for familiarizing themselves with the technicalities and legal obscurities with which lawyer-legislators have for venal purposes loaded the statutes of every country, is not greater than for learning successfully to cobble a worn pair of shoes. And yet there are ignoramuses preposterous enough to arrogate to themselves the infallibility of so many Daniels, merely because they have memorized the leading precepts of Blackstone. They seem to forget that their great authority, invaluable in his way, does not necessarily impart a knowledge of English literature; that because they are able to nose out a flaw in an indictment and cheat justice with her own tricks, is no absolute reason for their having a discriminating taste in the fine arts—yet in their eyes to be a lawyer is to be all that is desirable. Ridiculous as such claims must appear to all sensible people, they yield in folly to the weakness of those who are deluded into the belief that there is more in them than bombast; and who stubbornly persist in the belief that all lawyers must be oracles, and that all other people must be fools.

Young lawyers and doctors appear principally to base their pretensions upon a contemptible piece of tin, eighteen inches by six, which bears the curious inscription of "John Smith, attorney-at-law," or "Dr. John Jones." Yet it is really quite amazing, what a superstructure of arrogant assumption some of these learned gentlemen succeed in building upon so insignificant a foundation; and I am sorry to find so decided a disposition in some of our Southwestern States, to humor such absurd presumption. In the incomprehensible technicalities of the law, in the Latinized jargon of prescriptions, in drug-mixing and pill-rolling, I am free to acknowledge that the learned professions far excel the less enlightened portion of their countrymen. But, by what process they are presumed to monopolize *all* the cultivation and intellect of the country, continues one of those mysteries which fashionable calculations only can solve. So long as humanity is afflicted with such curses as lawsuits and sore shins, lawyers and doctors must be considered eminently useful members of society. But I am unwilling to concede that a man must necessarily be destitute of all taste and refinement, because he happens not to be familiar with the operation of pounding a mortar, or writing a deed.

It is a fact, of which the legal profession may be justly proud, that almost all of our greatest statesmen have commenced their career as lawyers. I acknowledge that the application to books, which is essential to their success as lawyers, often excites that love of general reading, which almost always produces an elegantly-cultivated mind. But, because an aspiring upstart has in his pocket a sheepskin permission to nonsuit his clients, that he must, in consequence, have a refined taste and brilliant intellect, is much more ridiculous in us to acknowledge, than for him to assert. But this is one of the hallucinations peculiar to new states, which time and more extended observation never fail to correct. Attaching such importance to mere pursuits is too much like the senseless respect of the English for birth. Because a man is a lawyer or doctor, is no better reason for his being an elegant and well-read gentleman, than for a descendant of the Duke of Marlborough being a hero.

Our republican institutions demand that *the man*, without regard to his father or his profession, should speak for himself. If he be deficient in mind or manners, a distinguished father or a learned profession ought not to save him from neglect; as humble birth and lowly pursuit ought not to hamper genius.

AN EXPLANATION.

The Church and State are as closely connected in abuses as in law. After reading of one, a person naturally looks for the other. I had most certainly intended to devote a considerable portion of my book to the corruptions under the British Government, but, in approaching them, I find I am unable to treat them with the attention they so richly deserve, and therefore prefer to omit them altogether, rather than to review them hastily. They are as numerous as startling, and would require a small book to expose them. But I cannot forego the hope of referring more fully at some future time to these outrages perpetrated by the State. My readers have a right, I confess, to expect some exposition here, and nothing but the want of space prevents my doing so. None but those intimately acquainted with their extent can realize the difficulty of compressing them into a chapter.

THE END.

Novels, Tales, &c.

AGUILAR, G.—A MOTHER'S RECOMPENSE. 12mo., paper, 50c.; cloth, 75c.

——— WOMEN OF ISRAEL. Two vols. 12mo., paper, $1; cloth, $1 50c.

——— VALE OF CEDARS. 12mo., cloth, 75c.; paper, 50c.

——— WOMAN'S FRIENDSHIP, cloth, 75c.; paper, 50c.

ADRIAN; OR, THE CLOUDS OF THE MIND. By G. P. R. James and M. B. Field. 12mo., cloth, $1.

CORBOULD'S HISTORY AND ADVENTURES OF MARGARET CATCHPOLE. 8vo., 2 plates, paper cover, 25c.

DUMAS' MARGUERITE DE VALOIS. A Novel. 8vo., 25c.

DUPUY, A. E.—THE CONSPIRATOR. 12mo., cloth, 75c.; paper, 50c.

ELLEN PARRY; OR, TRIALS OF THE HEART. 12mo., 63c.; paper, 38c.

ELLEN MIDDLETON. A Tale by Lady Fullerton. 12mo., paper, 50c.; cloth, 75c.

HEARTS UNVEILED; OR, "I KNEW YOU WOULD LIKE HIM." By Mrs. Saymore. 12mo., paper, 50c.; cloth, 75c.

HOME IS HOME; A DOMESTIC STORY. 12mo., paper, 50c.; cloth, 75c.

HELOISE; OR, THE UNREVEALED SECRET. By Talvi. 12mo., cloth, 75c.; paper, 50c.

HOWITT, MARY.—THE HEIR OF WAST WAYLAND. 12mo., paper, 38c.; cloth, 50c.

IO; A TALE OF THE ANCIENT FANE. By Barton. 12mo., 75c.

JAMES MONTJOY; OR, I'VE BEEN THINKING. By A. S. Roe. Two Parts, paper, 75c.; cloth, $1.

LIFE'S DISCIPLINE.—A TALE OF THE ANNALS OF HUNGARY. By Talvi, author of "Heloise," &c. 12mo., paper, 38c.; cloth, 63c.

LOVER, SAMUEL.—HANDY ANDY. 8vo., paper cover, 60c.

——— L. S. D., TREASURE TROVE. 8vo., paper, 25c.

MARGARET CECIL; OR, "I CAN, BECAUSE I OUGHT." By Cousin Kate. 12mo., paper, 50c.; cloth, 75c.

McINTOSH, M. J.—TWO LIVES; OR, TO SEEM AND TO BE. 12mo., cloth, 75c.; paper, 50c.

——— AUNT KITTY'S TALES. 12mo., cloth, 75c.; paper, 50c.

——— CHARMS AND COUNTER CHARMS. Paper, 75c.; cloth, $1.

MAIDEN AUNT (The). A Story. By S. M. 12mo., paper, 50c.; cloth, 75c.

Novels, Tales, &c.—Continued.

MANZONI.—THE BETROTHED LOVERS. 2 vols., 12mo., cloth, $1 50c.; paper, $1.

MARGARET MAITLAND; (Some Passages in the Life of). 12mo., paper, 50c.; cloth, 75c.

MAXWELL'S HILL-SIDE AND BORDER SKETCHES. 8vo., paper cover, reduced to 25c.

——— FORTUNES OF HECTOR O'HALLORAN. 8vo., paper cover, 50c.; 23 plates; boards, $1.

MORTON MONTAGUE; OR, YOUNG CHRISTIAN'S CHOICE. By C. B. Mortimer. 12mo., cloth, 75c.

NATHALIE. A Tale. By Julia Kavanagh, author of "Woman in France," "Madeleine," &c. 12mo., paper, 75c.; cloth, $1.

NORMAN LESLIE. A Tale. By G. C. H. 12mo., cloth, 75c.; paper, 50c.

ROSE DOUGLAS; OR, THE AUTOBIOGRAPHY OF A MINISTER'S DAUGHTER. By S. R. W. 12mo., paper, 50c.; cloth, 75c.

SEWELL, E. M.—THE EARL'S DAUGHTER. 12mo., cloth, 75c.; paper, 50c.

——— AMY HERBERT. A Tale. 12mo., cloth, 75c.; paper, 50c.

——— GERTRUDE. A Tale. 12mo., cloth, 75c.; paper, 50c.

——— LANETON PARSONAGE. A Tale. 3 vols., 12mo., cloth, $2 25c.; paper, $1 50c.

——— MARGARET PERCIVAL. 2 vols., cloth, $1 50; paper cover, $1.

——— WALTER LORIMER, and other Tales. 12mo., illus., 75c.

——— JOURNAL OF A TOUR, For the Children of a Village School. In Three Parts, paper, each 25c.

SOUTHWORTH, E. D. E. N. THE DESERTED WIFE. A Novel. 8vo., paper, 38c.

——— SHANNONDALE. A Novel. 8vo., paper, 25c.

——— THE MOTHER-IN-LAW; OR, THE ISLE OF RAYS. A Novel. 8vo., paper, 38c.

TO LOVE AND TO BE LOVED. A Story. By A. S. Roe, Author of "James Montjoy," &c. 12mo., cloth, 63c.; paper, 38c.

USES (The) *OF SUNSHINE.* By S. M., Author of "The Maiden Aunt," &c. 12mo., paper, 50c.; cloth, 75c.

VILLAGE NOTARY. A Romance of Hungarian Life. Translated from the Hungarian of Eotvos. 8vo., paper, 25c.

ZSCHOKKE.—INCIDENTS OF SOCIAL LIFE. 12mo., cloth, $1.

MISCELLANEOUS WORKS.

APPLETON'S Library Manual. 8vo. Half bound, $1 25.

——— Southern and Western Traveller's Guide. With colored Maps. 18mo. $1.

——— Northern and Eastern Traveller's Guide. Twenty-four Maps. 18mo. $1 25.

——— New and Complete United States Guide-Book for Travellers. Numerous Maps. 18mo. $2.

——— New-York City and Vicinity Guide. Maps. 38 cts.

——— New-York City Map, for Pocket. 12 cts.

AGNELL'S Book of Chess. A complete Guide to the Game. With Illustrations by R. W. Weir. 12mo. $1 25.

ANDERSON, WM. Practical Mercantile Correspondence. 12mo. $1.

ARNOLD, Dr. Miscellaneous Works. 8vo. $2.

——— History of Rome. New Edition. 1 vol., 8vo. $3.

——— History of the Later Roman Commonwealth. 8vo. $2 50.

——— Lectures on Modern History. Edited by Prof. Reed. $1 25.

——— Life and Correspondence. By the Rev. A. P. Stanley. 2d Edition. 8vo. $2.

AMELIA'S Poems. 1 vol., 12mo. Cloth, $1 25; gilt edges, $1 50.

ANSTED'S Gold-Seeker's Manual. 12mo. Paper, 25 cts.

BOWEN, E. United States Post-Office Guide. Map. 8vo. Paper, $1; cloth, $1 25.

BROOKS' Four Months among the Gold-Finders in California. 25 cts.

BRYANT'S What I Saw in California. With Map. 12mo. $1 25.

BROWNELL'S Poems. 12mo. 75 c.

CALIFORNIA Guide-Book. Embracing Fremont and Emory's Travels in California. 8vo. Map. Paper, 50 cts.

CARLYLE'S Life of Frederick Schiller. 12mo. Paper, 50 cts.; cloth, 75 cts.

CHAPMAN'S Instructions to Young Marksmen on the Improved American Rifle. 16mo. Illustrated. $1 25.

COOLEY, A. J. The Book of Useful Knowledge. Containing 6,000 Practical Receipts in all branches of Arts, Manufactures, and Trades. 8vo. Illustrated. $1 25.

COOLEY, J. E. The American in Egypt. 8vo. Illustrated. $2.

COIT, Dr. History of Puritanism. 12mo. $1.

CORNWALL, N. E. Music as It Was, and as It Is. 12mo. 63 cts.

COUSIN'S Course of Modern Philosophy. Translated by Wight. 2 Vols., 12mo. $3.

COGGESHALL'S Voyages to Various Parts of the World. Illus. $1 25.

DON QUIXOTTE DE LA MANCHA. With 18 Steel Engravings. 16mo. Cloth, $1 50.

EMORY'S Notes of Travels in California. 8vo. Paper, 25 cts.

ELLIS, Mrs. Women of England. 12mo. 50 cts.

——— Hearts and Homes; or Social Distinctions. A Story. Two Parts. 8vo. Paper, $1; cloth, $1 50.

EVELYN'S Life of Mrs. Godolphin. Edited by the Bishop of Oxford. 16mo. Cloth, 50 cts.; paper, 38 cts.

FAY, T. S. Ulric; or, The Voices. 12mo. 75 cts.

FOSTER'S Essays on Christian Morals. 18mo. 50 cts.

FREMONT'S Exploring Expedition to Oregon and California. 25 cts.

FROST, Prof. Travels in Africa. 12mo. Illustrated. $1.

FALKNER'S Farmer's Manual. 12mo. 50 cts.

GARLAND'S Life of John Randolph. 2 Vols., 12mo. Portraits, $2 50.

GILFILLAN, GEO. Gallery of Literary Portraits. Second Series. 12mo. Paper, 75 cts.; cloth, $1.

——— The Bards of the Bible. 12mo. Cloth, 50 cts.

GOLDSMITH'S Vicar of Wakefield. 12mo. Illustrated. 75 cts.

GOULD, E. S. "The Very Age." A Comedy. 18mo. Paper, 38 cts.

GRANT'S Memoirs of An American Lady. 12mo. Cloth, 75 cts.; paper, 50 cts.

GUIZOT'S Democracy in France. 12mo. Paper cover, 25 cts.

——— History of Civilization. 4 Vols. Cloth, $3 50.

——— History of the English Revolution of 1640. Cloth, $1 25.

HULL, Gen. Civil and Military Life. Edited by J. F. Clarke. 8vo. $2.

HOBSON. My Uncle Hobson and I. 12mo. 75 cts.

GOETHE'S IPHIGENIA IN TAURIS. A Drama in Five Acts. From the German by G. J. Adler. 12mo. 75 cts.

KAVANAGH, JULIA. Women of Christianity, exemplary for Piety and Charity. 12mo. Cloth, 75 cts.

KENNY'S Manual of Chess. 18mo. 38 cents.

KOHLRAUSCH'S Complete History of Germany. 8vo. $1 50.

KIP'S Christmas Holidays at Rome. 12mo. $1.

LAMB, CHAS. Final Memorials. Edited by Talfourd. 12mo. 75 cts.

LAMARTINE'S Confidential Disclosures; or, Memoirs of My Youth. 12mo.

MISCELLANEOUS WORKS—Continued.

LEE, E. B. Life of Jean Paul F. Richter. 12mo. $1 25.

LEGER'S History of Animal Magnetism. 12mo. $1.

LETTERS FROM THREE CONTINENTS. By R. M. Ward. 12mo. Cloth, $1.

LORD, W. W. Poems. 12mo. 75 c.

——— Christ in Hades. 12mo. 75 cts.

MACKINTOSH, M. J. Woman in America. Cloth, 62 cts.; paper, 38 cts.

MAHON'S (Lord) History of England. Edited by Prof. Reed. 2 Vols., 8vo. $4.

MICHELET'S History of France. 2 Vols., 8vo. $3 50.

——— Life of Martin Luther. 12mo. 75 cts.

——— History of Roman Republic. 12mo. $1.

——— The People. 12mo. Cloth, 63 cts.; paper, 38 cts.

MATTHEWS & YOUNG. Whist and Short Whist. 18mo. Cloth, gilt, 45 cts.

MILES on the Horse's Foot; How to Keep it Sound. 12mo. Cuts. 25 cts.

MILTON'S Paradise Lost. 38 cts.

MOORE, C. C. Life of George Castriot, King of Albania. 12mo. Cloth, $1.

NAPOLEON, Life of, from the French of Laurent de l'Ardeche. 2 Vols. in 1. 8vo. 500 Cuts. Im. mor., $3.

OATES, GEO. Tables of Sterling Exchange, from £1 to £10,000—from 1-8th of one per cent. to twelve and a half per cent., by eighths, etc., etc. 8vo. $3.

——— Interest Tables at 6 per cent. per Annum. 8vo. $2.

——— Abridged Edit. $1 25.

——— Interest Tables at 7 per cent. per Annum. 8vo. $2.

——— Abridged Edit. $1 25.

——— Sterling Interest Tables at 5 per cent. per Annum, from £1 to £10,000. 4to. $5.

O'CALLAGHAN'S History of New-York under the Dutch. 2 Vols. $5.

POWELL'S Living Authors of England. 12mo. $1.

REPUBLIC OF THE UNITED STATES; Its Duties, &c. 12mo. $1.

REID'S New English Dictionary, with Derivations. 12mo. $1.

RICHARDSON on Dogs. Their History, Treatment, &c. Cuts. 25 cts.

ROBINSON CRUSOE. Only complete Edition. 300 Cuts. 8vo. $1 50.

ROWAN'S History of the French Revolution. 2 Vols. in 1. 63 cts.

SOYER'S Modern Domestic Cookery. 12mo. Paper cover, 75 cts.; bd., $1.

SCOTT'S Lady of the Lake. 38 cents.

SCOTT'S Marmion. 16mo. 37 cts.

——— Lay of the Last Minstrel. 25 cents.

SELECT Italian Comedies. Translated. 12mo. 75 cts.

SPRAGUE'S History of the Florida War. Map and Plates. 8vo. $2 50.

SHAKSPEARE'S Dramatic Works and Life. 1 Vol., 8vo. $2.

SOUTHEY'S Life of Oliver Cromwell. 18mo. Cloth, 38 cts.

STEWART'S Stable Economy. Edited by A. B. Allen. 12mo. Illustrated. $1

SOUTHGATE (Bishop). Visit to the Syrian Church. 12mo. $1.

SQUIER'S Nicaragua; Its People, Antiquities, &c. Maps and Plates. 2 Vols., 8vo. $5.

STEVENS' Campaigns of the Rio Grande and Mexico. 8vo. Paper, 38 cts.

SWETT, Dr. Treatise on the Diseases of the Chest. 8vo. $3.

TAYLOR, Gen. Anecdote Book, Letters, &c. 8vo. 25 cts.

TUCKERMAN'S Artist Life. Biographical Sketches of American Painters. 12mo. Cloth, 75 cts.

TAYLOR'S Manual of Ancient and Modern History. Edited by Prof. Henry. 8vo. Cloth, $2 25; sheep, $2 50.

THOMSON on the Food of Animals and Man. Cloth, 50 cts.; paper, 38 cts.

TYSON, J. L. Diary of a Physician in California. 8vo. Paper, 25 cts.

WAYLAND'S Recollections of Real Life in England. 18mo. 31 cts.

WILLIAMS' Isthmus of Tehuantepec; Its Climate, Productions, &c. Maps and Plates. 2 Vols., 8vo. $3 50.

WOMAN'S Worth; or, Hints to Raise the Female Character. 18mo. 38 cts.

WARNER'S Rudimental Lessons in Music. 18mo. 50 cts.

WYNNE, J. Lives of Eminent Literary and Scientific Men of America. 12mo. Cloth, $1.

WORDSWORTH, W. The Prelude. An Autobiographical Poem. 12mo. Cloth, $1.

LAW BOOKS.

ANTHON'S Law Study; or, Guides to the Study of the Law. 8vo. $3.

HOLCOMBE'S Digest of the Decisions of the Supreme Court of the United States, from its commencement to the present time. Large 8vo. Law sheep, $6.

——— Supreme Court Leading Cases in Commercial Law. 8vo. $4.

——— Law of Debtor and Creditor in the United States and Canada. 8vo. $4.

SMITH'S Compendium of Mercantile Law. With large American additions by Holcombe and Gholson. 8vo. $4 50.

www.ingramcontent.com/pod-product-compliance
Lightning Source LLC
LaVergne TN
LVHW010153110826
845151LV00002B/506

* 9 7 8 1 4 2 5 5 3 6 8 7 9 *